UKIR
WAYANG KULIT
&
TOPENG

Inside the Puppet Box

A Performance Collection of Wayang Kulit at the Museum of International Folk Art

Felicia Katz-Harris

MUSEUM OF INTERNATIONAL FOLK ART
SANTA FE, NEW MEXICO

IN ASSOCIATION WITH

UNIVERSITY OF WASHINGTON PRESS
SEATTLE AND LONDON

The photographs of the wayang figures in this catalog are not necessarily intended as true contextual representations, but rather their poses are artistic interpretations of the characters that are presented.

Editor: Alice Davenport, Davenport & Schwintzer
Design: Skolkin + Chickey, Santa Fe
Indexer: Karla Knight
All studio photography by Blair Clark
Printed in Singapore
14 12 11 10 09   5 4 3 2 1

Distributed by the University of Washington Press
P.O. Box 50096, Seattle, WA 98145 U.S.A.
www.washington.edu/uwpress

Library of Congress Control Number: 2010929329

The paper used in this publication meets the minimum requirements of American National Standard for Information Sciences — Permanence of Paper for Printed Library Materials, ANSI

Contents

For my family

Acknowledgements

Many brilliant performers, artists, and scholars helped me wrap my head around this magnificently complex art form. I am in awe of those who have mastered each intricate facet of wayang, and I am immensely grateful to them for the little that I have learned.

A collection of wayang kulit acquired from Ki Purbo Asmoro serves as a basis for this book, complemented by that of Ki Enthus Susmono. My deepest gratitude goes to these extraordinary dhalang who generously shared their time, knowledge, and opinions and have continually made themselves accessible. In addition, Ki Purbo provided the core identifying information and structure for the catalog section – documentation that could only come from a true scholar with a spirit for collecting. It is an honor to know these two artists, each with a different performance approach, and I am privileged to have had the opportunity to work with them and attend their inspiring performances.

The research presented in this book was only possible with a lot of help from a lot of people and I am deeply grateful to the following individuals. Dr. Suyanto contributed the Preface and was available at my beck and call to answer countless questions. Kathryn Emerson devoted a seemingly unlimited amount of time (24/7), translated lakon titles, facilitated the project in a multitude of ways, and was an incredible source of knowledge; she made things happen. Honggo Utomo—a master of everything and dear friend—coordinated trips and interviews, shared his expertise and experiences, and accomplished in a blink what would have otherwise taken me weeks; he is also an excellent photographer and generously provided a number of images in this book. Midiyanto guided my initial research, introduced me to artists and dhalang, and generously shared his knowledge, skills, and time. Dr. Sumarsam—a truly gracious and giving teacher—read the manuscript and provided careful and constructive attention to the book's content; he clarified scores of questions, provided appropriate spellings for Javanese names and words as well as translations and interpretations for complex ideas, and gave invaluable advice throughout the course of this project.

I owe a debt of gratitude to Tri Suwarno, an accomplished wayang artist from Bantul, who took time away from his busy schedule and young family to take me, multiple times, all over Central Java to meet wayang artisans; he introduced me to the implausibly detailed process of making wayang kulit and the mind-blowing talent required; he also ran all over Yogya to find my lost camera and retrieve film that I inadvertently left behind. Amazing artists, Riyadi Dwi Susanto from Bantul; Marino, Thoyib, and Suyanto from Wonogiri District; and Hadi Siswanto from Klaten also provided hours of interview time, allowed me to observe them work, and took me into their homes.

I am very grateful for the time and expert knowledge freely shared by dhalang, Ki Anom Suroto, who also allowed the privilege of videotaping a demonstration on *sabetan*. Other artists, scholars, and friends who participated in interviews and/or gave their time and help include: Ki Sukasdi; Sukardi; Suyoto; Rejo Sumarto; Giyarno; Rukun Santoso; Sarjo; I Wayan Tunjung, SSN; RM Donny S Megananda of the Kekayon Museum; Dr. Kathy Foley; Dr. Martha Satz; and the families of: Tri Suwarno; Riyadi Dwi Susanto; Honggo Utomo; Ki Purbo Asmoro; Ki Enthus Susmono; Dr. Suyanto; and the family of Midiyanto. Mohammad Fadil translated the preface and translated and transcribed hours of recorded interviews—help that is very much appreciated. Special thanks go to Tadashi Kumagai for use of his beautiful photography. I am also very grateful to Dr. Widya Nayati and the late Prof. Dr. Hj. Endang Daruni Asdi for their help and hospitality. Many thanks to Jurusan Pedalangan at Institut Seni Indonesia, Solo and also to Pusat Studi Kebudayaan at Universitas Gadjah Mada.

At the Museum of International Folk Art, my talented and resourceful colleagues did an incredible amount to help realize this book and deserve heartfelt thanks. The beautiful color plates that illustrate the collection are the work of Blair Clark, who put in many hours photographing (and re-photographing) the wayang—exuberant and supportive all the while. Paul Smutko and Jay Pearson, problem solvers extraordinaire, quelled emergencies often and on the spot. Mark MacKenzie and Maureen Russell successfully preserved the collection as it traveled from Solo to Santa Fe. Rosemary Sallee researched and with Deborah King catalogued and numbered the entire collection with dedicated volunteers and interns Carol Martin-Davis, Charlotte King, and Bianca Pais. Thanks are also due to the cheerful Annabelle Mischler—my third, forth, and fifth hands; Aurelia Gomez and my predecessor, Dr. Frank Korom who read manuscript drafts and offered support; and David Skolkin for his guidance and optimism. I am very grateful to Dr. Joyce Ice, former Museum Director, for planting this seed, and for careful review and thoughtful comments on the manuscript; MOIFA Director Dr. Marsha Bol for seeing this project through to fruition and finding the budget to do so; and Angelina Maestas for keeping the budget on track. I am indebted to the Folk Art Committee of the Museum of New Mexico Foundation and the Santa Fe International Folk Art Market for funding this book, and Laurel Seth and the International Folk Art Foundation for their encouragement and financial support of my research.

This book would not have been a remote possibility without the emotional support, editorial advice, and (duly noted) extra parenting hours from my husband, David Harris. I am thankful to my daughter Maya (my in utero research companion) and my family who supported my work through the good, the bad, and everything in-between.

Dr. Suyanto, S.Kar., MA.
Translated by Mohammad Fadil, S.Pd.

Preface

In the world's eyes, Indonesia is one of the richest countries for artistic and cultural works. In this era of global competition, the arts are one of Indonesia's most important treasures. One art form in particular has obtained international recognition and that is *wayang* ("puppetry") arts and performance. On November 17, 2003, The United Nations' Educational Scientific and Cultural Organization (UNESCO) offered wayang world-wide recognition for its excellence, cultural significance, and importance by designating it as a Masterpiece of the Intangible Heritage of Humanity.[1] Therefore, appreciation for wayang extends outside of Indonesia. This designation has real consequences in terms of the attitude and behavior of the Indonesian people, who have been acknowledged by UNESCO as the keepers of this tradition.

Wayang is not only a source of pride for the Indonesian people; it can also encourage them to think introspectively, placing a personal value on wayang and making it more meaningful to their own life and to humanity, in general. *Wayang kulit* ("leather puppet") performances are very popular and provide a sense of identity for the Javanese people, giving them a medium of art and entertainment through which they can feel a sense of community. They generally think of wayang as "a mirror of life" (*wewayanganing urip*). Wayang in the Javanese language is also called *ringgit*. Words containing these root words (*ringgit* and *wayang*) have been in existence for a long time.

Wayang kulit emerged from ancient Javanese religious practices. The art form was considered an appropriate way to deliver divine messages.[2] Evidence suggests that wayang existed from at least the ninth century CE, and that wayang was performed for spiritual purposes. One example is an epigraph at Wukajana by King Balitung's administration (ninth century CE), it was stated: "*Hinyunakên tontonan mawidu sang tangkil hyang sinalu macarita bhima kumara mangigêl kicaka si jaluk macarita ramayana mamirus mabanyol si mungmuk si galigi mawayang buat hyang macarita ya kumara,*" which roughly means: The performance was held . . . telling the story of Bima Kumara and having a Kicaka dance. Through the medium of a masked dance, characters conveyed the story of the *Ramayana* . . . and a performance of shadow puppets conveyed the story of Bima Kumara for Hyang (the soul of ancestors).[3]

These examples show that during that period of time, performances, including wayang performances, were presented for the benefit of the ancestors' souls.[4] Thus, wayang kulit functioned as a ritual means of veneration.

Wayang stories existed and developed in Indonesia from the age of the Hindu Kingdom of Mataram to the Islamic Mataram, and continue to develop in contemporary times. In the era of the Hindu Kingdom of Mataram, many poets composed works of art based on the wayang stories, in the form of prose, songs, or poems. The wayang stories were adapted from Indian literary works such as the *Ramayana* and *Mahabharata*, or developed from the two. A number of other works did not refer to those two stories but were created by the poets to reflect Javanese culture during that time.

Information about the existence of, and response to, wayang performance in Indonesia can also be seen through other works of art from ancient times. One of these works is *Pupuh V* from *Cikarini*.[5] In reference to Serat Arjunawiwaha (the "Story of Arjuna Wiwaha" created by the poet, Empu Kanwa in the administration of the King Erlangga of Kediri, in the eleventh century CE), it explains that ". . . those who cried while viewing a shadow performance were rather obtuse since, in fact, they knew that the puppets were carved leather, moved and sounded by the puppeteer. They were chained by materialism and had lost their way. What they saw was untrue, like a magic . . . "[6] From this, it can be assumed that these shadow performances used wayang figures (made of carved leather) that were "moved and sounded by the puppeteer," and that the story touched the spectators' hearts so much that they cried. More importantly, it can be assumed that the shadow performances represented the emotions or situations of Javanese people's lives at that time.

Through the continued existence of wayang stories in performance arts, the role of wayang has developed in accordance with the development of Javanese cultures. The wayang stories mostly deliver messages such as the value of life, virtue, morality, humanism, and other important philosophies. Those matters are included in delicate and complex symbols. To understand all the symbolism in a wayang performance requires serious and deep contemplation.

One discipline that can be used to think about the matters presented in wayang performances is philosophy. Philosophical activity is contemplation, which is different from dreaming or speculative thinking. Its purpose is to construct a system of rational knowledge that can properly be used to understand either the world in which we live, or to understand ourselves.[7] Through philosophical contemplation, the values that exist in wayang stories can be understood and rationalized. Studying philosophy is an attempt to seek basic truth. Therefore, philosophical discussions of wayang will draw from three interrelated philosophical branches: "metaphysics of wayang"; "axiology of wayang"; and "epistemology of wayang."

From the point of view of metaphysics (the philosophical theory of being or existence), a wayang performance is symbolic of the search for Principle Truth; a search for the deepest existence. It is clear that through wayang stories and the performance of the stories, people can understand the essence of existence, unity, and truth. From the aspect of axiology (the philosophical theory of value), a wayang performance is an exploration of the value of life as it relates to human life and human culture. The values are transferred through storytelling, manifested by symbols in the performance. The symbols can be figures such as warriors, giants, gods, or animals, but they can also be symbols expressed through language in the form of the figures' dialogues and the puppeteer's narration. Epistemologically (the philosophical theory of knowledge), through wayang, we can derive knowledge and meaning from life (*kawruhing urip*).

In today's era of cultural development, the wayang kulit of Java (generally called *wayang purwa*) retains a wonderful presence. Wayang kulit performances cannot be separated from the creative capability of the puppeteers (*dhalang*), from wayang supporters, or from a broader society that cares deeply about wayang kulit. Dhalang of today, particularly in Java, apply various models and strategies in their approach to their art.

Within the whole body of wayang presentations, there are at least three styles of performance: traditional; contemporary; and a combination of traditional and contemporary styles. These three styles appeal to different spectators. In Javanese culture, traditional *pakeliran* (wayang performances) tend to be favored by older generations, more conservative audiences, and the upper-middle class with comparable education. Traditional style wayang is generally full of traditional Javanese cultural values, and mostly emphasizes self-internalization. For instance, this performance style can be seen in performances by Ki Purbo Asmoro from Surakarta, and is still widely enjoyed today. In reality, many dhalang who take a traditional approach, such as Ki Purbo, still incorporate some new and innovative features, at least to particular scenes.

Contemporary pakeliran mostly lean towards entertainment and popular appeal. Generally, the spectators of this style of wayang are the younger generations, lower-middle class communities, or those communities that have a different appreciation for, or interpretation of those traditional values, which may be perceived as old-fashioned or restricting. For example, the contemporary approach of Ki Enthus Susmono from Tegal is now very popular. Yet, even a dhalang such as Ki Enthus, who is considered radical and risqué, still bases his contemporary performance upon traditional stories, and communicates serious values (though the values reflect more modern times).

Meanwhile, wayang shows which combine traditional and contemporary styles are now widely presented by popular young puppeteers from certain areas. This mixing of the traditional and contemporary commonly exists among villagers or rural communities whose populations tend to have a mixed background. In such a village community, the older generation still prefers traditional puppet shows, and the younger ones prefer contemporary puppet shows. Faced with this situation, many dhalang take this moderate approach, following the supporting community's preferences. Accordingly, today's wayang performances involve not only traditional Javanese gamelan instruments, but also non-gamelan musical instruments and technology, pop-music such as *dangdut* and *campursari*, and are equipped with a light arrangement such as a disco ball. In this kind of show, onstage performers include not only the wayang figures, the dhalang, singers, and gamelan musicians, but also comedians and guest artists.

The existence of various versions of today's wayang performances can be seen as a manifestation of the cultural complexity of communities in Indonesia, particularly in Java. This existing diversity of styles can be seen not as a separate and destructive trend to the culture of wayang, but as a positive result of the nation's cultural development. Various interpretations of wayang kulit, by either the dhalang or by the wider society, can be considered an indicator of the life and the growth of wayang culture in Indonesia today.

Notes

1. UNESCO, 2003:2.

2. Zoetmulder, 1990:285.

3. Hariyana, 2005:176.

4. The root words *wayang* or *ringgit*, as noted in the epigraphic plates, refers to the performance of two-dimensional puppets made of hide with only two facial representations: left or right.

5. Cikarini is an ancient Javanese song. Pupuh is a collection of stanzas from song lyrics that form sentences; it is a part of the song.

6. Wiryamarta, 1990:81

7. Kattsoff, 2004:6

Dr. Suyanto is a dhalang (puppeteer and shadow master), originally from East Java. He is also a lecturer of puppeteering and wayang studies at Indonesia's prestigious art institute, Institut Seni Indonesia (ISI), Surakarta. He has a PhD in philosophy from Universitas Gadjah Mada, where he focused on philosophy in wayang.

Mohammad Fadil teaches English in the Language Center at Universitas Jember, East Java. He is currently pursuing his Master's Degree in Language and Arts at Universitas Negeri Surabaya, where his major is English.

Felicia Katz-Harris

Inside the Puppet Box

Wayang Kulit at the Museum of International Folk Art

Wayang kulit performances lie close to the heart of Javanese culture, and are one of the greatest storytelling traditions in the world. Wayang kulit figures are elaborately painted and intricately punched and carved flat rawhide puppets that cast dramatic shadows through a cotton screen during a performance. The stories are based on classical literature, but every performance also draws on contemporary themes, and teaches important moral, ethical, and philosophical ideas while entertaining the audience at times with roaring humor and special action-packed scenes. Traditional performances, which are always accompanied by a *gamelan* (a traditional Indonesian musical ensemble), last all night long, beginning in the evening and ending at dawn.[1] Abbreviated performances, however, may be geared toward tourists and also to younger Indonesians, who may prefer television and movies to this deep-rooted tradition.

As opposed to common Western notions of puppetry as children's entertainment, wayang kulit is considered one of the highest forms of art in Indonesia and is a world-renowned representation of Javanese cultural heritage. It is a highly sophisticated art form that has been performed in villages, cities, and royal courts for hundreds of years. Performances commonly celebrate or commemorate personal accomplishments, rites-of-passage, holidays and national events—but performances may also be arranged simply for entertainment.

Wayang kulit is generally understood to mean "leather shadow puppet" in the national Indonesian language (*Bahasa Indonesia*). There are various theories about the specific meaning and origin of the word *wayang* itself. *Wayang* can be used in two senses. It can mean "puppet," or it can mean a type of performance (usually the performance of the associated *Ramayana* and *Mahabharata* epics, or the performance of other Javanese stories as described further below). As the root word for the Javanese terms *wewayangan* and *wewayanganing urip*, the word *wayang* also connotes the shadow of human life.[2] Originally, audiences mostly viewed not the physical form of the wayang (that is, the puppet), but the shadow that penetrated the screen. The word *kulit* literally means "skin" and is also typically translated as "leather." Although wayang kulit are commonly presented as leather shadow puppets, in reality the material used to make the figures is rawhide (from water buffalo skin). This book uses the words *wayang* and *wayang kulit* to refer to both physical puppets and to the performance art, depending on the context.

There are numerous regional and stylistic variations of wayang performance, even within the wayang kulit tradition. This book focuses on the contemporary court-based Surakarta, or Solo, style that has become (in modern times) the most widely recognized and widely performed form of wayang within and outside Indonesia.[3] The more local, regional styles of Yogyakarta, East Java, Banyumas, Bali, and elsewhere are less represented outside of Java. To some extent, the Solo style of wayang kulit performance adapts or incorporates elements of other regional styles, and it has become the favored style of performance for audiences and performers outside of Solo. In fact, the Solo style has come to be the mainstream style of performance in Indonesia, serving as a reference point for other wayang kulit styles.[4] Historically, Solo's cultural traditions have strongly influenced traditions (including wayang kulit) of other nearby regions, probably due to the widespread cultural influence of Solo's *kraton* (royal palace). Perhaps the most significant reason for the popularity of Solo-style wayang kulit and performances is that this form is flexible: through techniques of dramatization, and through its humor and philosophy, this form can be adapted to cater to the audience in each community.[5]

Wayang kulit is an extraordinarily complex art form, which can take a lifetime to truly understand. Indeed, each aspect of the art form is a multifaceted topic, and each is worthy of a book in its own right. To explore all the equally important components of wayang kulit is well beyond the scope of this book, which instead provides a brief overview of some of the main aspects of wayang kulit and its performance, such as: how wayang kulit are made; *wanda* (mood and form of the wayang), *simpingan* (the arrangement of the wayang); various aspects of performance; the remarkable skills of the *dhalang* (shadow master and puppeteer); and the history and literary repetoire of wayang kulit. This book also offers an extensive visual reference that catalogs a particular performance set.

It is hoped that this introduction and visual reference for wayang kulit will offer the reader points of departure for further research. This overview is based on published sources, and on information that was collected through formal interviews, informal conversations, observations and correspondence with numerous wayang kulit experts—scholars, puppeteers, and artisans. Following this introduction, the catalog presents images of wayang kulit from a special collection of the Museum of International Folk Art in Santa Fe, New Mexico. This collection, a full performance set of Solo-style wayang kulit, was acquired for the Museum's award winning exhibition, *Dancing Shadows, Epic Tales: Wayang Kulit of Indonesia* (March 2009–March 2010) primarily from Ki Purbo Asmoro, a prominent dhalang based in Solo who is also a Professor of Puppeteering and Wayang at Institut Seni Indonesia (ISI) in Surakarta (the Arts Institute of Indonesia). Some additional pieces were acquired from the collection of Ki Enthus Susmono, a famous dhalang based in Tegal. The catalog presents provenance history for each item in the collection and basic information regarding the specific characters that are included in the set; information provided mostly by Ki Purbo Asmoro.

The collection and these two performers will be discussed in further detail in the last section of this introductory essay, which will also explain how the organization of the catalog reflects the placement of the wayang during a performance.

How Wayang Kulit Are Made

The intricate art of wayang kulit is an example of the high level of artistry found in Indonesia. Different methods for creating wayang kulit may be employed in various regions, but this section describes the typical process as it is executed in Central Java.

The shadow puppets are made from water buffalo hide, cut and punctured by hand, one hole at a time. Then they are painted in layers of water-based paints, heavily decorated with extraordinarily fine details, and often finished with gold and/or bronze leaf. The sticks attached to the base and the articulated limbs of the wayang kulit are made from water buffalo horn, wood, or both. The artists who create wayang kulit often learn their craft from family members and then apprentice with a master; but some have also studied in an arts program at the *kraton* (royal palace). Several artists are usually involved in the process of making wayang kulit—the artists who prepare the water buffalo skin, artists who carve and puncture the hide, the painters, and the horn carvers. Each artist might have the knowledge needed to create a puppet from start to finish; however, it is common for artists to work together and develop a specialization for a particular aspect of the process.

Fig. 1
Family members Tri Suwarno, Sukardi, and Riyadi Dwi Susanto (left to right) work together to create *wayang kulit*. Photograph by the author, Sewon, Bantul, 2007.

Fig.2

Fig.3

Fig.4

Fig.5

Fig.2
Suyoto is a trained carver of *wayang kulit*, but chose as his profession the preparation of rawhide (for handicrafts such as *wayang kulit*) because the job market is less competitive. He supplies many *wayang kulit* artists in the Yogyakarta area with prepared hide. Photograph by the author, Kasihan, Bantul, 2007.

Fig. 3
Suyoto washes and softens water buffalo hide in a local pond. Photograph by the author, Kasihan, Bantul, 2007.

Fig. 4
Suyoto begins scraping the first layer of skin from the hide. Photograph by the author, Kasihan, Bantul, 2007.

Fig. 5
Suyoto (right) and *wayang* carving artist, Sarjo (left) display a hide that is ready for making *wayang kulit*. Photograph by the author, Kasihan, Bantul, 2007.

Rawhide Preparation

The creation of the shadow puppets begins with the preparation of skin. Hide from young Sulawesi water buffalo is most desirable for wayang kulit.[6] Cultural groups in Sulawesi, such as the Toraja, slaughter water buffalos for ceremonial feasts. When the animal is slaughtered and skinned, the hide is washed, stretched on a frame, and left in the sun to dry for a number of weeks: this process helps decrease any unpleasant odors. The hide is otherwise left intact.

In Java, when the preparer receives a hide, he soaks it overnight in water (usually a pond or river) to soften and clean it. The leather is again stretched on a frame, and left to dry in the sun for twenty-four hours. Loose dirt is brushed from the hide. The first layer of skin is peeled with a scraper, thus removing all hairs from the hide. Shavings of this first layer are used by farmers in their fields to protect crops from pests. The hide is again set in the sun to dry. Next, the second layer of skin is scraped, and the shavings of this layer are fried and eaten as a snack called *krecek*, or used in tasty dishes such as *nasi gudeg*, a specialty of Yogyanese and Solonese cuisine. The skin is dried once again in the sun and the leather rawhide is then ready to be formed into shadow puppets or other crafts that utilize water buffalo hide.

One hide can typically accommodate fifteen small wayang characters or eight large-sized characters. Thicker pieces of hide are saved for larger wayang characters, such as the giants, whereas thinner cuts are used for female characters and for delicately framed, small wayang characters. During the dry season, the process of preparing the hide may take two to three days. In wetter seasons, the process may take longer.[7]

Creating Horn Puppet Sticks

Often overlooked are the artists who make the stick handles for the shadow puppet. Water buffalo horn is the most valued material, with white horn preferred over black horn. Wood may be used for purposes of economy, although many dhalang today prefer to use white water buffalo horn for the base handle and wood for the articulated limbs. This is because wood is sturdier for performance purposes, particularly for robust, aggressive performance techniques where the wayang are thrown up in the air and physically smashed against each other or twirled and held by these puppet sticks, as is typical in battle scenes.

Many horn artists make a variety of handicrafts from horn, but not all horn artists make wayang sticks. In fact, there are only a few artists in Central Java who supply wayang kulit makers with horn sticks.[8] The process of making the handles from water buffalo horn is quite involved and intriguing to watch. First, with a simple saw, the raw material (a whole water buffalo horn) is split length-wise into two pieces; next, these two pieces are split in half. Each quartered piece is cut down the middle, but not severed. The quartered, partially sliced horn is heated until it is pliable. Using iron tongs, the horn is gently pulled apart forming a V-shaped piece. With an adze, the rough outer layer of the horn is hacked away and filed down to remove the coarse edges. The horn is soaked in water to help it cool and harden for the next step.

The V-shaped piece of horn is sliced down the middle with the simple saw, following the angle or curve of the "V" shape, but the piece is not severed. The horn is heated again and the angles are straightened with the tongs; this action lengthens the horn into a long, straight stick, partially split down the middle. In the end, this piece becomes the base handle: the segment that holds the hide figure, which is inserted into the split stick. The process of firing, cutting, filing, and soaking will be repeated until the wayang handle is ready for the final stages, when it is smoothed, polished with leaves and natural chalk, and finished with carved decorative touches.[9]

Fig.6

Fig.7

Fig.8

Fig.9

Fig. 6
Hadi Siswanto, a water buffalo horn carver, quarters water buffalo horn (one of the beginning steps to making puppet sticks) outside his home and workshop. Photograph by the author, Polanharjo, Klaten, 2007.

Fig. 7
Rejo Sumarto, Hadi Siswanto's father, heats the sliced water buffalo horn in order to create a long stick. Photograph by the author, Polanharjo, Klaten, 2007.

Fig. 8
Rejo Sumarto hacks away at the rough outer layer of the water buffalo horn. This begins the process of cleaning and smoothing the sticks, which ultimately become shiny and slick. Photograph by the author, Polanharjo, Klaten, 2007.

Fig. 9
Hadi Siswanto uses a metal file to smooth the horn. Photograph by the author, Polanharjo, Klaten, 2007.

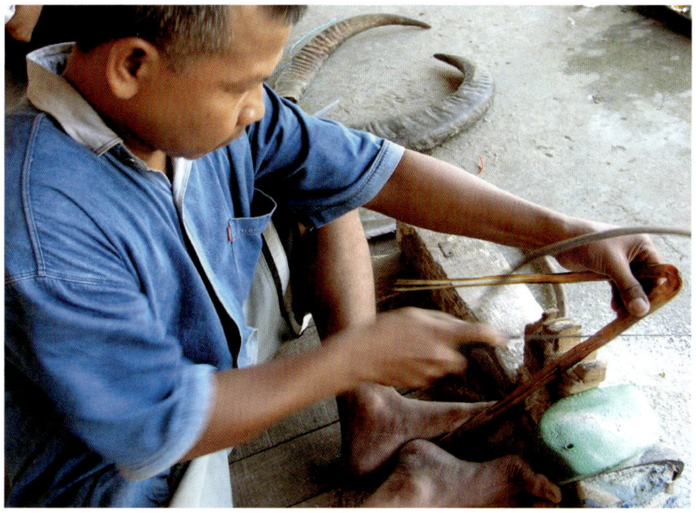

Fig.10

Fig.11

Fig.12

Fig.13

Fig. 10
Hadi Siswanto slices though the horn again, following the angle to create long thin sticks with slits where the *wayang* figure will eventually be inserted. Photograph by the author, Polanharjo, Klaten, 2007.

Fig. 11
Giyarno, Hadi Siswanto's brother, uses tongs to straighten out the bend in the horn over the flame. Photograph by the author, Polanharjo, Klaten, 2007.

Fig. 12
Giyarno finishes straightening the horn stick by heating it over a flame. Photograph by the author, Polanharjo, Klaten, 2007

Fig. 13
Hadi Siswanto finishes off a *wayang* base handle by polishing it with leaves and natural chalk powder. Photograph by the author, Polanharjo, Klaten 2007

Punching

The *penatah*, the artists who carve and puncture the leather, begin their work by scratching the outline of the wayang figure and the specific details of the character onto the hide. This drawing must be carefully executed, since the outline and the precise characteristics, especially the figure's posture, greatly influence the portrayal of the figure's personality, which is one of the most important marks of high quality wayang kulit. Subsequent carving and punching of the hide is guided by this sketch.[10]

The basic tools used to carve the rawhide include a *gandin* (mallet) and *tatah* (thin carving tools, similar to a nail or chisel with specially shaped points). Generally, the artists create the great variety of cutout shapes with only two kinds of tatah. They are *tatah datar* (flat) and *tatah lengkung* (curved), terms which refer to the tool's cutting edge. The mallet is used with these tools to tap the tatah and punch through the rawhide, in the same manner a sculptor might use a hammer and chisel, or an awl. Though the point of the tatah only comes in two basic shapes, the tools do come in various sizes. No matter the size, most punches require several turns of the tatah to achieve the desired detail in a single hole. This stage is the most time-consuming of the wayang making process, and is considered the most important to achieve accurate character portrayal.

Fig.14
Among a pile of *tatah*, the outline of this wayang figure has already been cut. The sketch of what will later become the carving details is seen on the rawhide surface. Photograph by the author, Eromoko, Wonogiri, 2007.

Fig. 15
A set of *tatah* (carving tools) belonging to the artist, Riyadi Dwi Susanto. Photograph by the author, Cabeyan, Bantul, 2007.

Fig.16 & 17
Thoyib, an artist (who is also a farmer) from Cemangkah Kidul, Wonogiri District, is an exceptional *wayang* carver. This series shows the artist punching the designs of a *wayang* figure. The leather is punched one hole at a time with the *tatah* (carving tool) and a mallet. Because of the intricacy of the carving, even small sections of high quality work like Thoyib's can take many hours to finish. Large shadow puppets can take several months to complete. Photographs by the author, Eromoko, Wonogiri, 2007.

Despite the seemingly infinite number of these punch shapes, only nine curved tatah and six flat tatah are used to create twelve distinct punch-patterns.[11] Each punch-pattern has a specific function. Combinations of curved and flat punches represent details such as clothing style, hairstyle, and personal ornamentation. For example, a pattern of short, straight lines (like dashes) might be used for the edging of a female character's *kain* (a general term for cloth, and the specific term for a skirt cloth). Or, in another example, rounded spirals represent hair.

Another type of carving detail is not achieved through punching, but by using the tools to push the hide surface into textured patterns that represent body or facial hair. Only select

Fig.16

Fig.17

Fig.18b

Fig.18c

Fig.18a

Fig. 18a
Wayang artists use specific patterns to create punch details of wayang figures (FA.2007.40.47). Photograph by Blair Clark.

Fig.18b
Detail of spiral punches that are used to represent hair.

Fig. 18c
Detail of straight line dashes that outline the edge of a characters *kain* (skirt cloth)

characters have this feature (see fig. 26). In deciding on the particular shapes, patterns, and details to use for a specific wayang character, artists must follow traditional rules and written guidelines for creating and decorating wayang kulit. Existing wayang figures, usually from kraton collections, serve as models; an artist can consult these older pieces, or standard drawings of these pieces, for carving and painting reference.

Painting

When the carving and punching are complete, painting is the next stage in the process of creating and decorating wayang kulit. The carved and punched wayang figure is smoothed with sandpaper: this prepares the skin for the first layer of color. The foundation color is usually white (in some locations yellow might be the base color of choice). This first layer of color evens out the hide's color tone and allows the overlayers of color to adhere well and to be shown at their best. This foundation coat covers the entire piece and is allowed to dry before it is burnished with a seashell and the second color is added.

Rarely do contemporary artists make and use natural pigments.[12] Today, the preferred paints are water-based colors, such as acrylics. Paints are mixed with an adhesive such as *ancur*, which in theory is a type of glue made from fish bones. In reality, however, the substance varies from artist to artist: sometimes it is a merely a carpenters' glue. Other types of paints are sometimes used (such as latex house paints or oil-based paints), much to the detriment of the wayang figures–for these paints are not durable and often peel off the hide. Water-based paints are the ideal medium because they are more easily absorbed by hide and their colors last longer than those of other paints.[13]

Colors are generally added in layers: color is first applied to the larger areas in a particular order, and then gold or bronze leaf is applied. Additional colors are painted on after the gilding process, and fine details, such as thin lines and tiny dots, are painted or stippled onto the design in the later stages.[14] Egg white is applied very carefully to the painted area, around the gold or bronze leaf (the metal leaf is not coated with egg white). *Sungging* refers to the process of coloring wayang, specifically to adding gradations of color. (At least three to five color gradients—light to dark—are needed for each hue, depending on the size of the wayang figure.)

Painters generally follow tradition, using standard colors and decorative patterns for specific attributes of specific characters. Artists do have some leeway in terms of individual

Fig. 19 & 20
Wayang painter, Tri Suwarno, sands an already carved and punched figure and prepares the hide for the first layer of paint. Photographs by the author, Sewon, Bantul, 2007.

Fig.19

Fig.20

Fig. 21–24
Wayang artist, Marino of Manyaran, paints details on a *wayang* figure in color gradients. Marino is a full time *wayang* artist, whose specialty is painting. Fellow painter Suyanto looks on (in Fig.21). Photographs by the author, Eromoko, Wonogiri, 2007.

Fig.21

Fig.22

Fig.23

Fig.24

Fig.25

Fig. 25
Garudha's face from a detail of a figure's hair ornament. Following tradition, this garudha glances to the side, has a blue face and white fangs (FA.2007.40.66). Photograph by Blair Clark.

Fig.26

Fig. 26
Gathutkaca has a black face and gold teeth, conforming to standard color schemes. Textured patterns represent facial hair, as do the spiral punches under the figure's chin. (FA.2007.40.16). Photograph by Blair Clark.

preferences and creativity, but for the most part, they must adhere to the traditional guidelines and choose colors suitable for the character they are creating.[15]

The following examples demonstrate a few of the many rules included in these artistic guidelines for making wayang. The *garudha* (a mythical bird) image is found in the hair ornaments and/or clothing of many characters and the image must be created with its eyes casting a somewhat sideways glance. The garudha's adornments should be gold, the teeth or fangs must be white, and the face of the bird should include gradients of red or of blue, or sometimes a shade of dark yellow.[16]

Another example is the color of the wayang figure's teeth. Wayang figures with black faces can only have teeth that are gold or red. Gold-faced characters will have black teeth, unless the character is a *raksasa* (demon-giant), in which case it will have white teeth. Raksasa with a red or blue face must have gold teeth.[17] These guidelines can be quite specific, and for non-specialists they may seem overly esoteric. In fact, not all wayang-makers (not even all dhalang) know the exact reasons for the rules; they only know that these rules exist. One wayang expert suggested that these explicit formulas (for patterning the punches and combining and/or juxtaposing particular colors) all help create an impressive visual impact.[18]

Fig.27

Fig. 27 & 28
Marino demonstrates the application of gold leaf, and examines his work at his home. Photographs by the author, Manyaran, Wonogiri, 2007.

Fig.28

On the other hand, sometimes the color of a figure's body and face can be a straightforward representation of personality or mood. Facial color is the strongest identifier, with the most common colors (at least for human characters) being gold, black, white, and red. A gold face signifies dignity and calmness; black can represent a strong character, or age; red symbolizes an intense, sometimes violent anger, or one who is easily upset or offended; and a white face indicates a person's youth, innocence, or honesty.[19] These are only a few of many such examples of the rich and complex iconography that exists in wayang kulit from the Solo tradition; and many other illustrations may be found in other regional wayang forms.[20]

Twenty-two karat gold or bronze leaf is used for finer pieces. The leaf is very delicate; it is prepared and applied with great care. Ancur is often mixed with gold colored paint to soften the gold leaf so it adheres smoothly. Certain colors are added after the gilding process, and fine details such as thin lines and tiny dots are then painted or stippled into the design. After fixing the articulated limbs to the figure's body with bone or metal fasteners (*gegel*), the final step in creating a wayang kulit figure is to attach the horn sticks. The horn sticks are heated over a small flame to mold the horn and to custom fit the stick around each individual shadow puppet's form. Finally, the wayang kulit is inserted into the handle and secured with a needle and thread. In the past, and still in some regions today, thread-like strips of rattan have been used to tie the sticks to the form.

In the end, wayang kulit are incredibly ornate works of art. Many people wonder why shadow puppets are so elaborately decorated when their purpose is to produce shadows. For one, people do see the physical puppet when they watch a performance from the dhalang's side of the screen. Furthermore, wayang kulit are important objects that represent important characters. It could be for the sake of the puppet that the figures are so beautiful. Most likely, the

Fig.29

Fig 29
Each figure has incredible detail, such as tiny dots and fine lines (FA.2007.38.10). Photograph by Blair Clark.

Fig.30

Fig.31

reason is that a dhalang desires an admirable set of wayang in the same way that a musician might desire a beautiful instrument. Not all dhalang can afford the best wayang collection; therefore, a high quality, gold (or even bronze) leafed set is indicative of the status, popularity and overall success of a particular dhalang.

Fig. 30 & 31
Wayang artist, Riyadi Dwi Susanto, heats a puppet stick (made from water buffalo horn) to fit a *wayang* figure. He thus creates a perfectly balanced *wayang* for a *dhalang's* use. After the figure is inserted into the pronged horn stick, Riyadi secures everything in place with a needle and thread. Photographs by the author, Sewon, Bantul, 2007.

Wanda: mood and form of the wayang characters

Wanda refers to the "inner mood" of certain wayang characters in different circumstances.[21] Wanda also refers to the physical manifestation or expression of that mood, as seen in a figure's face and posture.[22] So, several shadow puppets may be used in a performance to portray a single character. These various wayang figures are used to portray (or emphasize) the different personality traits of one character, and to express that character's emotional state as the performance progresses.

Physical features indicate the particular wanda of a character that is being portrayed, and the wanda, therefore, is dependent on the carving and painting of the wayang kulit. For example, the figure Kresna has several wanda. In a *jejer* scene, Kresna's demeanor would be respectful, formal, and humble.[23] These characteristics are best portrayed through his wanda Rondhon (Kresna with a black face and body of gold) and this is the version of Kresna that usually appears in such scenes (see plate 30 in the Simpingan Kanan section of the catalog). The physical characteristics that vary by wanda include face and/or body coloring; clothing; ornaments; hair style; position of the face or head (whether bent downward or held high); the size, shape, and position of the eye and the direction of its glare; the size and general posture of the body; the way in which the neck is positioned; the posture and balance of the shoulders; and the shape of the character's stomach.[24] Changes in such features can signal subtle or dramatic differences in a character's personality or mood, and these differences can be very important to the dhalang. For example, when dhalang Ki Enthus Susmono talks about different wanda, his whole body reacts and his facial expression changes: he gets a glint in his eyes; his jaw tightens; he straightens his posture. These are the types of facial or body expressions that represent emotions associated with various wanda.

In general, spectators who have a basic knowledge of wayang kulit and are familiar with wayang figures may recognize the different wanda of a single character in a performance, or at least particularly common wanda such as Kresna's wanda, Rondhon, as discussed above. Nevertheless, differences between a character's wanda are oftentimes so slight, that only the most astute observer can distinguish between them. In such instances, most audience members cannot tell the difference between the wanda, even if the viewers are seated only a few feet away from the stage. For example, it is very difficult for an audience to perceive the precise direction of a figure's glare, or whether a figure's head is bent a few millimeters lower than in another wanda representation. These subtle differences exist for the dhalang, the artists, and the experts—although even they cannot always distinguish between the various wanda, even when they view the pieces up close. Ki Purbo Asmoro notes that sometimes, dhalang cannot recognize the differences but may choose a particular wanda based on personal preference: for example, based on the perceived comfort in handling the figure, or whether the hide structure is flexible enough for use in battle scenes. Still, wanda also exist for the sake of the puppet and the story: wanda can illuminate the character's various moods and personality aspects; and a particular wanda may be necessary for the story according to the way it is interpreted by the dhalang. [25]

Like many aspects of wayang as an art form, the concept of wanda is open to interpretation, and a continuing discourse exists among dhalang and scholars that is part of a broader discussion about the nature of wayang kulit. Some dhalang claim that only certain characters may have numerous wanda, but other performers explain that if the dhalang believes it is necessary, he should be free to create a new wanda for any character. For example, Ki Enthus Susmono explains that if a character dies, the dhalang can create a *wanda mati* (that is, a wanda that expresses death). Innovation, such as creating new wanda, seems to be a popular trend in the wayang kulit tradition. Ki Enthus believes that a dhalang's personal interest, point of view, or interpretation of a story may also be expressed through wanda, which can amuse the spectators and strengthen the story, but he also notes these are his own ideas regarding wanda (perhaps on the progressive side) and that other performers may have different ideas. [26]

Dhalang, who lean toward the classicist end of the spectrum believe that such innovations are entertaining and creative but that with few exceptions, these trends do not generally last more than ten or twenty years. Therefore, traditionalists maintain that the newer, "invented" forms of wanda may be considered unique and unusual examples of wayang kulit, but are not actually a new "wanda." Ki Purbo Asmoro noted that the norms for using wanda are more relaxed today than in the past, particularly in performances by younger dhalang. But, as in the past, the most important use of wanda is still in *jejer* scenes (the beginning scene where there is a meeting with a king), in which the character is expected to behave in a particularly respectful and humble manner, and for most dhalang, only certain wanda will best portray those behaviors. [27]

Simpingan

During a performance, the wayang kulit are arranged in a relatively standard way on the *gedebog* (banana log).[28] This arrangement is referred to as the *simpingan*. At every wayang kulit performance, wayang figures are lined up to the right (*simpingan kanan*) and left (*simpingan kiri*) of the screen, and are set firmly into the gedebog, in ascending size order (with the smallest figures set closest to the dhalang who sits at the midpoint of the screen), and the figures face outward, away from the screen. The arrangement is viewed from the dhalang's side of the screen. A third group of wayang is kept apart by the dhalang; the *dhud-hahan* group. The dhudhahan group is not placed on the banana log.

The line of wayang on the gedebog is visually compelling, with overlapping pieces flanking the screen to the right and left, all lined up in order of size, and forming a diagonal line that brings the audience's focus to the center of the screen—the central performance space. The number of wayang "on the log" can range from fewer than fifty to more than two hundred, depending on the dhalang's artistic vision and collection, the sizes of the gedebog and the screen, the occasion of the performance, the performance space, and the sponsor of the event.

Simpingan Kanan-Kiri (Arrangement to the Right and Left of the Screen)

As mentioned above, the physical arrangement of wayang on the log for a performance is relatively standard. Placing specific characters on one side or another depends on aesthetics and tradition as well as the dhalang's interpretation and personal preferences.

A popular misconception about simpingan is that the placement of the characters on the gedebog is based primarily on the characters' moral fiber: that is, that characters with a generally good, polite, and refined disposition (*halus*) would be placed to the right (*simpin-gan kanan*) and those with a generally bad, rude, or coarse disposition (*kasar*) would be placed to the left (*simpingan kiri*). Characteristics such as halus and kasar are said to epito-mize Javanese world view, at least in terms of ideal behaviors.[29] However, there is more to the arrangement of the wayang than good and bad qualities, or polite and rude traits.

Most wayang characters (like most human beings) are not simply "good" or "bad." Good characters may do bad things, may be loud and coarse-mannered, or may have obliga-tions that lead to allegiances with the antagonists. Likewise, some characters are polite, loyal, and diplomatic, but are at the same time immoral or make poor decisions. Arguably, there are no purely good or bad characters in wayang, only shades of grey. For example, if any char-acter might be conceived as completely bad, Rahwana (a villain from the *Ramayana*) would be the one. However, Rahwana believed that possessing Sinta (a reincarnation of a goddess) would make him great: that is, Rahwana sought to better himself through his own actions

Fig. 32
Wayang kulit flank the screen to the right and left in an arrangement referred to as *simpingan*. Performance by Dhalang Ki Enthus Susmono. Photograph by Tadashi Kumagai, Central Java, July 2008.

Fig. 33
Detail from *simpingan kanan*, the right side. Photograph by Dr. Widya Nayati, Bantul, 2007.

Fig.32

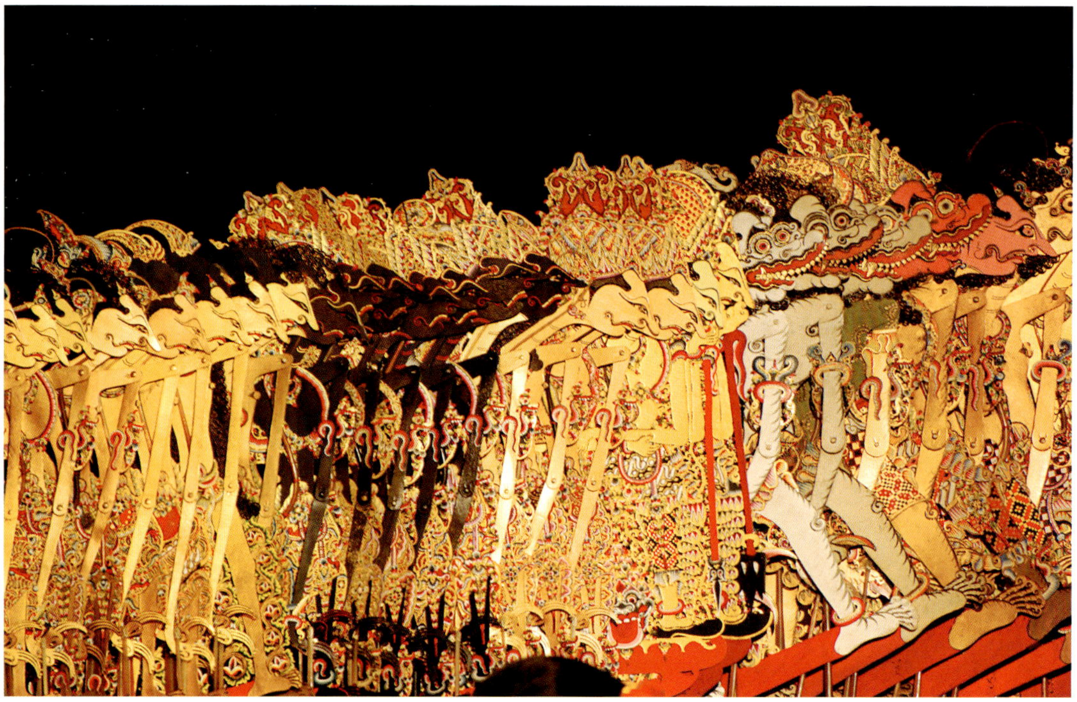

Fig.33

based on principles that he believed. Thus, even though there are many negative aspects to Rahwana's character, it can be argued that even this famous villain nevertheless has some positive traits and good intentions.[30] So the good-bad dichotomy does not completely define the wayang characters, and therefore (although a character's temperament may play a role) the good-bad divide does not alone influence how they are arranged on the banana log.

The arrangement of the wayang on the gedebog depends primarily on aesthetic balance and proportionality.[31] That is, the size and form of the characters set up to the right and to the left of the screen should be well balanced: the smallest characters should closely flank (or overlap) the screen on the right and left; and characters should gradually increase in size

Fig. 34
View of the *simpingan kiri*, the left side of the screen at a performance by dhalang Ki Anom Dwijo Kangko. Photograph by the author, Jebres, Solo, June 15, 2009.

as they extend out on the banana log, with the largest characters at the end of the lines. Gender also plays a role in the arrangement of wayang figures: female characters are displayed on the right side. Facial features and facial color are important factors in the arrangement of the wayang as well. For example, according to Ki Purbo, black and gold or yellow-faced wayang figures are placed on the right, and red and blue-faced wayang are placed on the left. Although facial color may indicate temperament, personality, or mood, the wayang are placed on a particular side based on how they look and groups of wayang with same-colored faces, of similar size, are usually placed together.[32]

The placement of the individual figures in the simpingan is also determined by regional style or the aesthetics of a particular region, which is probably related to the color of the wayang figures. For instance, in Solo and Klaten, the antagonistic character Duryudana (a figure with a black face) is often placed in the *simpingan kanan* (to the right), where many dhalang feel the character looks best aesthetically in the lineup. (Duryudana's facial features, facial color, and expression are close to those of his cousin, Bima—a figure usually placed on the right; see plates 4–7 and 11–12 in the Simpingan Kanan section of the catalog.)[33] However, in places like Pacitan, Duryudana is normally placed in the *simpingan kiri* (to the left of the dhalang).[34]

In summary, the exact placement of specific figures is not fixed, however, under normal circumstances, it is the overall look of the space—the visual balance— that is the major determinant of wayang placement, and that balance can be expected from show to show. In the end, the arrangement of the wayang on the gedebog is ultimately up to the dhalang.

Dhudhahan (Wayang Left Off the Gedebog)

Excluded from the simpingan kanan (right) and simpingan kiri (left) categories of characters are the wayang figures that fall into the *dhudhahan* group—meaning, "taken-out."[35] These are shadow puppets that remain in the dhalang's *kothak* (puppet box) or are kept within arms' reach at the dhalang's side.[36]

Wayang figures may be left off the gedebog (categorized as the dhudhahan group) if they are minor wayang figures (such as animals, ghosts, vehicles, armies, and weapons) and wayang figures that in some way confound or disrupt the aesthetic balance of the performance setting.[37] For example, if a character's physical form is too small, too big, or too fat they will not harmonize with the other figures displayed on the gedebog and may spoil the aesthetic balance in the simpingan arrangement. Such figures are therefore left out of the gedebog's right-left arrangement.

Also in the dhudhahan group are the puppeteer's most frequently used figures and the characters that appear in a given performance. Characters used in an evening's performance are not anchored to the log because retrieving a particular shadow puppet in mid-performance would be very disruptive.[38] The characters used in the evening's performance will be kept close to the dhalang's side, stacked on *eblek* (trays) in a very particular order. The trays are placed on top of the kothak, on the puppeteer's left (as he faces the screen) and on the lid of the box, to the puppeteer's right, where the dhalang has easy access to the pieces. The characters included in this scenario would depend on the particular story to be performed.

Performance

Wayang kulit performances are grand events that last throughout the night, accompanied all the while by a live gamelan orchestra. Hundreds of people gather to watch and enjoy these traditional theatrical performances.

Fig. 35
Ki Anom Suroto demonstrates how he brings the wayang to life. Performance elements include the screen and screen frame, banana logs, wayang kulit, the puppet box and box lid, a light source, and gamelan instruments. Photograph by the author, Solo, June 2007.

Elements of Performance

The fundamental components of the performance include the *dhalang* himself, *wayang kulit* figures, a *kelir* and *gawang* (screen and frame), a *blencong* (light source),[39] *gedebog* (banana logs), a *kothak* (the puppet box), and a gamelan orchestra. The gamelan performers include *pesindhen* (singers—usually female) and *gerong* (a male chorus).

The screen is the main focus of the performance area, with stationary wayang kulit figures flanking the right and left sides of the screen in the arrangement called the *simpingan*. The middle of the screen is the actual performance area. The dhalang sits front and center, directly facing the screen, and he remains in this spot throughout the performance. An assistant may be employed by some dhalang who sits behind and serves the dhalang by handing him puppets that are needed in each scene. The gamelan orchestra is set up behind the dhalang and the pesindhen sit beside him facing the audience.[40] An electric lamp, the *blencong*, is wired (into a light socket) and set up so that it hangs from a point above and behind the dhalang and hangs down into the screen's space. When the dhalang holds the shadow puppet in front of the screen, the light projects onto the puppet, passes through hundreds of perforations in the hide, and results in gloriously ornate shadows. The patterns of light and shadow show clearly against the screen and the audience can see also the shadow, or silhouette, of the wayang figures on the opposite side of the screen (referred to as the "shadow side of the screen" as opposed to the "dhalang's side of the screen"). A hint of color from the painted puppets can usually be seen through the screen as well. Shadows are manipulated by moving the wayang kulit to and from the screen and the light: shadow puppets touching the screen create a dark, well-defined, puppet-size shadow; while pulling the puppet away from the screen, towards the light source creates a very large, ethereal shadow.

In the past, the audience typically watched the show from the shadow side of the screen; spectators viewed the shadows, not the physical wayang figure, nor the performers. For many viewers the shadows are the most dramatic visual aspect of the wayang performance. But traditional performances were often informal, and audiences would walk around the screen to see all the action that took place behind the scenes—the dhalang, the wayang, and the gamelan musicians. However, this practice changed around 1945, the year when Sukarno (Indonesia's first president) took office. Sukarno encouraged the audience to watch wayang performances from the dhalang's side of the screen—the puppet side.[41] This remains the standard practice today. In fact, sometimes the screen is actually pushed up against a wall and the audience is prevented from watching the show from the shadow side.

Some see this shift in preference (the shift away from watching performances from the shadow side to watching performances from the dhalang's side of the screen) as an indication of serious philosophical changes in society. The shadow has traditionally been seen as a reflection, or shadow, of life—and some may say that the shadow is the soul. Today's preference to watch from the puppeteer's side, that is, to watch the performance of the physical puppets instead of only watching the shadows, may reveal a modern tendency to see, or a desire to experience, the immediate physical world, rather than an interest in reflecting on some deeper concept, like the state of the soul.[42]

Happily, the soul of wayang has not been completely lost, for there are still viewers who enjoy watching the shadows. Only nowadays, as mentioned, the majority of the viewers watch the performance from the dhalang's side of the screen, and those who wish to view the dancing shadows without the distraction of the dhalang, the wayang, and the gamelan

Fig. 36
Ki Enthus Susmono brings the puppet closer to the screen to produce a smaller, finer shadow. Photograph by the author, Patih, June 13, 2009.

Fig.36

Fig. 37
Ki Seno of Yogyakarta performs in Bantul. He creates grand, striking shadows by holding the *wayang* figure close to the light (away from the screen). Photograph by the author, Bantul, June 20, 2009.

Fig.37

must walk around to the "shadow side of the screen." Plus, the shadows are still an integral part of the performance, and still a prominent feature, even if the audience can only see them from the dhalang's side of the screen.

Occasions for Performance

Wayang kulit performances may occur for many reasons. They may be sponsored by an individual, a family, an organization, or by the government, as part of a broader celebration or ritual event.[43] Examples of the occasions for performances are almost limitless. Wayang performances can commemorate an important event: for example to honor the marriage of one's son or daughter; to commemorate a boy's circumcision;[44] to celebrate a new entryway to a neighborhood; to celebrate a village harvest; to kick off a political campaign; to promote social service programs; to celebrate Indonesia's Independence Day; or simply to entertain an audience.

The particular *lakon* (story-episode) presented and the messages conveyed are often, but not necessarily, relevant to the celebration or commemoration.[45] For example, a performance celebrating a birth might tell the story of the birth of a heroic or admired character.[46] Special scenes such as the *gara-gara* and *limbukan* (described further below) may make reference to the occasion, or to the honorees and their families. A sponsor may request a particular story, or may request that the dhalang choose the story. However, it is not considered appropriate for a dhalang to have one favorite story, or a favorite character, because he is expected to view and treat each lakon and each wayang character with equal attention and equal favor.[47] In practice, the dhalang usually chooses the story from a broad repertoire that seems most appropriate for the event.

Performances that are sponsored for ritual celebrations are not a part of the actual ceremony. For example, wayang kulit would not be performed during a wedding ceremony; instead, the performance might occur before or after the primary event. But performances of wayang kulit are not required for such ritual celebrations: performances are elaborate and expensive affairs, and not everyone has the financial means, the time, or the space to sponsor such an event. Therefore, the ability to hold a wayang kulit performance for such occasions usually reflects the high social status of the sponsors.

Performance for "Protection"

In the past, another occasion for wayang kulit performance may have been to offer a community protection: that is, an audience might feel a sense of safety and well-being when they attend a performance. The performance itself might be perceived as a "ritual defense" during times of crisis, and the audience might believe that, during the performance, the shadow puppets and the dhalang are charmed by protective or magical spirits.[48] Today, although some may still hold these traditional beliefs, most contemporary audiences see the dhalang as a human being who is capable of mistakes. Ki Enthus Susmono explains that audiences may feel protected for logical reasons; perhaps they feel connected to the philosophies presented by the dhalang or they relate to the story, but that it is not his practice as a dhalang to offer "magical" protection. Wayang kulit may also be performed for exorcism rites (*ruwatan*), which are very serious and specialized performances that are not part of this discussion.[49] But whatever the attitude of the puppeteer towards magic, people in the audience have their own perceptions and ideas. So even when a dhalang, such as Ki Enthus, explains that he does not have special powers, some in the audience may still believe otherwise.[50]

Ki Purbo Asmoro offers further insight into the issue of protection and wayang. He confirms that in the past, the dhalang was believed to have supernatural power (and he adds there are still some dhalang today who are thought to have special powers to ward off rain and the like). But today, according to Ki Purbo, performances are more about the dhalang's ability to perform wayang well and to "win the hearts of the spectators." In other words, it is the show itself that enraptures the audience to the point where those attending may feel hypnotized and safe or protected. At the same time, Ki Purbo notes that although wayang kulit performances attract large audiences (sometimes numbering thousands of people) very rarely do riots or acts of violence occur at these performances—as they might at other large events such as rock concerts. Ki Purbo speculates that this is likely in line with the character

Fig.38

Fig.39

Fig. 38
A performance as seen from the "dhalang's side of the screen," which is the more popular side for spectators. Performance of dhalang Ki Anom Dwijo Kangko. Photograph by the author, Jebres, Solo, June 15, 2009.

Fig. 39
A performance scene by dhalang Ki Enthus Susmono, as seen from the "shadow side of the screen." Spectators still enjoy the tradition of watching shadows. Photograph by Honggo Utomo, Manyaran, June 23, 2007.

Fig. 40
The "shadow side of the screen" of this performance by dhalang Ki Enthus Susmono faces a parking lot as most spectators today choose to watch from the "dhalang's side of the screen." Photograph by the author, Patih, June 13, 2009.

Fig.40

of the spectators, who are perhaps influenced by the philosophy and perspective of the dhalang. It is not "magic," but perhaps the personal aura and authority of the dhalang are not irrelevant. It is possible that the relatively calm atmosphere at wayang kulit performances is due to the dhalang's positive influence and the example he sets for the community.[51]

Performance Setting

Although traditional performances for specific events may be sponsored by individuals, particular organizations, or the government, when these performances take place in a village, everyone is invited to watch. Regardless of who sponsors the performance or the elaborateness of the staging (as in gold-leafed palace-style wayang, or special lighting effects), these performances remain very much an art of and for the people. As such, wayang kulit performances can take place anywhere people are found—from a royal palace to a small village.

Fig. 41
Performances occur for a wide variety of reasons. In this picture, people gather to watch a performance in Solo by Ki Anom Dwijo Kangko that was sponsored by a neighborhood cooperative to celebrate the new entry-way to their neighborhood. These fancy gates are painted with batik motifs that are special to Central Java. Photograph by the author, Jebres, Solo, June 15, 2009.

Furthermore, modern wayang performances that are staged at more elite venues are often broadcast on radio or television— providing an even greater number of people with access to this art form.

The milieu of a village performance is always lively. Crowds of people gather to watch the performance and to socialize. The performance area is usually set on a platform, and the approaches to this area are full of vendors selling souvenir shadow puppets, books on wayang, balloons and toys, coffee and tea, noodles, peanuts, satay, soups, electronics and more. Games, including gambling games, are also common. Unlike formal, sit-down performances in the West, audiences of wayang kulit are not expected to remain seated throughout the performance. People get up, walk around, view the performance from both sides of the screen, talk to one another, eat, drink coffee or tea, smoke cigarettes, nap, send text messages, leave, and come back. The majority of viewers are not "tuned in" for the whole night-long performance, nor are they expected to pay attention throughout the entirety of the show. Instead, audiences depend on cues from the dhalang (for example, his language or tone of voice, special musical compositions or songs, a joke, or the entrance of a particular character onto the stage). These cues pull the audience's attention back to the performance for important scenes or for important messages.

Fig. 42
The general atmosphere at typical *wayang kulit* performances. Photographs by the author.

Symbolism in Performance

Wayang kulit performances are highly symbolic and are sometimes considered a mystical representation of the universe. For example, the wayang kulit figures themselves may represent humanity; the wayang shadow is a shadow of life, a dreamlike or illusionary world, connoting the soul; the screen may be viewed as heaven or the universe; the gedebog (the banana log puppet base) may be viewed as the physical earth. The dhalang may symbolize the "Creator" in the world of wayang; a Great Authority who draws on his spiritual beliefs and his knowledge of humanity to bring the wayang and the story to life.[52]

Within each performance, there are three distinct acts, symbolizing an individual's life cycle. The first act symbolizes youth and immaturity; the second act corresponds to middle age and one's search for the right path in the face of temptations; and the final third act connotes old age, the defeat of enemies, and the achievement of inner peace and enlightenment.[53] These acts will be discussed further below.

The Gamelan Orchestra

The gamelan orchestra is indispensable to wayang kulit; without gamelan there is no wayang kulit performance. Music supports the all-night performance almost non-stop, though the number of instruments that play at a given time within the performance may vary.[54]

The music plays a vital role in punctuating the dhalang's narration, emphasizing the puppets' movements, aiding transitions between scenes, and generally stimulating the audience's imagination and encouraging an emotional connection to the story. In essence, the gamelan orchestra helps to set the mood for various scenes. Music creates intensity during battles; levity and excitement during humorous and spirited scenes; an atmosphere of romance during love scenes; and sadness during more tragic scenes.[55]

Different *gendhing* (gamelan compositions) may be suitable for different types of action in the performance. For example, some compositions may signal the entrance and exit of particular characters to the set, while other compositions may be played during battle scenes and journeys.[56] Hence, the gamelan musicians follow the show very closely in order to sup-

Fig. 43
The bonang section of a gamelan orchestra. Photograph by Honggo Utomo, Manyaran, June 23, 2007.

port dialogue and action with their musical performance: for example, by playing loud and lively music in some scenes and quietly providing soft background music (or no music) in others. Furthermore, certain modes of music are related to a character's childhood, youth, or old age and those modes are played in the corresponding acts (*pathet*).

Some people believe that gamelan orchestras serve a higher purpose as well. Similar to the belief that wayang kulit performances offer the audience "protection," there is also a belief that gamelan music itself could ensure the safety and well-being of those in attendance.[57] Historically, gamelan instruments (particularly palace collections of instruments) and wayang orchestras were believed to be magically charged.[58] Though today this belief may not be as widespread, people are still expected to act politely towards a gamelan orchestra; the physical instruments are highly valued by the culture and even considered by many to be sacred objects, treated with great care and respect.[59]

Performance Structure

The manner in which all wayang performances unfold is strictly structured and follows a standard outline. This is not to say that wayang kulit performances remain static over time; that is far from the case. However, the traditional structure of performance is maintained for most stories, despite the infusion of unique practices, interpretations, and personal innovations that each dhalang brings to his performance. So although the plots, characters, themes, and morals may differ from lakon to lakon, the way in which the story progresses is formulaic, and remains more or less the same. This also helps explain why an audience familiar with the performance structure can drift away and then be drawn back for important or favorite scenes.

The three acts of wayang kulit performance are known as *pathet*, a term which refers to the modes of music that characterize the different acts; they are: *Pathet Nem*, *Pathet Sanga*, and *Pathet Manyara*. Each act is broken down into distinct scenes, interspersed with smaller transitional and/or sub-scenes, all of which have specific names and functions. The following is intended to provide a general idea of how a plot progresses, and summarizes only some of the main events of the three main acts and a few entertaining scenes that have become a popular part of today's performances.

When the dhalang sits before the screen, the first puppet he uses is the *gunungan,* also known as the *kayon* (a cosmic mountain or tree of life figure). This mountain-shaped puppet is manipulated to flutter and "breathe" before the screen. The gunungan/kayon begins and ends every performance, and marks the beginning and end of each plot division and scene. It can also be used to represent the natural elements (fire, water, earth, and air), natural storms, special places or physical elements within a scene, and strong emotions. Only one gunungan/kayon is required, but the current trend is to utilize at least two or three of these puppet types (and often more are used) to create very beautiful and dramatic shadow imagery. (see figure 37)

Pathet Nem

The first act (*Pathet Nem*) is always set in a particular kingdom. The opening scene, called the *jejer* scene, takes place in the king's main audience hall of a *kraton* (royal palace). The central plot of the story is revealed through dialogue between the king and his princes, chief ministers and military personnel—all of whom make grand and elaborate entrances. Following a discussion of important matters, the king either appoints a messenger to carry out his wishes or assembles an army to do so. The king then usually enters the private chambers of the palace to relay information to the queen, and to have a feast.[60] Pathet Nem symbolizes the hero's youthful innocence as he begins his life journey.

LIMBUKAN: The *limbukan*, a scene that often occurs in the second scene of the first act, involves two comedic ladies-in-waiting. The characters (Limbuk and her mother Cangik) come onto the set and engage in a dialogue, which in a modern performance is usually unrelated to the main story. In this part of the show, the dhalang typically introduces the gamelan musicians, the *pesindhen* (singers), the sponsors, the honorees, and the occasion for the performance. This marks a great departure from the dhalang's relationship with his audience during the rest of the performance—in other parts of the performance the dhalang does not address or present himself to the audience. The limbukan is different; the dhalang has a more direct relationship with his audience. The limbukan is presented as a comedy routine with much witty banter, especially between the dhalang and the singers.

Originally the limbukan may have been a scene in which a newborn baby was nursed by Limbuk, and past dhalang did not always include a limbukan in their performance.[61] The limbukan, as it is known today, was popularized by Ki Nartosabdo (1925–1985), one of the most influential wayang performers of the late twentieth century, a man who made numerous innovations that have become standards in today's wayang performance. It was Ki Nartosabdo who transformed the limbukan scene from a short dialogue between mother and

Fig. 44
Pesindhen (singers) performing with dhalang Ki Anom Dwijo Kangko. Photograph by the author, Jebres, Solo, June 15, 2009

daughter palace servants to a whole comedy routine complete with contemporary music, special guest stars, and other trendy, cutting-edge attention-grabbers.[62] Today the limbukan is typically pure entertainment and it is one of two special humorous scenes. The other, the *gara-gara*, is discussed below.

THE ARMY DEPARTS: After the limbukan, the performance returns to the main story line, which is now set in an army camp. The army receives orders and departs from the kingdom. This departure scene, which always includes a soldier who leaves on horseback, is particularly captivating. Two separate puppets (a soldier and a horse) move gracefully and simultaneously, to create the impression that the character is riding a horse. After the departure scene, the army eventually arrives in a foreign, enemy kingdom. The scene is presented from the perspective of the antagonists; discussions take place between the enemy king and his entourage in the main audience hall of this king's palace. The enemy dispatches its messengers and sends its army (usually the giants) into battle. The opposing messengers or armies meet and engage in a battle (in which there are never any casualties) before the first act ends.[63]

Pathet Sanga

In traditional all-night performances, the second act, *Pathet Sanga,* usually coincides with the midnight hour. Two especially popular scenes occur during this act. One special scene is the *gara-gara*, in which the *punakawan* star (the punakawan are clown-servants to the gods and to royalty). The other special scene is the *perang kembang* (the "flower" or "blossom battle"). Pathet Sanga symbolizes middle age and the search for meaning in life.

GARA-GARA: The punakawan characters are uniquely Javanese and do not appear in the original Indian versions of the epics *Ramayana* or *Mahabharata*. The servants of the protagonists may meet up with the servants of the antagonists to relay messages from their overlord(s). Although the *punakawan* may appear in various scenes, the gara-gara is a scene specifically for these figures; today the gara-gara is most commonly presented as a separate scene, unrelated to the rest of the story.

Each punakawan character has a personal history and set of family relationships, and these figures are often the audience's favorite characters. The character Semar, for example, is loved for his wisdom, compassion, and his sound, balanced advice (despite his homely physical appearance and his uncontrolled flatulence). In fact, Semar is so highly revered that even the gods come to him for advice, for he is actually a manifestation of the high god, Sang Hyang Ismaya.[64] Semar is usually followed onstage by his three sons Gareng, Petruk, and Bagong, in that order.

The word *gara-gara* refers to a temporary disturbance of world order caused by the distress of a hero.[65] Formerly, at least in Solo, the gara-gara would only occur when a prince or hero was in a tumultuous state of mind, or if there was chaos in the natural world. The punakawan figures would make their appearance in this period of disorder (of mind or of nature), and with their antics and poignant words, they would help the hero refocus and bring order back to the world.

Today, in essence, the gara-gara is a narrative digression that can function as exuberant comic relief or may, at least, provide mental respite by bringing the audience back to reality from its immersion in the profound story line of the performance. In this scene, the punakawan might discuss the plot of the story from a philosophical perspective, but more often they have a story of their own to tell, or have matters to discuss that are unrelated to the

Fig. 45
Punakawan, Semar (left) and his sons during the *gara-gara* scene as seen from the shadow-side of a performance by Ki Enthus Susmono. Photograph by the author, Patih, June 13, 2009.

rest of the story (such as current events, politics, or other contemporary issues). The dhalang often uses this scene to interject his personal commentary and introduce novel practices, such as the use of contemporary popular music. In fact, during the gara-gara, some dhalang even include a drum kit and keyboards in their orchestras, which are not traditional gamelan instruments.[66] If a performance is sponsored by the government, the dhalang might be asked to disseminate some information to the audience about government programs: for example, information on reforestation or family planning. In such cases, the dhalang would present the information using neutral characters such as the punakawan.

Certain rules that govern the ways in which wayang characters may move about onstage and the ways in which the figures may be positioned on the gedebog are relaxed during this scene.[67] These rules are otherwise highly regarded and are usually closely observed, even by those dhalang who push the boundaries of convention.

The presentation of this scene in its current format (that is, somewhat of an interlude, unrelated to the main story) is a relatively recent innovation. The development of the gara-gara likely comes from the Yogyakarta performance tradition, which was incorporated into Solo-style performance in the early part of the twentieth century.[68] This style of presentation is now the norm in what is generally accepted as "Solo-style" performance, and the gara-gara is expected by most audiences. (It should be noted, though, that other regional performance styles may not follow this practice)[69] Although gara-gara existed in traditional Solonese performances in the past, today's performances of gara-gara are distinguished by the scene's inclusion in every performance, and, even more so, by the length of the scene. In the past, the gara-gara may have only lasted a half hour, but today the scene can go on for two or more hours.

The end of the gara-gara scene brings the play back to the main story line, where a hero confers with someone considered judicious, such as a respected seer, or a priest. These figures are usually hermits. They discuss best tactics for overcoming evil and finding peace, and the philosophies that underpin these quests.[70]

PERANG KEMBANG/CAKILAN: Later in the performance, but still in the second act, as the characters continue on their journeys another battle is portrayed: this is the *perang kembang* (the "flower" or "blossom battle"). Despite the reference to a flower, this is not a dainty battle; characters smash into each other and flip one another around the set. The *perang kembang* is perceived as "a spiritual battle within man between good and evil".[71] The flower connotation refers to the blossoming of the characters' lives on their journey towards their temporal and spiritual ideals.[72] The hero (for example, Arjuna or Abimanyu) is referred to as a *bambangan* character; the term *bambang* implies hope or expectation, and the young hero is expected by his elders to overcome hurdles in life and achieve something great. In every wayang performance, the refined, noble hero (the *bambangan* character) fights the antagonist forces in the *perang kembang* scene. These enemy forces consist of the ogre character, Buta Cakil, and his "mafia" of other enemy ogres, giants, and demons—who together represent obstacles to spiritual goals. The *perang kembang* scene (also referred to as the *cakilan* because Buta Cakil is inevitably involved) occurs in every performance and is the tipping point between positive and negative forces. The hero always wins—he defeats the buta characters, which means he overcomes those (spiritual) obstacles and continues on his journey towards enlightenment. The *perang kembang* is usually a favorite battle scene with the public, for audiences enjoy watching the intense action and the elaborate movements of the puppets in combat. These maneuvers are often considered some of the most beautiful and compelling movements in the performance.

Pathet Manyura

Finally, events in the third act, *Pathet Manyura*, may vary according to the specific *lakon* performed and the interpretation offered by the dhalang. Nevertheless, towards the end of the act, characters come on the set as they prepare for the final battle. After a gory and brutal battle scene, the heroes (usually) win and either Bima or Anoman (depending on the story) will dance around the screen in full glory. The problem is resolved and the heroes return to the kingdom of the victor. The king meets with his entourage for a final concluding scene in which the characters discuss the events that transpired and the goals that were achieved. The performance concludes with one last appearance of the *gunungan/kayon* figure, which at the very end is stabbed it into the gedebog by the dhalang, in the center of the screen. Pathet Manyura symbolizes older adulthood, enlightenment, and one's triumph over enemies and obstacles.

The Dhalang

As the star artist of a wayang kulit performance, it is the dhalang who makes the wayang figures and the story come alive, and it is the dhalang alone who manipulates each character. The dhalang also conducts the gamelan orchestra. The art of the dhalang is usually passed from generation to generation, and today many dhalang enhance their traditional artistic training by attending a formal art school. In fact, the most renowned art schools of Indonesia offer degree programs in dhalang studies.

Dhalang (who are commonly, but not exclusively, male) must develop a wide range of complex skills in addition to their innate talents. Characteristics that define an effective and successful dhalang include possession of a powerful speaking and singing voice and the ability to express a shadow puppet's personality by using skillful sets of movements (*sabetan*) and by using a distinctive voice for particular characters. The dhalang must have a good command

Fig. 46
Dhalang Ki Purbo Asmoro conducts a demonstration performance at the Museum of International Folk Art. Photograph by Blair Clark, Santa Fe, NM, August 29, 2009.

of the complex story lines and the elaborate, poetic language used in wayang performances; further, the dhalang must be able to clearly communicate intellectual concepts and philosophical ideas, while also showing a strong sense of humor and knowledge of politics and current affairs. The puppeteer presents serious ideas about the state of the world, human nature, and the like—but he also deftly intersperses such serious material with jokes and silly songs to provide lighter moments for the audience in what would otherwise be a long night of heavy philosophical contemplation. In addition, the dhalang must have the ability to conduct the gamelan orchestra and direct the *pesindhen* (singers) throughout the performance.

Some dhalang themselves also have the skills and knowledge to carve and paint wayang figures, although a dhalang with an active performance schedule rarely has the time to do so. Therefore, he may commission the figures. If other artists make the puppets, the dhalang might oversee the work, to ensure that the puppets meet his artistic standards. The dhalang is also usually responsible for the complicated task of organizing the wayang venue: for example, by coordinating the supporting artists (musicians and singers) and the sound and light engineering, especially if the setting is particularly elaborate, or hiring someone to handle these logistics.

A dhalang can draw on over a hundred episodes (*lakon*) for his wayang kulit performance. A dhalang can (and usually does) add his own innovations, interpretations, humor, and commentary, yet he must also be careful to maintain the integrity of the story and the art form. Therefore, the dhalang must have a firm grasp of the stories he presents so that he does not stray too far from the story line (which he narrates in his own words, from his own perspective, and usually without a written script).

Singing is a major part of a wayang performance. The many song interludes, together with the extensive sections of gamelan music, are responsible for the many hours required for traditional performances.[73] The dhalang sings different types of songs to mark different events, to communicate a mood, or to augment the overall feeling of a particular scene. One type of song is the *sulukan*—a general term referring to different types of phrases sung, or chanted, by the dhalang.[74] The sulukan musically describes the setting and atmosphere of a scene—although the lyrics of the individual song might not relate directly to what is happening. That is, the text of a particular sulukan might include quotations from ancient literature that have little to do with the events taking place in the scene, but the music supporting the sulukan conveys the mood.[75]

As a storyteller, the dhalang must be able to present a story with great detail and clarity. Wayang kulit performance can be understood as an "art of speaking" that is accompanied by the physical appearance of wayang kulit.[76] As with song, different types of narration serve different purposes. Only a few examples are given here. *Janturan* is a narration that describes what is happening in the moment and involves slow, soft background music: the janturan may describe a particular scene, introduce the characters, and explain the characters' personalities. *Pocapan* is a narration that describes past, present, or future events or situations with minimal music (perhaps only the *gendér*—a metallophone used in gamelan orchestras—is played). These types of descriptive narration enhance the audience's experience by providing the viewers with information to help them visualize a more detailed scene, especially since the only objects on set are the wayang figures performed against a standard white screen.

The dhalang further shows his vocal and narrative skills in the dialogue between the wayang characters (called *antawecana*). He demonstrates a character's unique personality and status by using different voices and dialects, and by choosing the most suitable language (perhaps Old Javanese or Modern Javanese) and language level (formal, middle, or informal) for particular characters in given situations.[77] Some characters have such a distinct voice that the sound is recognizable in all performances, by all audiences, regardless of the dhalang. The character, Buta Térong (see plate 23 in the Dhudhahan I section of the catalog) is known throughout Java for his mumbled, nasal voice caused by his eggplant-shaped nose (*térong* means eggplant). Male or female, rude or polite, high-ranking or common—each wayang figure has a different personality and the tone, dialect, and pitch of the dhalang's voice changes for many of the characters.

At the same time the dhalang gives the wayang kulit performance, he is also conducting the gamelan orchestra without using eye contact or obvious verbal signals. Through practice and experience with a particular dhalang, the musicians often know what music to play and when to play it. Nevertheless, gamelan musicians also follow certain musical and verbal cues embedded within the performance: for example, they listen for certain words or phrases from the dhalang, or for special percussive effects when the dhalang strikes the hammer-like *cempala* or the metallic *kepyak* plates.[78]

The way in which wayang kulit are placed, handled, manipulated, and put into motion during a performance by the dhalang is called *sabetan*. The greater the ability of the dhalang to make the puppets walk, dance, prostrate themselves, show fear, and (perhaps most importantly) to battle one another, the more the performance, the story, and the characters come to life for the audience. And to make all of these actions conform with the tempo of the music, as the dhalang is required to do, requires a high level of skill.

As with many aspects of wayang kulit, there are special guidelines for sabetan. The movement and handling of the wayang may vary according to the personality of a particular character. Though there are many fascinating aspects of these rules for moving the wayang during a performance, only a few examples are presented here. There is a precise way to place the wayang on the gedebog during a performance: this affects the physical stance or posture of the wayang figure and its communication and interaction with the other characters. There are also specific guidelines for the way a character enters and exits a scene, and standards for how a particular character moves, behaves, and speaks. All of these guidelines help the dhalang to best show the personality and disposition of the wayang figure. For example, a bumbling giant will move and speak differently than a sophisticated and gracious knight. In other examples, some wayang characters walk with a permanent limp, some characters are infamous for suffering from chronic gas, and yet other characters exude confidence and strength in their gait.

The last aspect of sabetan to be touched on is battle. Battle scenes feature exciting action onstage as the opponents fight fiercely, thrashing and tossing one another across the battlefield. The dhalang physically batters the puppets against each other and flips them so they seem to do somersaults in the air. However, even here there are limitations to the actions that can be taken. For example, royal characters who wear a crown can never be turned upside down, unless that royal figure is a demon. Another interesting example is that low-ranked characters can never touch the head of a higher-ranked character (as determined by the age and status of a character in wayang society).[79]

One final requirement for a dhalang is that he must have the physical and emotional strength to give an entire wayang performance. As previously mentioned, traditional wayang kulit performances last all night, without any intermission or break. The dhalang remains seated, in a cross-legged position through the night; he sits facing the screen in front of him and does not even take a break for the restroom. During the whole performance, the dhalang's voice must remain strong and clear to hold the audience's attention. The work is not easy, especially when performed for such long stretches of time. The ability to simply get through the performances—let alone to perform the final scenes with as much gusto as the beginning scenes—demonstrates the stamina and strength of the individual dhalang. The eighth-generation Solo-based dhalang, Ki Anom Suroto, explains that because he has had so much experience watching performances and has been performing himself since he was fourteen years old, he is simply accustomed to enduring traditional all-night performances. In fact, Ki Anom says it is more difficult to present a short two-hour show when he performs abroad, because he has to summarize the story, the setting and the atmosphere—whereas a traditional show is less restricted with more room for interpretation and allows him to communicate the many layers of meaning inherent in wayang.[80]

Because of their abilities and philosophical insights, dhalang are highly respected within their own culture. A performance by an expert dhalang is focused and profound, embedded with "esoteric knowledge about God, the world, and nature."[81] It is no wonder that dhalang are looked upon as especially spiritual individuals. Truly, the dhalang is a master. He is a master of puppets, of shadows, of music, and of literature and linguistics. He is also a leader who has the ability to manage his own tasks and to oversee the work of others. However, the dhalang's most important role is that of teacher; his foremost responsibility is to educate people about wayang kulit—for example, the symbolic characteristics of the puppets, the philosophy embodied within the stories, Javanese cultural values, and prescriptions for a moral, ethical life.

In Java, wayang kulit is not a theater specifically designed for children, as puppet shows often are in the West. In contrast, wayang audiences are made up of people of all ages. However, performances may be best understood and appreciated by elders because the philosophies and moral dilemmas that are presented are sophisticated; "these stories and the performance of these stories speak to a lifetime of experience." [82] Nevertheless, it is the duty of the dhalang to reach all audience members, in various stages of life, so that youth, as they mature, can draw on the lessons of wayang to learn Javanese virtues and to lead lives enriched by the tradition of wayang. It is the dhalang's ability to bring the wayang and their stories to life (and to make innovations without ignoring respected traditions or changing the story line) that gives the dhalang the power to captivate his audiences and to ensure that the totality of the art form remains relevant to all generations.

Wayang Purwa: History and Repertoire

Wayang purwa refers to traditional Javanese plays that are often considered a continuum: a series of epics. The two most popular and commonly performed wayang purwa epics are the *Ramayana* and the *Mahabharata*.

History

The *Ramayana* and the *Mahabharata* are clearly literary products of India's ancient Hindu culture, and the epics may have emerged in India as far back as the eighth century BCE. These epics appeared in Java around the ninth century CE and were recited in the form of wayang kulit as an established court-based form of theater.

In Java, despite the great importance of Islam (the country is home to the world's largest Muslim population), the Indian epics have retained an essentially Hindu character and have remained a popular and significant part of Javanese art and culture.

This relationship between Javanese culture, Hindu stories, and the Islamic religion developed gradually over time. The origin of wayang kulit is unclear, but shadow puppetry may have developed in Java in pre-Hindu times for ancestor worship and animist rituals, or the art form may have originated in China or India.

Hinduism spread to Indonesia from India through trade around the beginning of the current era and remained a predominant religion of Java for a number of centuries. The Hindu stories merged with local shadow puppet traditions and created a uniquely Javanese art form. The Javanese versions of these epics are distinct and differ in numerous ways from the original Indian texts. For example, there are no comic *punakawan* characters in the Indian version, nor are there special characters like Buta Cakil or Buta Térong; *buta* and *punakawan* characters are indigenous to Java and typically appear in every performance. The names and life stories of a number of epic characters in Java differ from their Indian counterparts (sometimes the difference is slight and sometimes great). Furthermore, in the Javanese versions, the Indian stories were assigned a Javanese setting: for instance, in Java, the

Ramayana and the *Mahabharata* are closely tied to legends about the history of Java and the ancestry of the Javanese people. The wayang epics are filled with ideas specific to Java and suggest that important characters (including gods) lived in specific places in Central Java.[83]

Fig. 47
Dhalang and wayang kulit maker, I Wayan Tunjung, SSN showing the author his collection of Balinese wayang kulit. The Balinese form of *wayang* more closely resembles human form than their Javanese counterpart. It is possible that Javanese *wayang* figures had a similar, more realistic look before Islam became Java's predominant religion and *wayang kulit* became more stylized to avoid cultural and religious restrictions on the representation of the human form. Photograph by the author, Mas, Bali, June 6, 2007

Muslim traders brought Islam to the Indonesian region, and the religion slowly spread throughout Indonesia between 1200 and 1600 CE. Islam grew in popularity and became stronger, particularly in the northern coastal regions of Java after the fall of the Majapahit Empire (the last great Hindu empire in Java) and with the rise of the Mataram Empire (between the sixteenth and seventeenth centuries).[84] However, many Javanese people held onto certain Hindu and animist traditions that were intertwined with Javanese culture. Conflict emerged between those followers of Islam who stayed close to the religion's Middle Eastern roots, and those who wanted to maintain elements of Javanese cultural traditions. The Nine *Wali* (Muslim saints who helped spread Islamic teachings in the fifteenth and sixteenth centuries) sought to resolve the issue.[85] One of these saints, Sunan Kalijaga (also known as Raden Mas Said), a prominent Wali from Java, drew on established elements of Javanese art and culture in order to encourage the spread of Islam on the island. Wayang kulit was accepted and used as one way to convey Islamic teachings, allowing Javanese people to convert to Islam without losing their heritage.[86]

It is likely that during the period of Islamization in Java, wayang kulit took on their current physical form. In their original form, the Javanese figures may have resembled the relatively realistic relief sculptures on Hindu temples in East Java, which date between the tenth and fourteenth centuries or the wayang kulit figures found today in Bali, where Hinduism is still the main religion.[87] After Islam became the predominant religion of Java, the puppets' appearance changed to the stylized version used today, in order to avoid cultural and religious restrictions on the representation of the human form.[88]

In addition to the physical appearance of wayang, Islam also influenced the wayang stories. Wayang stories in contemporary Java, though Hindu in nature, include values and philosophies that are important in Islam. And, according to Ki Purbo Asmoro, in some contemporary wayang scenes (in certain lakon), the Hindu gods are not presented as godlike, sacred figures, but are merely special figures who "reside in heaven." Ki Purbo further points out that the Hindu gods are not always portrayed in the best light. That is, they scheme, they have faults, and they sometimes behave like children—behaviors that are not associated with God.[89] Moreover, today, in Java, the stories are generally appreciated not as a religious text, but rather as important legends and valued literature; the Hindu gods are viewed as cultural icons and heroes, not as holy figures to be worshipped. Therefore, the wayang stories (that include multiple Hindu gods) do not conflict with the core Islamic belief in one God.

Literary Cycles

The wayang epics comprise well over one hundred *lakon* (distinct and self-contained, yet related episodes). Each episode is presented in a single nine-hour performance in Central

Java. Wayang stories are characteristically about the moral and ethical dilemmas faced by heroes and their antagonists in love, in war, and in the greater journey of life. To say the subject of the stories is good versus evil is true—but it is also a great oversimplification. The epics explore the existential struggle between right and wrong with great sophistication and in great depth. The stories consider the ways to live a virtuous, noble life and they search for the meaning of life. But the plays do not give clear cut solutions to these classic human philosophical challenges. Because good characters may possess negative traits and because not all bad characters are entirely immoral, we sometimes empathize with the villain; and we are sometimes disappointed in the behaviors and decisions made by the hero. Whatever the circumstances of the characters, wayang stories always ask compelling truth-seeking questions.

Wayang purwa is considered the "first generation" of epics.[90] As noted above, the most commonly performed cycles of wayang purwa are the *Ramayana* and the *Mahabharata*. The latter is more frequently requested for wayang kulit because it includes the most lakon, and the great number of episodes offers many choices and allows more room for interpretation by the dhalang. The following paragraphs are only very simple summaries of these very complex epic stories.

The *Mahabharata* is a complex story full of family feuds, political action, love triangles, gruesome battles, and terrible wars that occur over many generations. Throughout this epic tale, heroes and villains seek truth and face major moral dilemmas. In the course of the story, the characters have great adventures and learn important life lessons.

The *Mahabharata* focuses on the lives of the five righteous Pandhawa brothers and their erring cousins, the hundred Kurawa brothers. The Pandhawa heroes are the sons of Pandhu Déwanata, King of Hastina, who died young; they are the rightful heirs to the Hastina Kingdom. The antagonist characters in this story are the Kurawas, the children of Drestarastra (Pandhu's blind brother) who succeeded Pandhu as King. When both groups of brothers came of age, King Drestarastra was supposed to give the crown to Puntadéwa, Pandhu's eldest son. However, Drestarastra unjustly gave his hundred impetuous children control of the Kingdom of Hastina, naming his eldest, Duryudana, the king.

Although they are the villains of the story, not all of the Kurawas (or the characters who side with them) are entirely bad or immoral characters—and a number of these characters find themselves in rather tragic situations. As a whole, the Kurawas represent the flaws of humankind. The cousins' hostility and aggression towards each other—and their dispute over power in Hastina—culminate in a great war, called the Bharatayuda. In the end, the Pandhawas prevail. It is because they are symbols of justice, virtue, and spiritual purity that the eventual victory of the Pandhawas is assured: it is the will of the gods.

The *Ramayana* is a story about a kidnapping that involves romance, adventure, battle, and swashbuckling heroism. Prince Rama is the hero of this morality tale. The hero was banished from his kingdom, Ayodya, to the forest for fourteen years, along with his wife, Sinta, and his half-brother, Laksmana. Rama's father was manipulated by his secondary wife to order this exile. While living in the forest, Rama's beloved Sinta was tricked and abducted by Rahwana, the Demon-King of Alengka, a character despised for his greed, insatiable lust, and vicious disposition. The kidnapping begins Rama's great quest to find and rescue his wife—a period of many years that is filled with numerous trials and tribulations. Rama is aided by his loyal brother and faithful companion, Laksmana, by the brave and devoted white monkey-hero Anoman, and by an army of monkeys. In the story, during Sinta's captivity, Rahwana repeatedly tries to seduce her, but the villain is always unsuccessful. As the story progresses, the villains are defeated, the evil Rahwana is killed, and Sinta is freed. The heroes return to their kingdom and Rama becomes King of Ayodya. But although Sinta is reunited with Rama, her fidelity is questioned. She must undergo numerous trials to prove her chastity. Like *Mahabharata*, *Ramayana* also involves numerous generations, and provides the audience with insights into the background of the characters, from a time before Rama was born. In this way, the audience comes to understand the motives of (and maybe even feel some sympathy for) the villain, Rahwana.

Another epic cycle comprises a "second generation" of wayang known as *wayang madya* or middle-period stories. This cycle of stories is about the Javanese kings that ruled after the eras of the *wayang purwa* tales. The kings are believed to be descendents of characters from wayang purwa, particularly the descendents of the virtuous Pandhawa family. The "third generation" of stories is known as *wayang gedhog*. These tales originated around the sixteenth century and tell the story of twelfth-century Javanese heroes such as Prince Panji.[91] Today, the second and third generations of wayang stories are hardly performed as wayang kulit. Instead, the stories are kept alive through other modes of performance—such as dance, *wayang beber* (illustrated scrolls), or other puppet forms (for example, flat, wooden puppets called *wayang klitik*).[92]

The Collection at the Museum of International Folk Art

In 2007, the International Folk Art Foundation purchased a set of classical Surakarta court-style wayang kulit for the permanent collection of the Museum of International Folk Art, Santa Fe, New Mexico (MOIFA). This set includes approximately 230 individual shadow puppets, made with gold and bronze leaf, which had been used in hundreds of wayang performances in Indonesia. This collection is considered a full performance set of wayang kulit by the puppeteers from whom the pieces were purchased. Although this is a contemporary set, some individual pieces are quite old. For example, the oldest shadow puppet in the collection, Bathara Indra (the god of sky and winds; see plate 2 in the Dhudhahan II section of the catalog), is from the Kartasura Era (1680–1755).

The set was assembled primarily by dhalang Ki Purbo Asmoro of Surakarta, and the framework of this catalog relies heavily on the detailed and valuable information that he provided with the collection. This information includes a character list, a basic description of the characters (identification of *wanda*; familial or political relationships; interesting comments about the character; etc.), special notes about individual wayang figures (including the names of the artists who made the puppets; place and date of manufacture; names of puppeteers who previously owned or used specific shadow puppets; and commentary on special characteristics of the wayang figure), as well as examples of lakon in which a particular character would appear (not to be read as a comprehensive list of lakon for each character).[93] The following catalog is also structured around Ki Purbo's preferences in the organization of the figures.

A modest selection of wayang kulit from the collection of dhalang Ki Enthus Susmono of Tegal is also included in this set. These pieces were all designed and performed by Ki Enthus, and he too provided information such as who made the piece, where, and when. The wayang by Ki Enthus complement Ki Purbo's collection and include some of the main characters from the *Ramayana*, popular Buta (ogre) characters, and two classic *kayon/gunungan*. The selection of these wayang figures from Ki Enthus's collection were based on Ki Purbo's original character list and his advice.

One extraordinary piece, a *kayon/gunungan* with a contemporary theme, was purchased directly from the wayang maker (who also performs as a dhalang), Ki Sukasdi of Sukoharjo,

Fig. 48
Kothak designed by Ki Purbo Asmoro (FA.2007.40.217v). Photograph by Blair Clark.

whose work is in high demand by dhalang in Central Java (see plate 34 in the Dhudhahan II section of the catalog).

This assemblage includes the wayang figures that these contemporary Central Javanese puppeteers believe are necessary to perform a significant and diverse repertoire of stories. In addition, the two dhalang (Ki Purbo Asmoro and Ki Enthus Susmono) drew on their own professional and aesthetic judgment to incorporate into the set interesting or unique wayang figures that reflected their own personal preferences. Some of the shadow puppets are unusual and rarely seen in other sets; some figures were made by well-known artists for important wayang performers. Completing the set is a beautifully hand-carved *kothak* (puppet box) in which Ki Purbo Asmoro stored his wayang kulit. Ki Purbo personally designed the motif that adorns the puppet box.

In the end, the collection presented here was put together by acclaimed Javanese dhalang—seasoned "performer-maker-scholars" with a deep knowledge of the art form as a whole. The wayang kulit in this collection were not created for outsiders, as tourist or collectors' items, but for wayang practitioners who live and breathe wayang. These experts have

Fig. 49
Ki Purbo Asmoro. Photograph by the author, Surakarta, 2007.

compiled the figures for specific purposes, and for the most part the shadow puppets have been heavily used. This factor adds immense cultural value and significance to MOIFA's collection. In addition, with so much input from the artists, MOIFA's wayang kulit collection is both a beautifully crafted set of figures and an important source of information for researchers.

The Collectors

Dhalang Ki Purbo Asmoro

As noted above, the majority of wayang in this set were acquired from the popular Surakarta-based dhalang, Ki Purbo Asmoro (b. 1961), who is known for combining an intellectual approach and traditional style of performance with humor and innovation, particularly in the clown scenes. In addition to his heavy performance schedule, Ki Purbo is an esteemed Professor in the Puppeteering and Wayang (*Pedhalangan*) program at *Institut Seni Indonesia*, Surakarta (the Arts Institute of Indonesia, Surakarta).

Each wayang kulit figure in Ki Purbo's collection was handpicked, or was personally designed and commissioned, over the course of almost twenty years. Most of the shadow puppets in Ki Purbo's collection were purchased in Central Java from other dhalang or from families of deceased dhalang. Ki Purbo carefully recorded this provenance for MOIFA. One shadow puppet in Ki Purbo's collection belonged to the late Ki Nartosabdo (1925–1985), one of the most famous and respected dhalang of all time in Indonesia (see the character, Bima, in his *wanda* Jagur; (plate 6 in the Simpingan Kanan section of the catalog).

For the wayang kulit he designs or commissions, Ki Purbo Asmoro uses a signature logo at the puppet's foot—his own name in red and green, framed by yellow scrollwork patterns.

Fig. 50
Detail of Ki Purbo Asmoro's signature logo. Photograph by Blair Clark.

The hand-carved pattern of Ki Purbo's *kothak* (see Figure 48) bears the same scrollwork motif he uses in his logo and is also found in the architectural details of his home in Solo.

According to Ki Purbo Asmoro, it is the overall form and the detail of the carving that are the most important characteristics of high quality wayang. The fineness of the painting (though important) is not as crucial to him as the form, the posture, and the way in which the characters' personalities emerge in the rawhide puppet forms. That is, even if the paint wears off a shadow puppet, the figure can still provide a spectacular shadow. In this collection, it is the shadow puppets' balance—the shape and proportions, the detail, and the weight—that satisfies him. For Ki Purbo, even the way the horn-support bends around a character's body contributes to a character's look, the way a personality is portrayed, and the feel (the balance) of the wayang in his hands.[94]

Regarding his position as a dhalang, Ki Purbo says that he most enjoys the endless opportunity to learn about wayang kulit and its performance—in fact, he says everything about the art form is interesting. The dhalang explained that even after years of study and practice, one might only partially understand an individual character (each character can involve years of exploration). There are so many aspects to wayang (the gamelan orchestra, dramatic technique, aesthetics, iconography, politics, literature, and philosophy) that Ki Purbo believes it is impossible to become bored with the art form. But beyond his scholarly interests, this puppet master is also interested in the important role a dhalang plays in society. Ki Purbo explains that a dhalang is a teacher, an entertainer, an actor, a painter, and a vocalist with a responsibility to offer moral values to his audience—even if those values are not applied to individual lives, and even if those values are not acted upon by the broader society. As he sees it, the most important aspect to being a dhalang is that he offers, or communicates, those values to society.[95]

Dhalang Ki Enthus Susmono

Also included in the set presented in this publication are pieces from the collection of the famous dhalang from Tegal, Ki Enthus Susmono (b. 1966). Ki Enthus is known throughout the archipelago for his contemporary approach to performance. His performances sometimes radically depart from tradition by mixing wayang kulit, *wayang golek* (rod puppets), dancers, and actors—sometimes Ki Enthus even reveals himself to the audience as the puppeteer or as a character in the play. Ki Enthus is also well known for his unique, contemporary style of puppet-making (for example, puppets in his series, *Wayang Orang Rai* have humanlike features, rather than the highly stylized features found in classical examples). He is sometimes referred to as *dhalang gila* (the crazy dhalang) for his many innovations—a term that was also applied to preceding wayang innovators whose performance styles gradually became the norm. Ki Enthus also performs classical wayang kulit, and it is from his classical collection that MOIFA acquired several figures that serve as complementary pieces to Ki Purbo Asmoro's collection. Ki Enthus designed and drew these meticulously executed, gold leaf pieces for his own personal use. The pieces are of extraordinary artistic quality.

Fig. 51
Ki Enthus Susmono. Photograph by Honggo Utomo, 2006.

In addition to his classical wayang examples, the Museum also acquired two of Ki Enthus's contemporary innovations (*kreasi baru*) from what he calls his *Wayang Planet* Series. These include George W. Bush and Saddam Hussein puppets that were made in 2001 and used in numerous performances that questioned the effectiveness and consequences of war.

As a dhalang, Ki Enthus believes that all his artistic skills are equally important for puppeteering: for him being a dhalang is an organic whole that requires knowledge, experience, and practice. One of the aspects that Ki Enthus most appreciates about puppeteering is that it serves as a platform for expression. For this dhalang, expressing his own views or revealing his own perspective sometimes presents problems, particularly when he finds himself challenging the government or the conventions of traditional wayang.[96] Ki Enthus Susmono has his share of critics because he pushes boundaries, yet he is a true artist with a creative vision and a master performer with clear respect for wayang. He sees his role in the world of wayang as one of motivation—of moving with the times and encouraging audiences to think while maintaining the integrity of Javanese values.

A Peek Inside the Box

The wayang kulit in the collection of the Museum of International Folk Art are not only stunning artistic creations, but comprise one of the most comprehensive and documented collections of contemporary Surakarta-style wayang in American museum collections. Because of its detailed provenance information, this acquisition holds great research potential for scholars who are interested in wayang kulit or related topics. The collection, as a whole, reflects contemporary notions of, and standards for wayang kulit, and its performance history represents important and beloved dhalang in Central Java.

Staying true to a dhalang's organization of characters, this catalog presents the wayang kulit in this particular set based on their position in the *simpingan* (that is, their position on the banana log, as they are arranged for a performance) according to Ki Purbo Asmoro.[97]

Fig. 52
George W. Bush and Saddam Hussein *wayang kulit* figures, from the series, Wayang Planet by Ki Enthus Susmono (FA.2007.17.1; FA.2008.4.1). Photograph by Blair Clark.

That is, this presentation follows Ki Purbo's organization of the wayang kulit in this set. The plates are grouped as *Simpingan Kanan* figures (those displayed to the dhalang's right); *Simpingan Kiri* figures (displayed to the dhalang's left); and the *Dhudhahan* groups (figures that are typically placed within easy arm's reach during a performance, not displayed on the banana log).

It should be noted that all sets of wayang (that is, the characters found in any given set) vary with the individual needs and unique interests of the dhalang who assembles and uses them. For instance, this set does not include figures that other puppeteers may consider essential and does include figures deemed unnecessary by others.[98] Therefore, this presentation is not intended to be definitive of wayang kulit collections; rather it serves as an example of a set used by a practicing dhalang. Furthermore, this presentation is not in any way intended as an encyclopedia of wayang characters, but merely an introduction to the characters that these figures portray; it is an overview of the characters that are found in this set.

This is, in essence, a peek inside a puppet box.

Notes

1. A gamelan includes a variety of instruments such as gongs, drums, metallaphones, xylophones, stringed instruments—and vocalists as well.

2. In the Javanese language (which is distinct from Bahasa Indonesia), *wewayangan* means "shadow"; *wewayanganing urip* means "the shadow of life."

3. Surakarta is a city in Central Java, commonly referred to as Solo; the two names are used interchangeably.

4. Personal conversation with Dr. Suyanto, S.Kar., MA, dhalang and Professor of Puppeteering and Wayang (*Pedhalangan*) at ISI-Surakarta, Surakarta, April 2007; interview with Dhalang Ki Enthus Susmono, Surabaya, June 14, 2009.

5. Interview with Ki Purbo Asmoro, dhalang and Professor of Puppeteering and Wayang (*Pedhalangan*) at ISI-Surakarta, Surakarta, June 17, 2009.

6. These hides may be utilized for a number of purposes, wayang kulit being one.

7. Interview with Suyoto, leather preparer, Bantul, May 20, 2007.

8. Personal conversation with Tri Suwarno, a wayang kulit artist, Bantul, June 2007.

9. Observation and interviews with Hadi Siswanto, Giyarno, and Rejo Sumarto, water buffalo horn artists, Klaten, June 17, 2007.

10. Observation and interview with wayang artist Riyadi Dwi Susanto, Bantul, May 20, 2007.

11. Interview with Riyadi Dwi Susanto, Bantul, May 20, 2007

12. Interviews with Riyadi Dwi Susanto and wayang artist Sukardi, Bantul, May 20, 2007.

13. Interview with Ki Purbo Asmoro, Surakarta, May 4, 2007.

14. Interviews with Thoyib, Marino, and Suyanto, wayang artists from the Wonogiri District, Eromoko, June 30, 2007. Also in Ki Marwoto Panenggak Widodo, *Tuntunan Ketrampilan Tatah Sungging Wayang Kulit* (Surabaya: PT. Citra Jaya Murti, 1990), 91–99.

15. Contemporary artists, such as dhalang (and wayang designer) Ki Enthus Susmono, are developing artistic innovations that step far outside convention. For instance, in his series, "Wayang Planet," Ki Enthus does not restrict himself to the "rules." The traditional characters in this set sport space suits and goggles and carry laser guns—yet the classical characters are clearly recognizable to Ki Enthus's audiences. Other sets by Ki Enthus, such as "Wayang Orang Rai," include figures with realistic human faces and proportions, a style of wayang that is a radical departure from tradition.

16. Ki Marwoto Panenggak Widodo, *Tuntunan Ketrampilan*, 99-101.

17. Ibid., 101-102.

18. Interview with Tri Suwarno, Bantul, May 20, 2007.

19. James Brandon, *On Thrones of Gold* (Cambridge: Harvard University Press, 1970), 50; K.R.M.H. Wirastodipuro, BcAP, *Ringgit Wacucal, Wayang Kulit, Shadow Puppet* (Surakarta: Press Solo, 2006), 435.

20. Iconography also differs from region to region.

21. Jan Mrázek, *Phenomenology of a Puppet Theatre: Contemplations on the Art of Wayang Kulit* (Leiden: KITLV Press, 2005), 53.

22. Interview with Ki Enthus Susumono, Surabaya, June 14, 2009.

23. A *jejer* scene is the beginning scene of a performance where the king meets his allies in the main audience hall of a palace.

24. Widodo, *Tuntunan Ketrampilan Tatah*, 107.

25. Interview with Ki Purbo Asmoro, Surakarta, June 17 and 18, 2009.

26. Interview with Ki Enthus Susumono, Surabaya, June 14, 2009.

27. Interview with Ki Purbo Asmoro, Surakarta, June 17, 2009.

28. The *gedebog* is a trunk of a banana tree used as a mount for displaying the wayang figures during a performance. The banana trunk is a relatively soft, spongy substance, yet is heavy enough to support the wayang kulit. The shadow puppet's handle has a pointed tip to pierce the banana log and keep the shadow puppet in place. Several logs are lined up under the screen. The *dhalang* uses the *gedebog* to mount figures to the right and left of the screen (an arrangement called *simpingan kanan and simpingan kiri*), and to set directly in front of him (in the center of the screen) those characters that are engaged in a particular scene. The characters' position on an upper or lower log defines their status.

29. Clifford Geertz, *The Religion of Java* (Chicago: University of Chicago Press, 1960), 232.

30. Interview with Dr. Suyanto S.Kar., MA, Surakarta, June 22, 2009.

31. According to Ki Purbo Asmoro the arrangement of wayang on the gedebog is based on aesthetic balance; in his opinion, characters such as Durga, Subali, and Duryudana all belong in the *simpingan kanan* (to the puppeteer's right) because that is where they aesthetically fit best into the *simpingan*. However, if temperament were the determining factor, then these characters would all go in the *simpingan kiri* (to the puppeteer's left). Interview with Ki Purbo Asmoro, Surakarta, July 4, 2007. Ki Enthus Susmono explains that the arrangement of wayang on the banana log depends primarily on proportionality, and secondarily on the preference of the dhalang. Ki Enthus notes that a character's placement may also vary from time to time and from place to place. Interview; Surabaya, June 14, 2009.

32. Interview with Ki Purbo Asmoro, Surakarta, July 4, 2007.

33. In the *Mahabharata*, Duryudana is the eldest of the antagonistic Kurawa brothers and fights against the righteous Pandhawa brothers; Bima is the second of the five virtuous Pandhawa brothers.

34. Interview with Ki Purbo Asmoro, Surakarta, June 25, 2009.

35. Brandon, *On Thrones of Gold*, 39.

36. During a performance, the *kothak* or (puppet) box used for storing wayang kulit is placed on the dhalang's left and the lid to the kothak is placed on the dhalang's right. The box and lid help keep the wayang organized during a performance. The dhalang also uses the kothak (on his left) with kepyak and cempala, instruments discussed further below.

37. Interview with Ki Purbo Asmoro, Surakarta, July 4, 2007.

38. Wayang in the *simpingan* may be pulled off the banana log by an assistant or even a dhalang during the performance, if necessary. However, most dhalang prefer not to have to do this.

39. In the past, the *blencong* (light source) was an oil lamp. The lamp was often ornately carved from wood or cast in bronze. Common forms included a *gunungan/kayon* (cosmic mountain/tree of life) and Garudha (a mythical bird). Oil lamps were very hot to work under and gave off sparks that often would singe the wayang kulit and/or the puppeteer. Today, Javanese dhalang prefer to use an electric light bulb (often placed in an ornate electrical fixture in *gunungan/kayon* and Garudha forms). In Bali (and in Java for wayang performances that occur for exorcism rituals) oil lamps are still used.

40. The placement of *pesindhen* (singers) in Solo-style performances to the right of the dhalang and facing the audience is a relatively recent development.

41. Interview with dhalang Ki Anom Suroto, Surakarta, May 24, 2007.

42. Interview with Dr. Suyanto S.Kar., MA, Surakarta, June 22, 2009.

43. Ward Keeler, *Javanese Shadow Plays, Javanese Selves* (Princeton: Princeton University Press, 1987), 5.

44. Male circumcision (*Sunatan*) is an important ritual related to Islamic ideas of purification. The ritual traditionally takes place when a boy is between the ages of ten and fourteen, although it can be held at a much younger age. Geertz, *The Religion of Java*, 51.

45. Lakon are distinct, self-contained, but related episodes of epic stories (for example, an episode from the *Mahabharata* and *Ramayana*). One lakon (episode) is presented in a singular, nine hour performance.

46. Brandon, *On Thrones of Gold*, 15.

47. Interview with Ki Anom Suroto, Surakarta, May 24, 2007.

48. Clifford Geertz, *The Religion of Java*, 269.

49. Not all dhalang are versed in the techniques of exorcism performances (*ruwatan*), which require specialized skills. Dhalang who may perform *wayang ruwatan* usually come from a special genetic lineage and are selected to be trained as a *dhalang ruwatan* by a senior dhalang of this line. *Wayang ruwatan* does not present stories from the *Mahabharata* or *Ramayana*, but instead the Javanese story, *Murwakala*.

These performances are serious matters and do not involve humor. Interview with Dr. Suyanto, S.Kar., MA., Surakarta, June 22, 2009.

50. Interview with Ki Enthus Susmono, Surabaya, June 14, 2009.

51. Interview with Ki Purbo Asmoro, Surakarta, June 17, 2009.

52. Brandon, *On Thrones of Gold*, 18; Benjamin Brinner, *Music in Central Java: Experiencing Music, Expressing Culture* (New York: Oxford University Press, 2008), 106; K. G. P. A. A. Mangkunagoro, VII, *On the Wayang Kulit (Purwa) And its Symbolic and Mystical Elements*, trans. from the Dutch, Claire Holt, Southeast Data Paper no. 27 (Ithaca, N.Y.: Cornell University, 1957), 3-4; interview with Ki Anom Suroto, Surakarta, May 24, 2007; interview with Suyanto S.Kar., MA, Surakarta, June 22, 2009.

53. Interview with Ki Anom Suroto, Surakarta, May 24, 2007; interview with Suyanto S.Kar., MA, Surakarta, June 22, 2009; Mangkunagoro. *On the Wayang Kulit*, 3–4; Brandon, *On Thrones of Gold*, 18.

54. For a thorough discussion of gamelan in the context of wayang kulit, see: Brinner, *Music in Central Java*; Sumarsam, "Gendèr Birung: Its Technique and Function in the Context of Javanese Art." *Indonesia* 20 (1975): 161-171; Sumarsam, "Gamelan Music and the Javanese Wayang Kulit," in *Aesthetic Tradition and Cultural Transition in Java and Bali*, ed. Stephanie Morgan and Laurie Jo Sears (Madison, WI: Center for Southeast Asian Studies, 1984), 105-116; Sumarsam, *Gamelan: Cultural Interaction and Musical Development in Central Java*. Chicago: University of Chicago Press, 1992.

55. Sumarsam, "Gamelan Music and the Javanese Wayang Kulit," in *Aesthetic Tradition and Cultural Transition in Java and Bali*, ed. Stephanie Morgan and Laurie Jo Sears (Madison, WI: Center for Southeast Asian Studies, 1984), 105-116; Wirastodipuro, *Ringgit Wacucal*, 439.

56. Ibid.; Brinner, *Music in Central Java*, 105.

57. Brinner, *Music in Central Java*, 98.

58. Sumarsam, *Gamelan: Cultural Interaction and Musical Development in Central Java*, (Chicago: University of Chicago Press, 1992), 7.

59. Interview with Dr. Suyanto S.Kar., MA, Surakarta, June 22, 2009.

60. Wirastodipuro. *Ringgit Wacucal*, 443; Brandon, On Thrones of Gold, 21.

61. Interview with Ki Anom Suroto, Surakarta, May 24, 2007. In the past a servant who cared for children may have acted as a wet nurse. This practice is outdated in contemporary society and such scenes are almost unheard of in contemporary wayang.

62. Mrázek, *Phenomenology of a Puppet Theatre*, 401. For a thorough discussion of contemporary aspects of wayang kulit see: Mrázek, *Phenomenology of a Puppet Theatre*; and Mrázek, *Puppet Theatre in Contemporary Indonesia: New Approaches to Performance Events*. Ann Arbor: University of Michigan Press, 2002.

63. Brinner, *Music in Central Java*, 113; David Irvine, *Leather Gods and Wooden Heros: Java's Classical Wayang* (Singapore: Marshall Cavendish International [Asia] Private Limited, 2005), 167; Brandon, *On Thrones of Gold*, 23; Sumarsam, "Gamelan Music," 113.

64. Sumarsam, *Gamelan*, 6.

65. Mangkurnagoro, *On the Wayang Kulit*, 11.

66. According to Ki Anom Suroto, 1997 saw a dramatic change in wayang gamelan musical performances when modern instruments, such as keyboards and drum kits, began to be used alongside classical gamelan instruments. These modern instruments are used by some dhalang to attract young people (particularly young men) and others who are losing interest in wayang performance. However, not all dhalang feel it necessary to go to such lengths to attract the younger generation. Interview with Ki Anom Suroto, Surakarta, May 24, 2007.

67. Jan Mrázek, Phenomenology *of a Puppet Theatre*, 366.

68. Irvine, *Leather Gods*, 167.

69. Mrázek, "Javanese Wayang kulit in the times of comedy: Clown scenes innovation, and the per-

formance's being in the present world. Part One," *Indonesia* 68 (1999): 38-128; Mrázek, *Phenomenology of a Puppet Theatre.*

70. Sumarsam, "Gamelan Music," 105–116.

71. Mangkurnagoro, *On the Wayang Kulit*, 3, quotes R.M.Ir. Sarsita (May 1932 lecture).

72. Interview with Dr. Suyanto S.Kar., MA, Surakarta, June 22, 2009.

73. Interview with Ki Anom Suroto, Surakarta, May 24, 2007.

74. Sumarsam, *Gendèr Birung*, 165; Wirastodipuro, *Ringgit Wacucal*, 445.

75. Phone communication with Dr. Sumarsam, Professor of Music at Wesleyan University, Middletown, CT, August 3, 2009.

76. Interview with Dr. Suyanto S.Kar., MA, Surakarta, June 22, 2009.

77. Wayang kulit is performed in the Javanese language. The Javanese language uses three levels of language for various social contexts. *Krama* is the highest, most formal level; *madya* is the middle level; and *ngoko* is the lowest level (reserved for intimate friends, or when someone is speaking to people of a lower status). For the most part, in wayang kulit performance, modern Javanese is used, but throughout the performance, the dhalang may also engage very formal Old Javanese. Not all Javanese audiences understand Old Javanese, so it is the responsibility of the dhalang to interpret the meaning for the audience. He may translate sections he knows the audience may not understand, or he may explain certain special word connotations. Some scenes—for example, a clown scene may also incorporate the Indonesian national language (*Bahasa Indonesia*, which is different from Javanese). In fact, Ki Enthus Susmono believes that Bahasa Indonesia should be used more often and encourages young dhalang to perform in Bahasa Indonesia so that people from all over Indonesia (not just those who speak Javanese) can understand and become engaged in the performance (lecture at Universitas Negeri Semarang. Semarang, June 14, 2009).

78. The *cempala* is a hammer-like instrument the dhalang uses to knock on the *kothak* (the wood box to the left of the dhalang that stores the puppets). The sound of the cempala is a signal for the gamelan to change tempo or play a different composition. The *kepyak* is a set of four or five bronze or steel plates hanging on the *kothak*. The dhalang bangs the plates with his foot while he sits cross-legged, thus creating a very loud and dramatic effect.

79. Wirastodipuro, *Ringgit Wacucal*, 457.

80. Interview with Anom Suroto, Surakarta, May 24, 2007.

81. Mangkunagoro, *On the Wayang Kulit*, 12.

82. Interview with Ki Anom Suroto, Surakarta, May 24, 2007.

83. Interview with Ki Purbo Asmoro, Surakarta, June 18, 2009; Ki Purbo Asmoro referred to *Pustoko Rojo Purwo*, a nineteenth-century manuscript recorded by Ronggowarsito.

84. David P. Chandler, et al., *In Search of Southeast Asia: A Modern History*, ed. David Joel Steinberg (Honolulu: University of Hawaii Press, 1987), 83; James L. Peacock, *Purifying the Faith: The Muhammadijah Movement in Indonesian Islam* (Monographs in Southeast Asian Studies; Program for Southeast Asian Studies, Arizona State University: 1992), 15-17.

85. David P. Chandler, et al., *In Search of Southeast Asia*, 83-84.

86. Interview with Dr. Suyanto S.Kar., MA, Surakarta, June 22, 2009; Personal conversation with Honggo Utomo, Director of Panglima Arts Management and Manager for Dhalang Ki Enthus Susmono, Surabaya, June 14, 2009.

87. Pandam Guritno, Haryono Guritno, Teguh S. Djamal, and Molly Bondan, *Lordly Shades: Wayang Purwa of Indonesia*, (Jakarta: PT Jayakarta Agung Offset.,1984), 7, 100–101.

88. Reid, *Southeast Asia*, 205.

89. Interview with Ki Purbo Asmoro, Surakarta, June 17, 2009.

90. Interview with Dony Suryo, Director of the Kekayon Museum, Yogyakarta, May 2007.

91. Ibid.; Irvine, *Leather Gods*, 22.

92. Wayang beber and wayang klitik are forms of wayang that are rarely performed today. Wayang beber is a form of wayang whereby the dhalang narrates (through word and song) a story presented in a scroll painting. The dhalang unrolls the scroll as the story progresses.

93. In this catalog, descriptions of *wanda* are either literal or connotative translations from the Javanese language, which differs from Bahasa Indonesia. These translations were provided from a number of sources, including Ki Purbo Asmoro, Ki Enthus Susmono, Kathryn Emerson, Dr. Sumarsam, Dr. Suyanto S.Kar, MA., and Honggo Utomo. Examples of lakon, which were provided by Ki Purbo Asmoro, were translated by Kathryn Emerson.

94. Interview with Ki Purbo Asmoro, Surakarta, May 4, 2007.

95. Interview with Ki Purbo Asmoro, Surakarta, June 17, 2009.

96. Interview with Ki Enthus Susmono, Surabaya, June 14, 2009.

97. Wayang kulit figures may be organized in other ways, depending on the story to be performed and the preferences of individual dhalang. This presentation is intended to provide the reader with one idea of how a dhalang might arrange his puppet collection for a performance.

98. For example, there are no specifically designated Drupadi or Gendari figures in this set. Instead, when those characters were needed, the puppeteer would choose a *putren* figure (a generic female character) whose physical characteristics match the specific needs of the character (the figure would have the right hairstyle or hold her head in a particular position). Male figures may also be used interchangeably as long as they exhibit the right physical features. Rama and Pandhu Déwanata, for instance, share enough such features that each could be an acceptable substitution for the other.

This section presents wayang kulit that would be set up on a banana log base, to the dhalang's right, as he sits facing the screen, during a performance. These figures are listed in order, beginning with the figure farthest from the dhalang's right (the largest), and ending with the figure closest to the dhalang's right (the smallest). Set up on the log, these figures all face right.

Simpingan Kanan

1. Brahala Putih

FA.2007.39.2

Ki Enthus Susmono Collection

Performer and Designer: Ki Enthus Susmono

Artist: Rasimin

Place and Date Made: Surakarta, 1992

Water buffalo hide and horn, water-based paint and dyes, *ancur*, gold leaf, wood

H: 126, W: 68 (cm)

Brahala Putih (Very Large White Giant) is the character Puntadéwa, the eldest of the five Pandhawa brothers. Puntadéwa is said to have white blood and the ability to transform into the fierce but rational Brahala Putih.

In the *Mahabharata* episode, "Déwa Amral" [The Story of Déwa Amral; Puntadéwa Transformed into a Giant] Puntadéwa becomes Brahala Putih to spiritually connect with the mighty Brahala Ireng (see plate 1, Simpingan Kiri), who is Kresna transformed into a furious Black Giant. Kresna and Puntadéwa are cousins and close friends. Brahala Putih is able to calm Brahala Ireng, bring him back to his senses, and stop him from destroying everything in his path. Brahala Putih also appears in "Pandhawa Pitu" [The Seven Pandhawas: The Story of Sumbadra and Srikandhi].

Brahala Putih and his counterpart, Brahala Ireng, are from the Yogyakarta tradition. Today, they are popularly used by many Solo-style dhalang who enjoy them either for display on the banana log or for use in performances.

2. **Anoman Triwikrama**

FA.2007.40.1

Performer: Ki Purbo Asmoro; also: Ki Arif Sarjono

Artist(s) unknown

Place and Date Made: Wonogiri, 1994

Water buffalo hide and horn, paint, *ancur*, gold leaf

H: 105, W: 50 (cm)

Certain wayang characters, such as Anoman, have the ability to become physically larger versions of themselves and gain extraordinary powers through meditation or when overcome by extreme anger. Triwikrama refers to this ability. In one example, transformed into Anoman Triwikrama, Anoman escapes from being burned at the stake and sets fire to the Kingdom of Alengka in the lakon, "Anoman Dhuta" [Anoman Serves as Messenger], from the *Ramayana* (the only lakon in which Anomon Triwikrama appears). Here, the Anoman figure has hair of fire and his size is larger than when he is in a normal mood.

Bima is the son of Pandhu Déwanata and Déwi Kunthi. He is the second of the five Pandhawa brothers and is known for his large physique, great strength, extreme willpower, and his deadly thumbnail—his *pancanaka*. Through lessons with the god Déwa Ruci, Bima learns the meaning of life and the secrets of the universe. To remind him to stay on the Right Path he wears a checkered cloth of black, red, and yellow (or gold). These colors represent vices that interfere with righteousness and nobility. White, the fourth color, represents positive forces and spiritual purity.

Bima and the monkey-warrior Anoman share a connection to Bathara Bayu (god of the winds).[1] Consequently, they share certain features, such as their *pancanaka*, a checkered cloth, and particular types of jewelry.

The figure of Bima portrays his strength of character, in part, through the shape of his eyes; a shape which is different from that of his brothers', but that can also be found on other wayang characters. Though Bima can be stubborn, he is devoted to and protective of his family and his people. His honesty, courage, and expert battle skills place him among the greatest heroes in the *Mahabharata*. He is a noble character and an audience favorite.

1. Bathara Bayu is said to have raised Anoman, and is said to be Bima's spiritual father.

3. **Tuhu Wasésa**

FA.2007.40.2

Performer: Ki Purbo Asmoro

Artist: Wiji Sutikno; Designer: Marsono

Place and Date Made: Sragen, 1996

Water buffalo hide and horn, paint, *ancur*, gold leaf

H: 120, W: 57 (cm)

Bima took the name Tuhu Wasésa when he briefly became King of Gilingwesi. The figure appears only in the *lakon* "Tuhu Wasésa" [Bima becomes King Tuhu Wasésa] from the *Mahabharata*.

4. **Bima, also known as Werkudara**

(*wanda* [inner mood]: Lintang)

FA.2007.40.3

Performer: Ki Purbo Asmoro; also: Ki Mauta Darsana

Artists: Wiji Sutikno (leather carver), Murdiyonto (painter); Designer: Marsono

Place and Date Made: Sragen, 2000

Water buffalo hide and horn, paint, *ancur*, gold leaf

H: 107, W: 54 (cm)

Lintang means "star," and this particular version of Bima is shown with eyes looking slightly towards the sky. Bima plays an important supporting role in many *Mahabharata* cycles, but this wayang is the central figure in *lakon* such as "Déwa Ruci" [Ruci: The Inner Spirit] and "Bharatayuda" [The Great Bharatayuda War]. The figure may be used for battle scenes, in part because his black-colored body indicates strength.

5. **Bima, also known as Werkudara**

(*wanda*: Lindhu)

FA.2007.40.4

Performer: Ki Purbo Asmoro; also: Ki Bambang Suwarno

Artist(s): unknown

Place and Date Made: unknown; acquired by Ki Purbo Asmoro in Sukoharjo, 2004

Water buffalo hide and horn, water-based paint, *ancur*, bronze leaf

H: 110, W: 49 (cm)

Lindhu means "earthquake" and the direction of Bima's glare is downward, he is watching the earth move. This version of Bima may be used to emphasize his respect for others; it is not used for battle scenes. This wayang kulit appears in the *lakon*, "Bima Suci" [Bima as Priest] and "Déwa Ruci" [Ruci: The Inner Spirit].

3

4

5

6. **Bima, also known as Werkudara** (*wanda*: Jagur)

FA.2007.40.5

Performer: Ki Purbo Asmoro; also: Ki Nartosabdo (1925–1985)

Artist: Yatna Tentrem (painter)

Place and Date Made: unknown, c. 1980; acquired by Ki Purbo Asmoro in Klaten, 1994

Water buffalo hide and horn, wood, water-based paint, *ancur*, gold leaf

H: 115, W: 54 (cm)

Jagur means "robust" or "big for one's age"; it may be used in any episode from the *Mahabharata* in which Bima appears, and is a popular version for use in battle scenes. This puppet was previously owned and used by the late Ki Nartosabdo, one of Indonesia's most famous dhalang.

6

7. **Bima, also known as Werkudara** (*wanda*: Mimis)

FA.2007.40.6

Performer: Ki Purbo Asmoro; also: Ki Bowo; Ki Manta

Artists: Wiji Sutikno (leather carver); Murdiyonto (painter)

Place and Date Made: Sukoharjo, date unknown; acquired by Ki Purbo Asmoro in Sragen, 2002

Water buffalo hide and horn, paint, *ancur*, gold leaf

H: 109, W: 56 (cm)

Mimis means "bullet," suggesting this *wanda* was invented at least after firearms existed. In this mood, Bima is fiery, strong, and fast (like ammunition) and the puppet is often used in battle scenes in *Mahabharata* stories. Bima's strength is emphasized by his black-painted body.

8. **Jagal Abilawa**

FA.2007.40.7

Performer: Ki Purbo Asmoro; also: Ki Puntana

Artist: Supena; Designer: Ki Mulyanta

Place and Date Made: Solo, 1993

Water buffalo hide and horn, paint, *ancur*, bronze leaf

H: 113, W: 50.5 (cm)

The character Jagal Abilawa is Bima in disguise. Puntadéwa, the eldest of the Pandhawa brothers, loses the brothers' kingdom in a game of dice with their cousins, the Kurawas. After this loss, the five Pandhawa brothers go into exile and conceal their identities for thirteen years. In his assumed identity as Jagal Abilawa, Bima grows his hair long and works as a butcher in the country of Wirata. This wayang appears in the *Mahabharata* episode, "Adon-Adon Rajamala" [Rajamala Enters the Ring] and "Wiratha Parwa" [The Story of the Kingdom Wiratha].

9. **Bratasena** (*wanda*: Bedhil)

FA.2007.40.8

Performer: Ki Purbo Asmoro; also: Ki Suryanta

Artist: Sriyadi

Place and Date Made: Wonogiri, 2001

Water buffalo hide and horn, paint, *ancur*, metal leaf (gold or bronze)

H: 112.5, W: 52.5 (cm)

Bratasena is Bima as he was known in his youth; his long and loose hairstyle is a clue to his age. *Bedhil* means rifle. In the *Mahabharata*, Bratasena appears in *lakon* such as "Babad Wanamarta" [The Clearing of the Amarta Forest], "Balé Si Gala-Gala" [The Firetrap Villa], and "Bima Bumbu" [Bima Served-Up as a Side Dish]. This particular piece is somewhat larger than typical depictions of Bratasena.

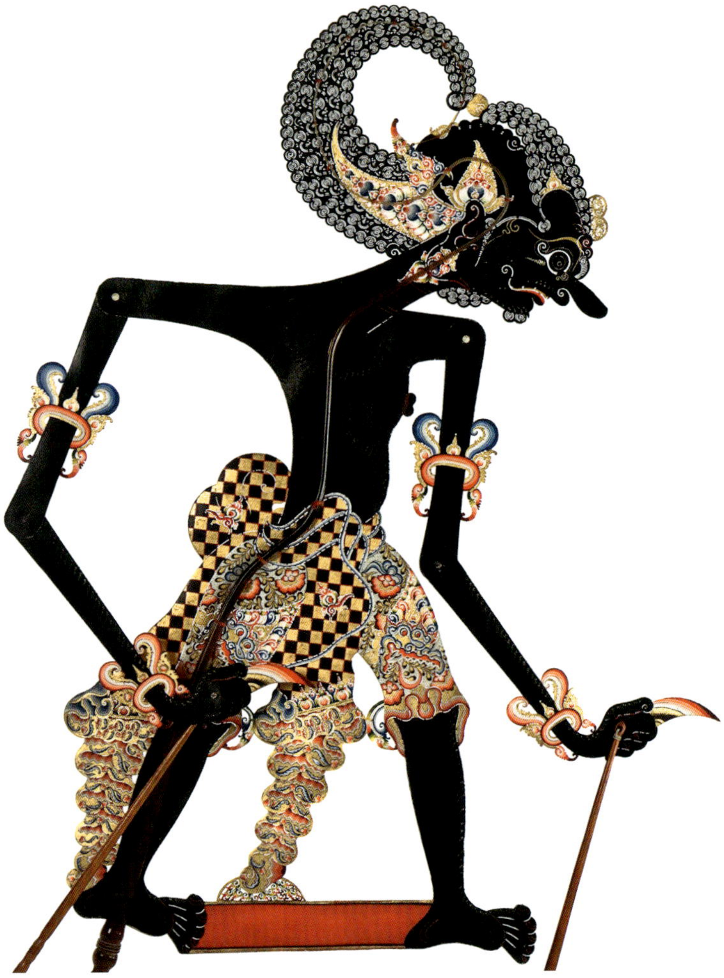

7

8

9

10. **Ramabargawa**

FA.2007.40.9

Performer: Ki Purbo Asmoro; also: Ki Purwanta

Artist: Ki Pringgo Satata

Place and Date Made: Boyolali, 1994

Water buffalo hide and horn, paint, *ancur*, bronze leaf

H: 97, W: 46 (cm)

The son of a wise and spiritual ascetic, Ramabargawa is an incarnation of the god Wisnu. He plays a prominent role in *lakon* such as "Ramabargawa" [The Story of Ramabargawa], "Kresna Dhuta" [Kresna Serves as Arbitrator] and "Lahiré Harjuna Sasra" [The Birth of Arjuna Sasrabahu].

10

Duryudana goes by other names at times, including Kurupati, Jaka Pitana, and Suyudana. In the *Mahabharata*, Duryudana is the eldest of the one hundred Kurawa children. His parents are the blind King Drestarastra and his conniving wife, Gendari (also known as Anggendari).

When he is growing up, Duryudana studies the noble ways of knighthood with the court teachers Durna and Bisma. At the time, Duryudana studies alongside his siblings and his rival cousins, the five Pandhawa brothers. However, the relationship between the two sets of cousins is plagued by conflict, competition, and deception. When he grows up, Duryudana becomes King of Hastina, though the position rightfully belonged to his cousin, Puntadéwa. The battles that ensue between the Pandhawa and Kurawa cousins eventually lead to a great war, the Bharatayuda.

12. detail

12. detail

11

11. **Duryudana**

FA.2007.40.10

Ki Purbo Asmoro Collection

Performer: Ki Purbo Asmoro; also: Ki Sunarna

Artist: Endratmi

Place and Date Made: Klaten, c. 2000

Water buffalo hide and horn, oil paint, *ancur*, imitation gold leaf

H: 101, W: 42 (cm)

This depiction of Duryudana shows him as the King of Hastina (evidenced by his crown), and the figure makes appearances in *lakon* from the *Mahabharata* such as "Bharatayuda" [The Great Bharatayuda War] and "Kresna Dhuta" [Kresna Serves as Arbitrator].

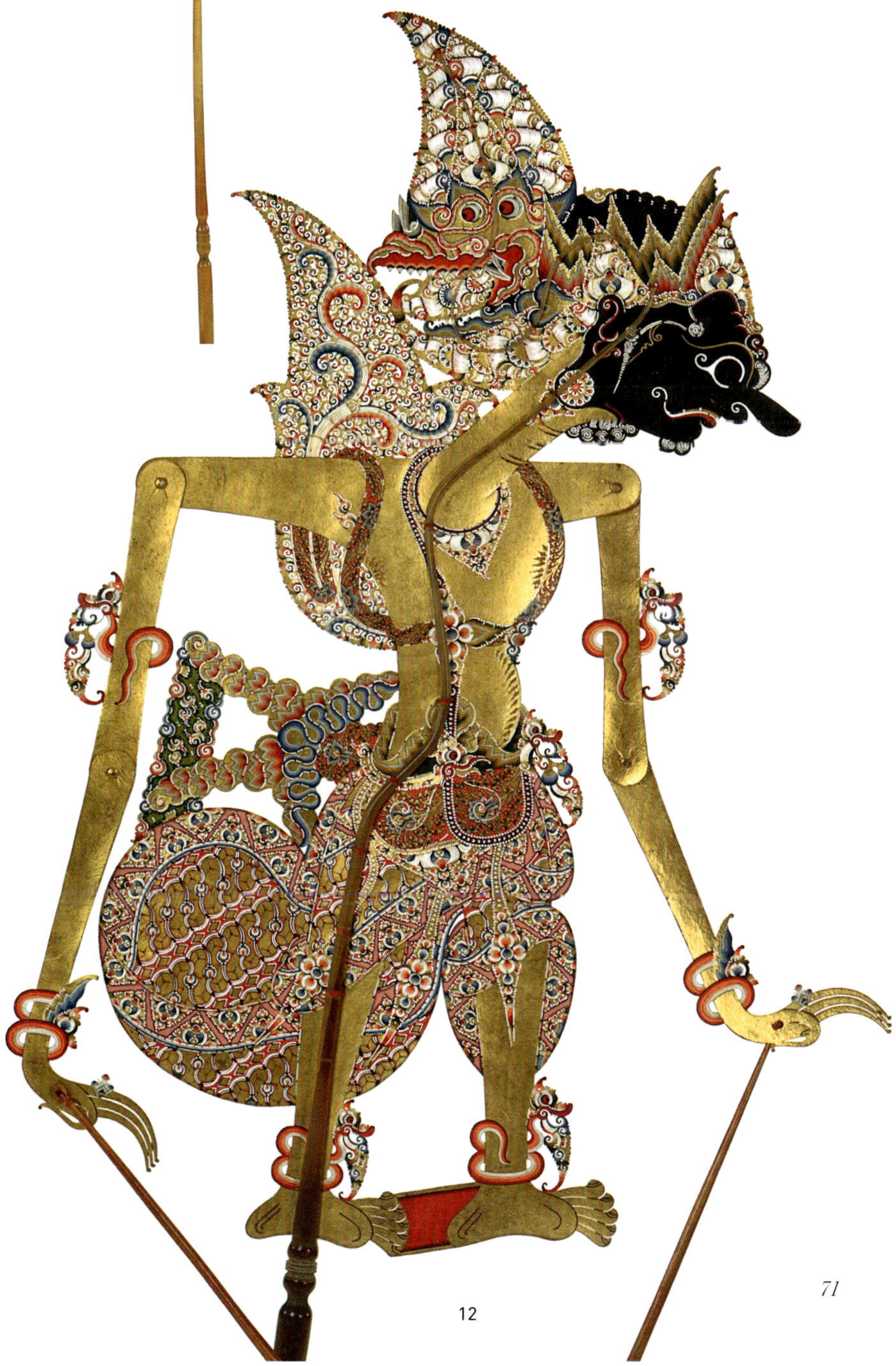

12

12. **Duryudana** (*wanda*: Jangkung)

FA.2007.40.11

Ki Purbo Asmoro Collection

Performer: Ki Purbo Asmoro; also: Ki Sudarsana

Artist: Ki Joko

Place and Date Made: Karang Anyar, date unknown; acquired by Ki Purbo Asmoro in Wonogiri, 2005

Water buffalo hide and horn, paint, *ancur*, metal leaf (gold or bronze)

H: 106, W: 46 (cm)

Jangkung means "a tall person." This puppet represents Duryudana without a crown, probably before he became King of Hastina. The figure appears in many *lakon* from the *Mahabharata* cycle of stories.

13. detail

13. **Danapati**

FA.2007.40.12

Performer: Ki Purbo Asmoro

Artist: Wiji Sutikno

Place and Date Made: Sukoharjo and Solo, date unknown

Water buffalo hide and horn, paint, *ancur*, metal leaf (gold or bronze)

H:96, W: 45 (cm

Danapati is the King of Lokapala. Although he is a large character with an imposing build, he is known for his polite disposition. He is the child of Bagawan Wisrawa, and was killed by his half brother, the terrible Rahwana. When Danapati dies, he becomes a god (Bathara Danapati). Danapati appears in *Ramayana* stories such as "Alap-Alapan Sukèsi" [The Marriage of Sukèsi], "Bedah Lokapala" [The Fall of Lokapala], and "Kembang Déwa Retna" [The Déwa Retna Flower].

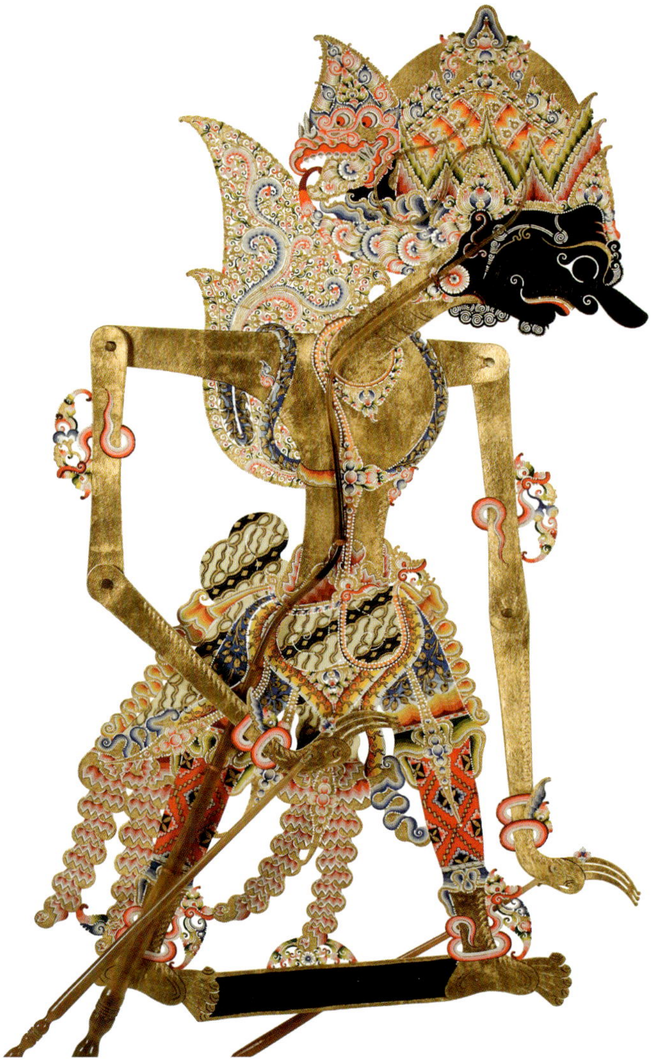

13

14. **Gandamana**

FA.2007.40.13

Performer: Ki Purbo Asmoro; also: Ki Sajali

Artist: Ki Diyo; Designer: Darmo Pithut

Place and Date Made: Klaten; acquired by Ki Purbo Asmoro in 2000

Water buffalo hide and horn, paint, *ancur*, bronze leaf

H: 88, W: 41 (cm)

This character is the son of Gandabayu (King of Pancala). Gandamana was the student of Pandhu Déwanata (the father of the Pandhawas). Gandamana is a character from the *Mahabharata* and plays a supporting role in several *lakon*. However, he plays a central role in "Gandamana Sayembara" [Gandamana Designs a Competition] and "Gandamana Luweng" [Gandamana is Buried Alive].

14

Antareja is one of Bima's children with Nagagini (Bima's wife, who is part human and part serpent), known to have the ability to walk through the earth's surface. This wayang figure belongs to a category called *srambahan*, which means it may be used for a number of characters with similar physical traits.

15

15. **Antareja**

FA.2007.40.14

Performer: Ki Purbo Asmoro

Artist: Tugimin

Place and Date Made: Sukoharjo, 2001

Water buffalo hide and horn, paint, *ancur*, bronze leaf

H: 90, W: 45 (cm)

This version of Antareja appears in *lakon* from the *Mahabharata* such as "Rabiné Antareja" [The Wedding of Antareja] and "Antareja Takon Bapa" [Antareja's Search for his Father].

16

16. **Antareja**

FA.2007.40.15

Performer: Ki Purbo Asmoro; also: Ki Heri Sutrisno

Artists: Yatna Tentrem (leather carver), Murdiyanto (painter)

Place and Date Made: Klaten, 2003

Water buffalo hide and horn, paint, *ancur*, gold leaf

H:85.5, W:41 (cm)

This is a younger version of Antareja than the previous example. It is used in *lakon* such as "Antareja Lahir" [The Birth of Antareja] and "Sumbadra Larung" [Sumbadra is Sent Downstream], from the *Mahabharata*.

In the *Mahabharata*, **Gathutkaca** is Bima's son with Arimbi. He is born to be a warrior, for his great strength and the ability to fly give him an obvious edge in battle. Like his father, Gathutkaca is known for his devotion to his family and his people, and he is particularly close with his cousin, Abimanyu.

17.detail

17

17. **Gathutkaca** (*wanda*: Gandrung)
FA.2007.40.16

Performer: Ki Purbo Asmoro; also: Ki Tristuti

Artists: Wiji Sutikno (leather carver), Diyono (painter)

Place and Date Made: Sukoharjo, 1994

Water buffalo hide and horn, paint, *ancur*, gold leaf

H: 92, W: 41 (cm)

Gandrung, means "infatuated; to fall deep in love." This version of Gathutkaca is used in the *lakon* "Gathutkaca Krama" (The Marriage of Gathutkaca)). The figure is wearing flowers in his *sumping* (ear ornaments; see detail).

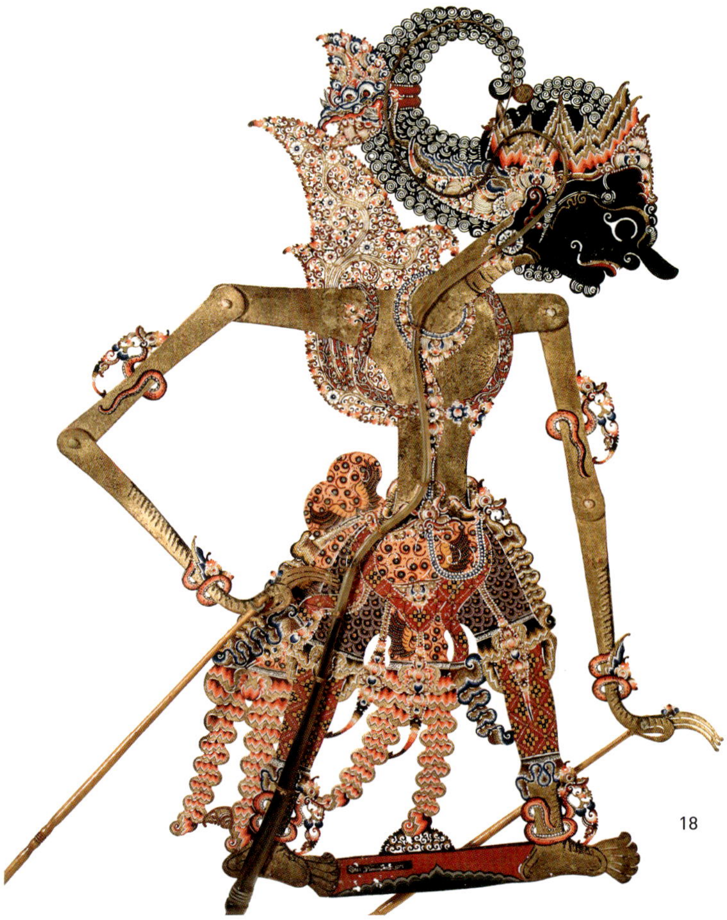

18

18. **Gathutkaca** (*wanda*: Guntur)
FA.2007.40.17

Performer: Ki Purbo Asmoro

Artist unknown

Place and Date Made: Sukoharjo, 2003

Water buffalo hide and horn, paint, *ancur*, bronze leaf

H: 91.5, W: 43 (cm)

Guntur means "thunder" and this version of Gathutkaca shows the character's strength and dignity.

19

19. detail

19. **Gathutkaca** (*wanda*: Thathit)

FA.2007.40.18

Performer: Ki Purbo Asmoro; also: Ki Sunarno; Ki Suryanta; Ki Pantono

Artists: Jono (leather carver), Sukasdi (painter)

Place and Date Made: Wonogiri (carved) and Sukoharjo (painted), date unknown; acquired by Ki Purbo Asmoro in 1989

Water buffalo hide and horn, water-based paint, *ancur*, bronze leaf, wood

H:90, W:45 (cm)

Thathit means "a flash of lightening." This version portrays Gathutkaca as quick, strong, and ready for battle, characteristics that are emphasized by the coloration of his body.

20

20. **Antasena**

FA.2007.40.19

Performer: Ki Purbo Asmoro; also: Ki Heri Sutrisno; Ki Pantono; Ki Joko

Artists: Tugimin (leather carver), Murdiyonto (painter)

Place and Date Made: Sukoharjo, 2004

Water buffalo hide and horn, water-based paint, *ancur*, imitation gold leaf

H: 84, W: 38 (cm)

Another of Bima's sons (with Urang Ayu), Antasena comes from the Yogyakarta tradition of wayang kulit but has over the years been incorporated by most dhalang who employ the Solo style. He appears in *Mahabharata* episodes.

In early chapters of the *Ramayana*, **Subali** and his brother, **Sugriwa**, become monkeys when they jump into a lake in pursuit of a magic box. Their father throws the box into the lake in a jealous rage, when he discovers that his wife has received the box from an admirer—Bathara Surya (god of the sun). The tainted water turns the boys into monkeys. Their sister, Anjani (Anoman's mother), only touches the water, thus only partially taking the form of a monkey. Subali and Sugriwa are Anoman's uncles.

After failed attempts to return to his human form, Subali is given a gift (a special mantra) by the gods to help him succeed in battle. When the villain Rahwana hears of this gift, he allies himself with Subali—and this eventually divides the two brothers. Sugriwa subsequently joins forces with Rama.

Sugriwa is the younger brother. In these wayang figures, this is shown by the extra tuft of hair on Sugriwa's forehead (compared to the Subali figure, whose hairline is receding). This pair appear in numerous *Ramayana* episodes, but star in the *lakon*, "Sugriwa Subali" [The Story of Sugriwa and Subali], which depicts the characters when they are young and have recently become apes. Ki Purbo Asmoro designed the cloth worn by these figures. An elder version of these two characters was also collected by Ki Purbo Asmoro and these are presented in the *Simipingan Kiri* section (plates 16–17) of this catalog.

21. **Sugriwa**

FA.2007.40.20

Performer: Ki Purbo Asmoro

Artists: Wiji Sutikno (leather carver), and Murdiyanto (painter); Designer: Karnodiharjo

Place and Date Made: Sukoharjo, 2000

Water buffalo hide and horn, water-based paint, *ancur*, gold leaf, wood

H: 85, W: 39 (cm)

21

22

22. **Subali**

FA.2007.40.21

Performer: Ki Purbo Asmoro

Artists: Wiji Sutikno (leather carver), and Murdiyanto (painter); Designer: Karnodiharjo

Place and Date Made: Sukoharjo, 2000

Water buffalo hide and horn, water-based paint, *ancur*, gold leaf, wood

H:87.5, W:39 (cm)

Anoman is a white monkey warrior and the commander of an army of monkeys; he is a main character in the *Ramayana* and also appears in the *Mahabharata*. The son of the god Bathara Guru and the monkey-woman Anjani (Subali and Sugriwa's sister), he symbolizes dedication, purity, and bravery; Anoman's life mission is to fight evil. He is widely recognized by his *pancanaka* (his deadly thumbnail) and checkered cloth, which are also associated with Bima and their connection to Bathara Bayu (god of the winds). Anoman and Bima also share other decorative elements, including particular types of armlets and bracelets.

In the *Ramayana*, Anoman becomes a close companion to the brothers Rama (the exiled Prince of Ayodya) and Laksmana. When Rama's wife, Sinta, is abducted by Rahwana (the Demon-King of Alengka), Rama sent Anoman to find her. After a long and dangerous search, Anoman discovers that she is held captive in Rahwana's palace. Anoman and his monkey army support Rama during many trials. When Rama finally defeats and decapitates Rahwana, Anoman places a mountain on top of the head, so that this vestige of Rahwana will be buried forever. For his valiant deeds, Anoman is rewarded with a long life.

23. **Anoman, also known as Hanuman**
(*wanda*: Barat)

FA.2007.40.22

Performer: Ki Purbo Asmoro;
also: Ki Bowo

Artists: Wiji Sutikno (leather carver), and Murdiyonto (painter)

Place and Date Made: Sragen, 1998

Water buffalo hide and horn, water-based paint, *ancur*, gold leaf

H: 83.5, W: 41 (cm)

Wanda Barat, means "wind" and depicts Anoman in shades of red, which indicates he is agitated and in battle mode. *Wanda* Barat follows the Mangkunegaran and Wonogiri style of wayang kulit.

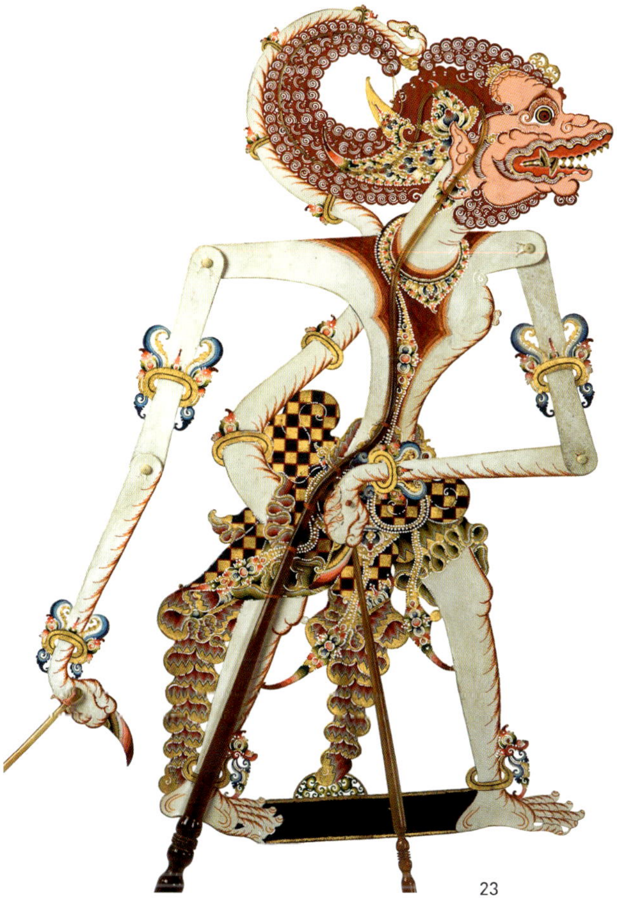

23

24

24. **Anoman, also known as Hanuman**

FA.2007.40.23

Performer: Ki Purbo Asmoro;
also: Ki Mauta Darsono

Artists: Wiji Sutikno (leather carver), and Murdiyonto (painter)

Place and Date Made: Sragen, 1998

Water buffalo hide and horn, water-based paint, *ancur*, gold leaf, wood

H: 83.5, W: 41(cm)

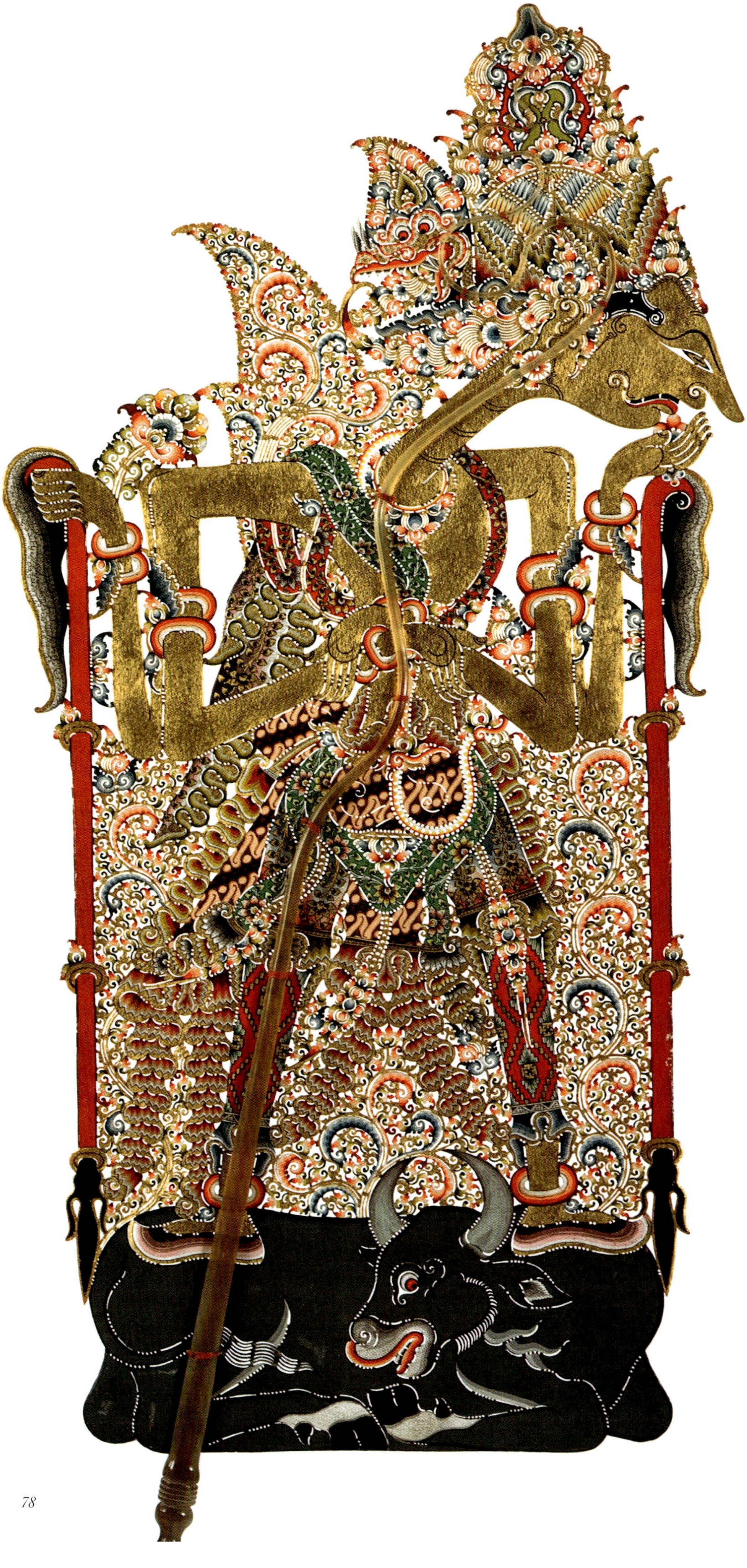

25. **Bathara Guru, also known as Siwa**

FA.2007.38.10

Performer and Designer: Ki Enthus Susmono

Artist: Rasimin

Place and Date Made: Surakarta, 1997

Water buffalo hide and horn, water-based paint and dyes, *ancur*, gold leaf, wood

H: 80, W: 29.5 (cm)

Bathara Guru is a high god whose name means "divine teacher." Like other gods, he resides in heaven. The wayang kulit figure of Bathara Guru has no articulated limbs but he is represented with four arms; he holds a trident and he rides the bull, Nandi.

26. **Bathari Durga, also known as Pramoni** (*wanda*: Gedrug)

FA.2007.40.24

Performer: Ki Purbo Asmoro

Artist: Ki Yatno

Place and Date Made: Klaten, date unknown; acquired by Ki Purbo Asmoro in 1994

Water buffalo hide and horn, water-based paint, *ancur*, gold leaf, wood

H: 81.5, W: 27 (cm)

Durga is a consort of Bathara Guru. The Javanese tradition describes Durga as the queen of the devils: she is the goddess of evil, darkness, and destruction. *Wanda* Gedrug portrays this character with her head bent downwards. The word *gedrug* means "stomping around" in Javanese, and suggests that the character is throwing a fit. This wayang figure has been used in *lakon* from the *Mahabharata* such as "Wisanggeni Lahir" [The Birth of Wisanggeni], "Sudamala" [Disease and Despair Reduced— which may also be translated as The Cleansing of Impurities], and other episodes.

26

27. **Rama**

FA.2007.38.4

Performer and Designer: Ki Enthus Susmono

Artist: Rasimin

Place and Date Made: Surakarta, 1992

Water buffalo hide and horn, water-based paint, batik pigments, *ancur*, gold leaf, wood

H: 85, W: 35 (cm)

Rama is the hero of the *Ramayana* and is an incarnation of the god Wisnu. As a young man, this Prince of Ayodya is banished to a forest for fourteen years, along with his half-brother Laksmana, and his wife, Sinta. Rama's own father, who was manipulated by his secondary wife, ordered the banishment. While Rama is in exile, his beloved Sinta is deceived and abducted by Rahwana, the Demon-King of Alengka. Rama sets off to rescue his wife. He encounters numerous adventures and engages in great wars, supported by his loyal brother Laksmana, his faithful companion Anoman, and other important allies. Rama takes different titles in different times of his life, as do many wayang characters. For example, when this hero returns to Ayodya and becomes king, he is called "Rama Wijaya" [Rama the Great].

27

27. detail

29. detail

28. **Arjuna Sasrabahu, also known as Harjuna Sasra**

FA.2007.40.25

Performers: Ki Purbo Asmoro; also: Sri Joko Raharjo

Artists: Wiji Sutikno (leather carver), Murdiyonto (painter)

Place and Date Made: Sukoharjo, 2000

Water buffalo hide and horn, water-based paint, *ancur*, gold leaf

H:81, W:31 (cm)

Arjuna Sasrabahu, or Harjuna Sasra, is the King of Maespati. He is the son of Kartawirya. This character has appeared in *lakon* such as "Sumantri Ngèngèr" [Sumantri as an Apprentice], "Sumantri Gugur" [The Death of Sumantri], and other episodes that belong to the Arjuna Sasrabahu part of the *Ramayana* cycle (set before Rama's birth).

The features and shape of the physical form of the Arjuna Sarabahu figure are such that it is appropriate to use the figure to represent other characters, such as Rama and Pandhu Déwanata (the father of the Pandhawa brothers from the *Mahabharata*).

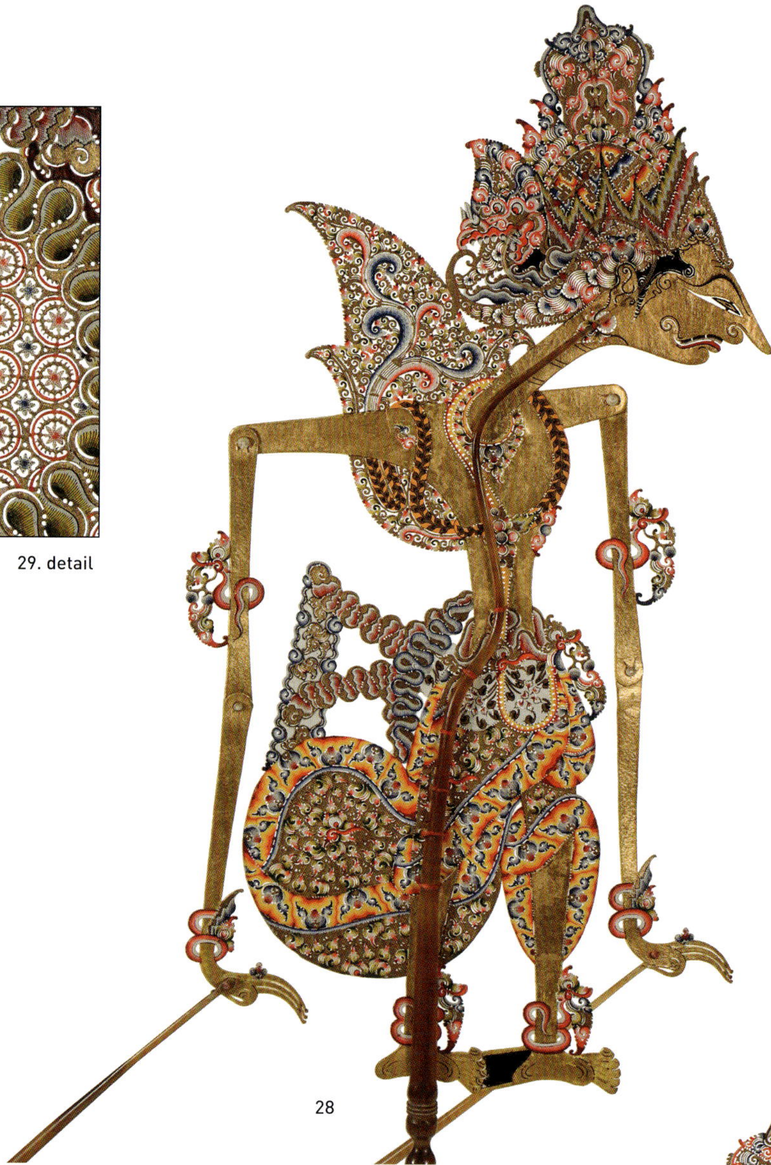

28

29. **Parikesit**

FA.2007.40.26

Performer: Ki Purbo Asmoro

Artists: Tugimin (leather carver), Murdiyonto (painter)

Place and Date Made: Sukoharjo, 2000

Water buffalo hide and horn, water-based paint, *ancur*, gold leaf

H: 80, W: 34 (cm)

This character stars in in *lakon* such as "Parikesit Grogol" [Parikesit Goes Hunting] and "Pandhawa Muksa" [The Spirit of the Pandhawa Rise to the Heavens] from the *Mahabharata*. Parikesit is Abimanyu's son with Déwi Utari, and he is Arjuna's grandson. Parikesit fights in the final wars between the Pandhawas and their cousins, the Kurawas, in the conclusion of the *Mahabharata*. Parikesit is ultimately named King of Hastina by Puntadéwa (his father's uncle) when Puntadéwa retires and enters heaven.

29

Kresna is an incarnation of the god Wisnu. Kresna is one of the most important characters in the *Mahabharata* and appears in numerous episodes.

Kresna's birth name is Narayana, and his father is Basudéwa, King of Mandura. His brother, Baladéwa, succeeds Basudéwa as King of Mandura, and his sister Sumbadra marries Arjuna. Kresna himself becomes King of Dwarawati. King Basudéwa's sister is Déwi Kunthi, the mother of the Pandhawa brothers, which makes Kresna her nephew.

More than just a cousin to the Pandhawa brothers, Kresna was also a great friend and their key advisor. Kresna is known as a skillful diplomat and an outstanding strategist. His role as advisor to the Pandhawas is assigned by the gods, who at the same time forbid Kresna to take part in actual, physical fighting.

Kresna's aim in everything he does and says is to carry out the will of the gods, whether that means manipulating a situation, breaking rules, or telling blatant lies as means to that end. His actions are always met with approval because they ensure that righteousness prevails he fulfils his promises to the gods.

30. **Kresna** (*wanda*: Rondhon)

FA.2007.40.27

Performer: Ki Purbo Asmoro; also: Ki Panut Darmoko

Artists: Wiji Sutikno (leather carver), Murdiyonto (painter)

Place and Date Made: Sukoharjo, unknown date; acquired by Ki Purbo Asmoro in Sragen, 2000

Water buffalo hide and horn, water-based paint, *ancur*, gold leaf

H: 83, W: 28 (cm)

In *wanda* Rondhon, (the word *rondhon* means "leaf"), Kresna's body is gold. This version is used in a *jejer* scene, the first scene in a wayang performance when the king meets with his allies in the main audience hall of a palace. Here, Kresna's demeanor is respectful, formal, and attentive.

31. **Kresna** (wanda: Mawur)

FA.2007.40.28

Performer: Ki Purbo Asmoro; also: Ki Joko Riyanto; Ki Tristuti

Artists: Wisnu (leather carver), Slamet (painter)

Place and Date Made: Boyolali, date unknown; acquired by Ki Purbo Asmoro in Boyolali, 1993

Water buffalo hide and horn, water-based paint, *ancur*, gold leaf

H: 80, W: 29 (cm)

In *Wanda* Mawur, the character is slightly mischievous.

32. **Kresna** (wanda: Botoh)

FA.2007.40.29

Performer: Ki Purbo Asmoro; also: Sri Joko Raharjo

Artist: Pardi (painter)

Place and Date Made: Sukoharjo, date unknown; acquired by Ki Purbo Asmoro in Sragen, 2003

Water buffalo hide and horn, water-based paint, *ancur*, gold leaf

H: 79.5, W: 30 (cm)

Wanda Botoh depicts Kresna as a supporter. He is the main advisor to the Pandhawas and he plays a major role supporting the Pandhawas during the great war, known as the Bharatayuda.

30

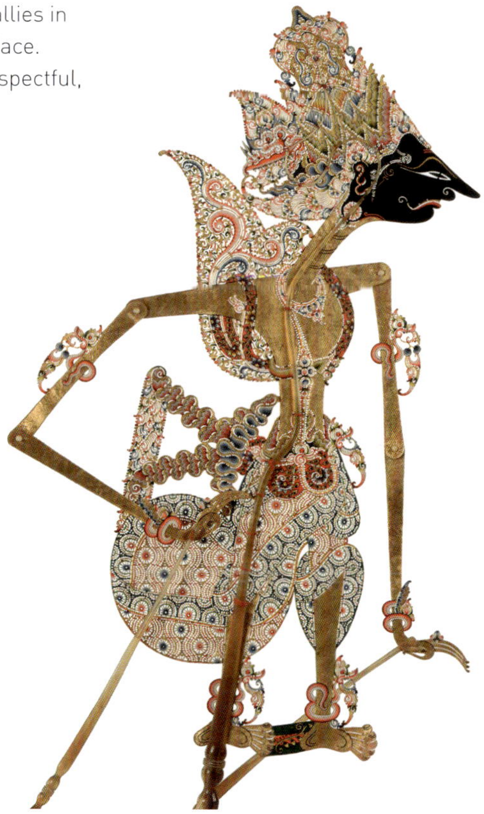

31

32

33. **Puntadéwa, also known as Yudhistira** (wanda: Panuksma)

FA.2007.40.30

Performer: Ki Purbo Asmoro; also: Ki Mulyono

Artists: Ki Mulyono (leather carver), Sukadi (painter)

Place and Date Made: Semarang, date unknown; acquired by Ki Purbo Asmoro in Semarang, 1993

Water buffalo hide and horn, water-based paint, *ancur*, gold leaf

H: 77, W: 28 (cm)

Puntadéwa (who is known as Yudhistira later in life) is the son of Pandhu Déwanata and Déwi Kunthi. He is the eldest of the five Pandhawa brothers and rightful heir to the Kingdom of Hastina, but the crown is given instead to his cousin Duryudana (the eldest Kurawa brother). Because of the rivalry between the two groups of cousins, Puntadéwa's uncle, Drestarastra, offers undeveloped land (the Amarta Forest) to the Pandhawa brothers for them to clear and build their own Kingdom Amarta. Puntadéwa becomes the King of Amarta.

Puntadéwa embodies the ideal character traits of virtuous Javanese men: he is scholarly, polite, humble, pure of heart, calm, and always just. However, he is friendly and accommodating to a fault, and his Kurawa cousins take advantage of him. Puntadéwa is tempted into an infamous game of dice by the Kurawas and gambles away the Kingdom of Amarta, all his possessions, his brothers' freedom, his own freedom, and even his wife's freedom. Nevertheless, in the end, the Pandhawas win the great war, known as the Bharatayuda and Puntadéwa becomes the King of Hastina.

Wanda Panuksma implies a state of intense meditation, with one's senses turned towards the inner soul. This version of Puntadéwa makes an appearance in *lakon* such as "Déwa Amral" [The Story of Déwa Amral], "Sesaji Raja Suya" [The Grand Offering of the Kings], and "Wahyu Dharma" [The Gift of Great Responsibility]," episodes from the *Mahabharata*.

34

34. **Sekutrem**

FA.2007.40.31

Performer: Ki Purbo Asmoro

Artists: Sadipon (leather carver), Murdiyonto (painter)

Place and Date Made: Sukoharjo, 1997

Water buffalo hide and horn, water-based paint, *ancur*, imitation gold leaf

H: 78, W: 28 (cm)

Sekutrem, the son of Manumayasa, is a scholarly sage with mystical powers whose line descends from Bathara Guru. Sekutrem is the great, great, great grandfather of the Pandhawa brothers and their cousins the Kurawas. As a skillful warrior, Sekutrem is called by the gods to defend heaven, and with his mystical powers, Sekutrem turns his enemies into magical weapons and special talismans. These items were passed down to his descendants and eventually inherited by the Pandhawa brothers.

Sekutrem appears in *lakon* such as, "Sakri Rabi" [Sakri's Wedding], from the *Mahabharata*.

35

35. **Palasara**

FA.2007.40.32

Performer: Ki Purbo Asmoro; also: Ki Toto Atmojo

Artists: Sadipon (leather carver), Murdiyonto (painter)

Place and Date Made: Sukoharjo, 1997

Water buffalo hide and horn, water-based paint, *ancur*, imitation gold leaf

H: 74.5 W: 29 (cm)

Palasara is the son of Sakri, and the grandson of Sekutrem. Palasara marries Durggandini and fathers Abiyasa, the common grandfather of both the Pandhawas and the Kurawas. He appears in *lakon* such as, "Abiyasa Lahir" [The Birth of Abiyasa] and other episodes from the *Mahabharata*.

Arjuna is the son of Pandhu Déwanata and Déwi Kunthi; the third of the five Pandhawa brothers in the epic, *Mahabharata*. Like many wayang characters, Arjuna goes by different names at different stages of his life: he is called Premadi in his youth; and Janaka in his later years. Arjuna exemplifies some of the most desirable traits of a Javanese man. He is slim and delicate in build, yet he is a consummate warrior with extraordinary archery skills, mental focus, and strength of will. To top it off, Arjuna is handsome, gallant, and attractive to women. Arjuna has a close relationship with his cousin Kresna, (advisor to the Pandhawas) who imparts to him the knowledge of the Bhagavad Gita—an important philosophy of the ways of men and gods and their relationships to one another.

Arjuna appears in many *lakon*, but he is the main character in episodes such as "Ciptoning" [Arjuna's Deep Meditation] and "Parta Krama" [Arjuna's Wedding] from the *Mahabharata*.

36. **Arjuna, also known as Janaka**
(*wanda*: Kinanthi)

FA.2007.40.33

Performer: Ki Purbo Asmoro;
also: Ki Toto Atmojo

Artist: Noto Carito

Place and Date Made: Klaten, date unknown; acquired by Ki Purbo Asmoro in Sukoharjo, 1994

Water buffalo hide and horn, water-based paint, *ancur*, gold leaf

H: 79, W: 27 (cm)

Noto Carito (d. 2004) was a well known and respected wayang maker and teacher. He left his maker's mark, a single hole punch, near this figure's eye.

Kinanthi means "accompanied by," or "to carry along." This version of Arjuna is a popular choice for dhalang, according to Ki Purbo Asmoro, because its form is flexible and it may be used in palace scenes as well as in battle scenes. This version of the character can appear in any *lakon* that involve the Pandhawa brothers.

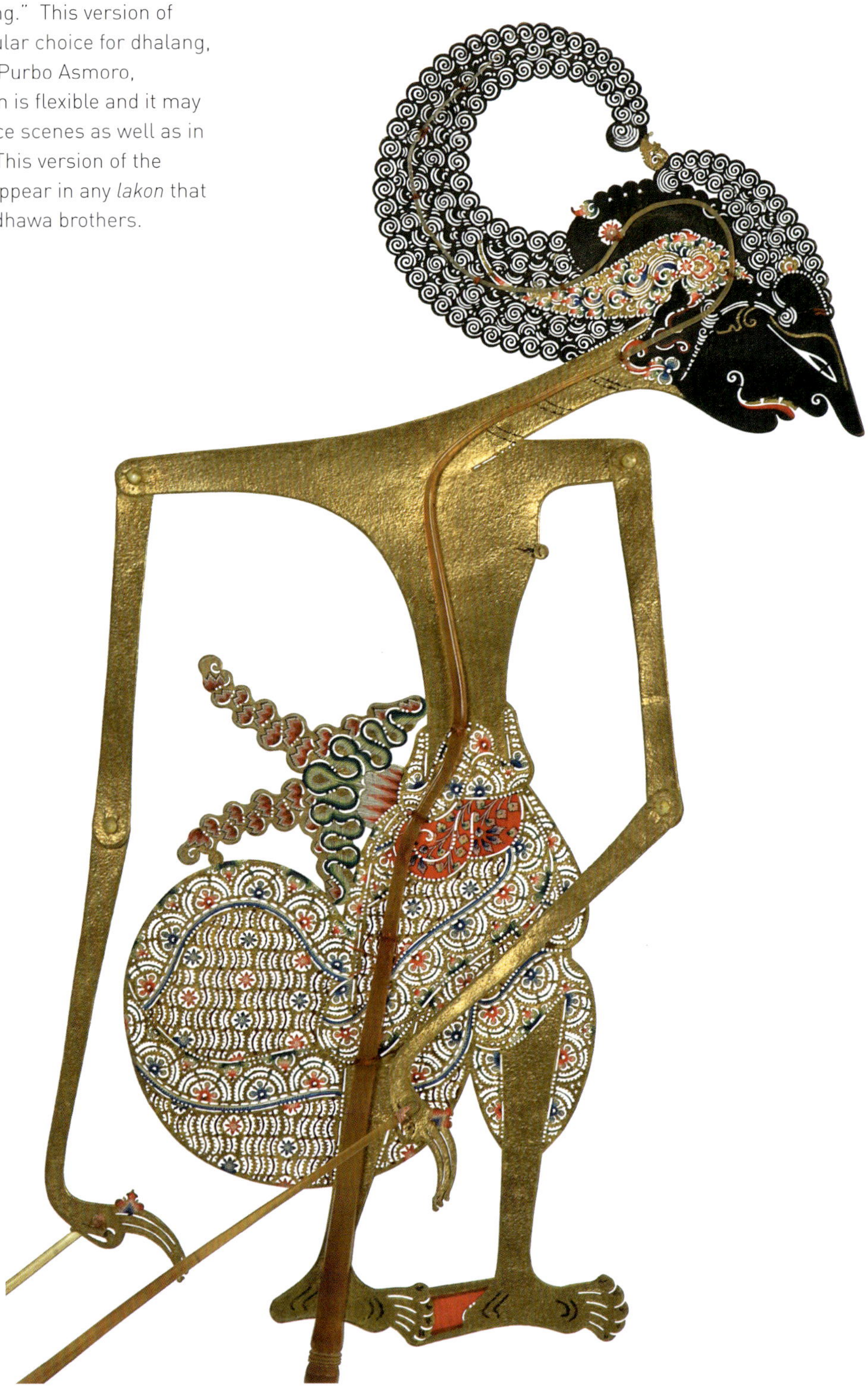

37

37. **Arjuna, also known as Janaka**
(*wanda*: Muntab)

FA.2007.40.34

Performer: Ki Purbo Asmoro;
also: Ki Puntono

Artist: Suwandi (leather carver)

Place and Date Made: Sukoharjo, date unknown; acquired by Ki Purbo Asmoro in 1990

Water buffalo hide and horn, water-based paint, *ancur*, gold leaf

H: 80, W: 27 (cm)

Muntab means "angry." In this version, Arjuna holds his head high, and compared to the other Arjuna figures, the eye on this wayang is open wide, glaring with rage. This is the version of Arjuna that might be chosen for the *lakon*, "Bharatayuda" [The Great Bharatayuda War].

38

38. **Arjuna, also known as Janaka**
(*wanda*: Janggleng)

FA.2007.40.35

Performer: Ki Purbo Asmoro;
also: Ki Suyono; Ki Sukanto

Artist: Noto Carito

Place and Date Made: Klaten, date unknown; acquired by Ki Purbo Asmoro in Sukoharjo, 1994

Water buffalo hide and horn, water-based paint, *ancur*, gold leaf

H: 76, W: 27 (cm)

Wanda Janggleng portrays Arjuna as somewhat confused, and looking downward. The artist's signature hole-punch is found near the figure's eye.

39. **Wibisana**

FA.2007.40.36

Performer: Ki Purbo Asmoro; also: Ki Mulyanto

Artist: Jono (leather carver)

Place and Date Made: Wonogiri, date unknown; acquired by Ki Purbo Asmoro in Wonogiri, 1999

Water buffalo hide and horn, water-based paint, *ancur*, gold leaf

H: 78, W: 28 (cm)

Wibisana is the son of Wisrawa and the brother of Rahwana (the Demon-King of Alengka) and Kumbakarna. When Rahwana kidnaps Sinta, both of Rahwana's brothers (Kumbakarna and Wibisana) condemn Rahwana for the act. However, only Wibisana chooses a higher moral path and fights against Rahwana in Rama's army. Wibisana is a righteous and rational character and appears in *Ramayana* episodes such as "Kumbakarna Gugur" [The Death of Kumbakarna] and "Wibisana Tundhung" [Wibisana is Exiled].

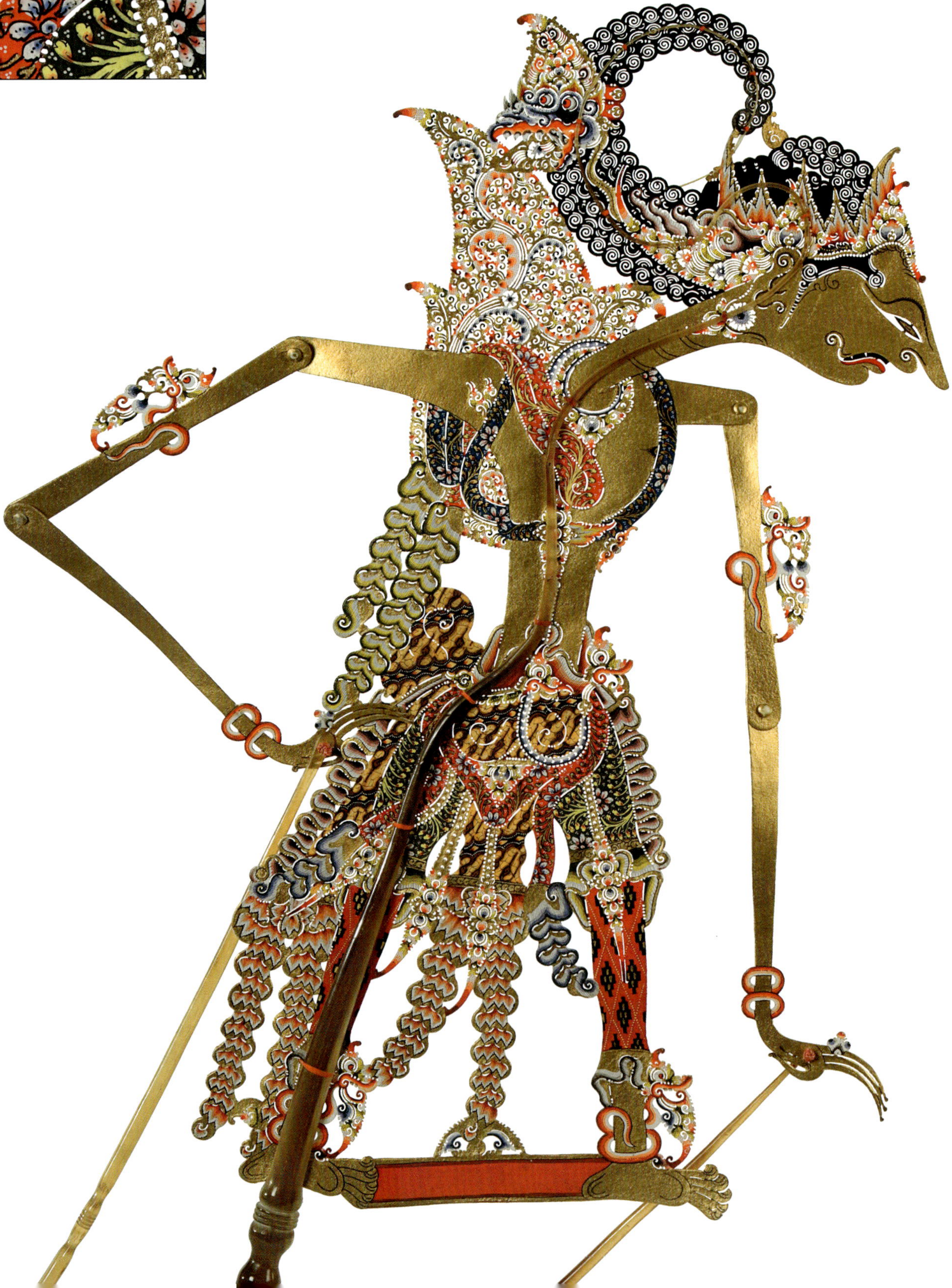

40

40. **Déwa Srani**

FA.2007.40.37

Performer: Ki Purbo Asmoro

Artist: Jono (leather carver)

Place and Date Made: Wonogiri, date unknown; acquired by Ki Purbo Asmoro in Wonogiri, 1999

Water buffalo hide and horn, water-based paint, *ancur*, bronze leaf

H: 78, W: 28 (cm)

Déwa Srani is the King of Tunggul, Malaya. His mother is Bathari Durga. The term *srani* means "Christian" in the Javanese language. This character appears in *lakon* such as "Wisanggeni Lahir" [The Birth of Wisanggeni] and "Wahyu Tohjali" [The Gift of Greatness].

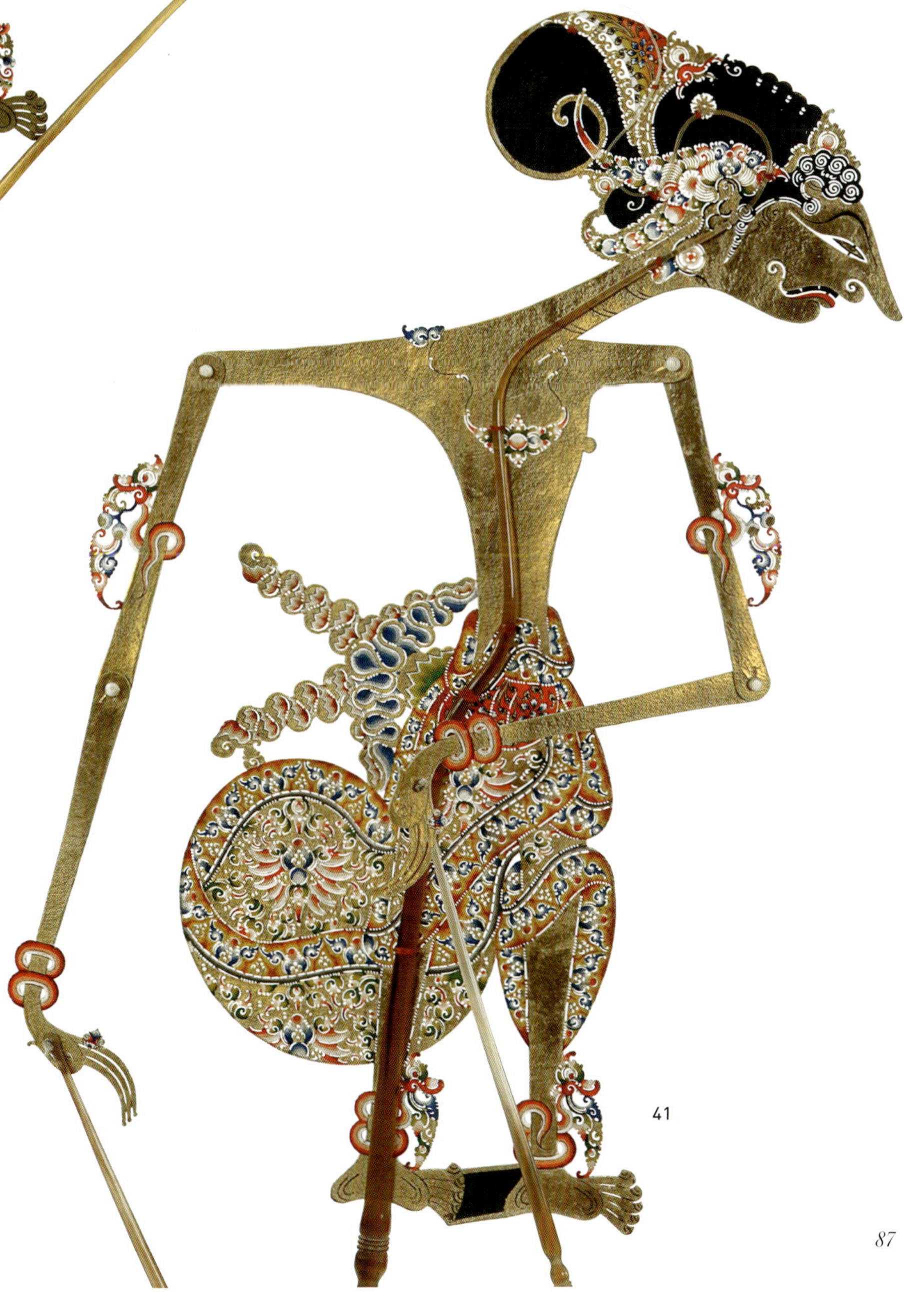

41

41. **Puntadéwa Enom**

FA.2007.40.38

Performer: Ki Purbo Asmoro; also: Ki Tristuti; Sri Joko Raharjo

Artists: Wasono (leather carver), Murdiyonto (painter)

Place and Date Made: Sragen, 1995

Water buffalo hide and horn, water-based paint, *ancur*, gold leaf

H: 77, W: 27 (cm)

Puntadéwa Enom is Puntadéwa (also known as Yudhistira) as he is known in his youth. (In the Javanese language, *enom* means "young.") Compared to his older self, Puntadéwa Enom wears more jewelry and has a different style of dress (it is not uncommon for wayang characters to dress in a more flashy fashion in their youth compared to their older ages); his face is colored gold and he also has a fuller hairline. Puntadéwa Enom is used in *lakon* such as "Babad Wanamarta" [The Clearing of the Amarta Forest] and "Gandamana Sayembara" [Gandamana Designs a Competition], from the *Mahabharata*.

Premadi is the youthful Arjuna from the epic, *Mahabharata*. Premadi wears more jewelry and has a fuller hairline than in his more mature form. The figure of Premadi is depicted with a gold or white face. *Wanda* Pengasih means "one who is compassionate." Premadi is the age-appropriate version of Arjuna in *lakon* such as "Parta Krama" [Arjuna's Wedding], "Bima Bumbu" [Bima Served-Up as a Side Dish], "Babad Wanamarta" [The Clearing of the Amarta Forest], and "Kresna Kembang" [Kresna Marries Rukmini].

43. **Premadi** (*wanda*: Pengasih)
FA.2007.40.40
Performer: Ki Purbo Asmoro
Artist: Ki Sukasdi
Place and Date Made: Sukoharjo, date unknown
Water buffalo hide and horn, water-based paint, *ancur*, gold leaf
H: 76, W: 28 (cm)

44. detail

42. **Premadi** (*wanda*: Pengasih)
FA.2007.40.39
Performer: Ki Purbo Asmoro; also: Slamet Gotri
Artists: unknown
Place and Date Made: unknown; acquired by Ki Purbo Asmoro in Boyolali
Water buffalo hide and horn, water-based paint, *ancur*, gold leaf
H: 74, W: 28 (cm)

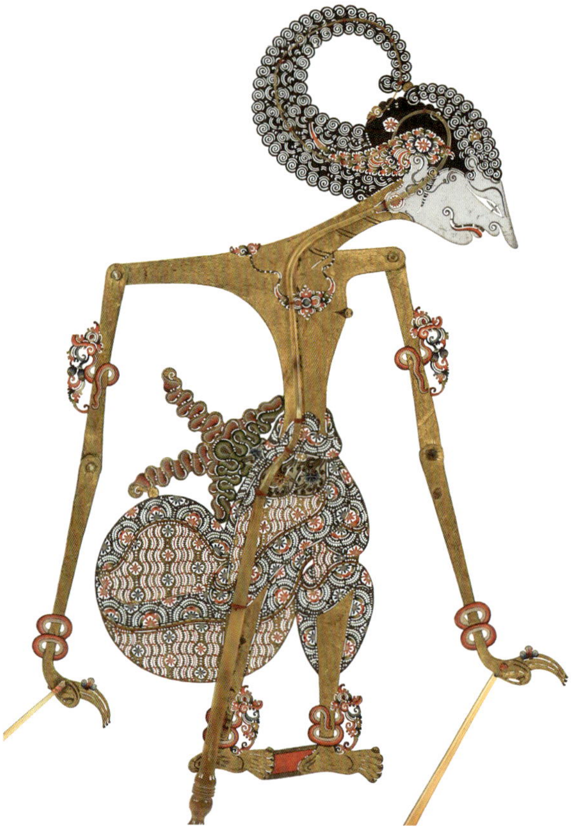

43

44. **Premadi** (*wanda*: Pengasih)
FA.2007.40.41
Performer: Ki Purbo Asmoro; also: Ki Sumarno
Artist: unknown
Place and Date Made: Wonogiri, date unknown
Water buffalo hide and horn, water-based paint, *ancur*, bronze leaf
H: 74.5, W: 28 (cm)

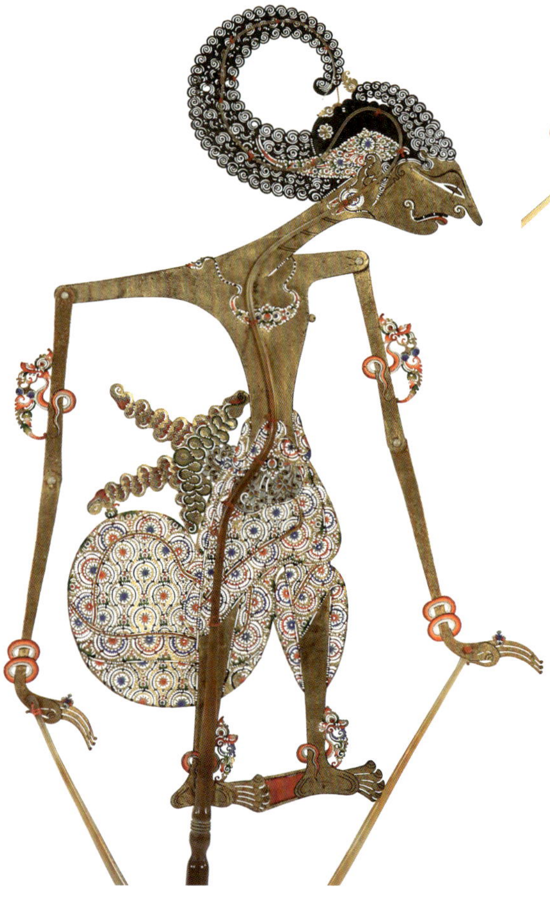

42

44

45

45. **Irawan**

FA.2007.40.42

Performer: Ki Purbo Asmoro

Artist: Tugimin

Place and Date Made: Sukoharjo, 2005

Water buffalo hide and horn, water-based paint, *ancur*, bronze leaf

H: 69, W: 25 (cm)

Irawan is Arjuna's son with Déwi Ulupi. He appears in *lakon* such as "Irawan Rabi" [Irawan's Wedding] and "Irawan Gugur" [The Death of Irawan] from the *Mahabharata*.

46

46. **Pancawala**

FA.2007.40.43

Performer: Ki Purbo Asmoro

Artists: Yatna Tentrem and Diman

Place and Date Made: Klaten, date unknown

Water buffalo hide and horn, water-based paint, *ancur*, bronze leaf

H:70, W: 27 (cm)

Pancawala is Puntadéwa's son with Déwi Drupadi. His stories include "Pancawala Rabi" [Pancawala's Wedding] and "Aswatama Nglandak" [Aswatama Digs a Tunnel] from the *Mahabharata*.

47. **Abimanyu**

FA.2007.40.44

Performer: Ki Purbo Asmoro;
also: Ki Puntana; Ki Sajali

Artist: Ki Sajali (painter)

Place and Date Made: Klaten, date unknown; acquired by Ki Purbo Asmoro in Klaten, 2000

Water buffalo hide and horn, water-based paint, *ancur*, gold leaf

H: 70, W: 27 (cm)

Abimanyu is the son of Arjuna and Sumbadra. Abimanyu's son, Parikesit, eventually inherits the crown of the Kingdom Hastina. Abimanyu, like his father Arjuna, embodies the ideals of the *satria* ("noble knights"). However, Abimanyu is tragically killed in battle. He plays a prominent role in the *Mahabharata* episodes "Wahyu Cakraningrat" [Cakraningrat: A Boon from the Gods] and "Abimanyu Ranjab" [Abimanyu is Pierced to Death] (which is also known as "Abimanyu Gugur" [The Death of Abimanyu]).

47

48. **Laksmana, also known as Lesmana**

FA.2007.38.5

Performer and Designer: Ki Enthus Susmono

Artist: Rasimin

Place and Date Made: Surakarta, 2005

Water buffalo hide and horn, water-based paint and dyes, *ancur*, gold leaf

H: 74, W: 28 (cm)

Laksmana is a main character in the *Ramayana* and the half-brother of Rama, the exiled Prince of Ayodya. Laksmana accompanies Rama through many adventures in the quest to rescue Rama's wife Sinta, who has been kidnapped by Rahwana, the Demon-King of Alengka. Laksmana is most admired for his unswerving loyalty and devotion to his brother Rama. In the Javanese adaptation of the *Ramayana*, Laksmana is celibate.

48

49

49. **Déwi Banowati** (*wanda*: Berok)

FA.2007.40.45

Performer: Ki Purbo Asmoro

Artists: Tugimin and Murdiyonto

Place and Date Made: Sukoharjo, 2006

Water buffalo hide and horn, water-based paint, *ancur*, bronze leaf

H: 68.5, W: 25 (cm)

Banowati is the daughter of King Salya of Mandraka, a noble man who nevertheless supports the Kurawas. Banowati is refined, graceful, and smart, but her life has tragic elements. She is married off to Duryudana, the eldest of the Kurawas, despite her lifelong love for Arjuna, a Pandhawa. After Duryudana is killed, she marries Arjuna, which is perceived by the Kurawas as treachery and Banowati is murdered.

Wanda Berok refers to the figure's large size. Banowati plays a role in *Mahabharata* episodes, such as "Rubuhan" [The Demise of a Kingdom] and "Gathutkaca Sungging" [Gathutkaca is Wounded].

49. detail

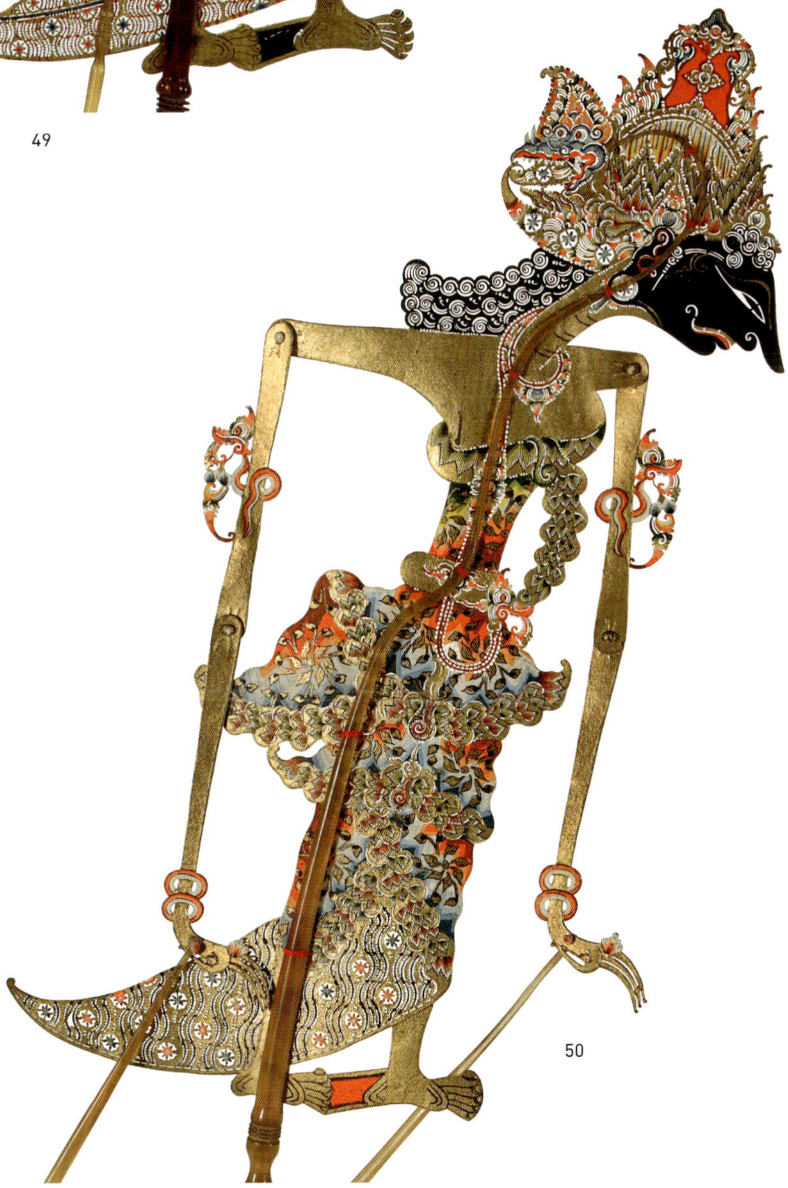

50

50. **Déwi Jembawati**

FA.2007.40.46

Performer: Ki Purbo Asmoro; also: Ki Sudarsono

Artists: Wisnu and Bambang Sucahyo

Place and Date Made: Solo, 1993

Water buffalo hide and horn, water-based paint, *ancur*, bronze leaf

H: 68, W: 22 (cm)

Déwi Jembawati is Kresna's first (primary) wife, and she is known for her absolute dedication, kindness and compassion. Déwi Jembawati is the daughter of Jembawan and Déwi Trijatha, characters from the *Ramayana*. Déwi Jembawati appears in *lakon* from the *Mahabharata* such as "Alap-Alapan Jembawati" [The Marriage of Jembawati], which is rarely performed. Jembawati also plays an important role as Sumbadra's bridesmaid in "Parta Krama" [Arjuna's Wedding], which takes place when Déwi Jembawati and Kresna are engaged to be wed.[2]

2. E-mail communication with Kathryn Emerson, wayang scholar and gamelan musician, August 18, 2009

51. **Déwi Rukmini**

FA.2007.40.47

Performer: Ki Purbo Asmoro; also: Ki Sudarsono

Artists: Wisnu and Bambang Sucahyo

Place and Date Made: Solo, 1993

Water buffalo hide and horn, water-based paint, *ancur*, bronze leaf

H: 64.5, W: 23 (cm)

Rukmini is the daughter of King Bismaka, and is one of Kresna's wives. Her main role is in the *lakon*, "Alap Alapan Rukmini" [The Marriage of Rukmini] of the *Mahabharata*.

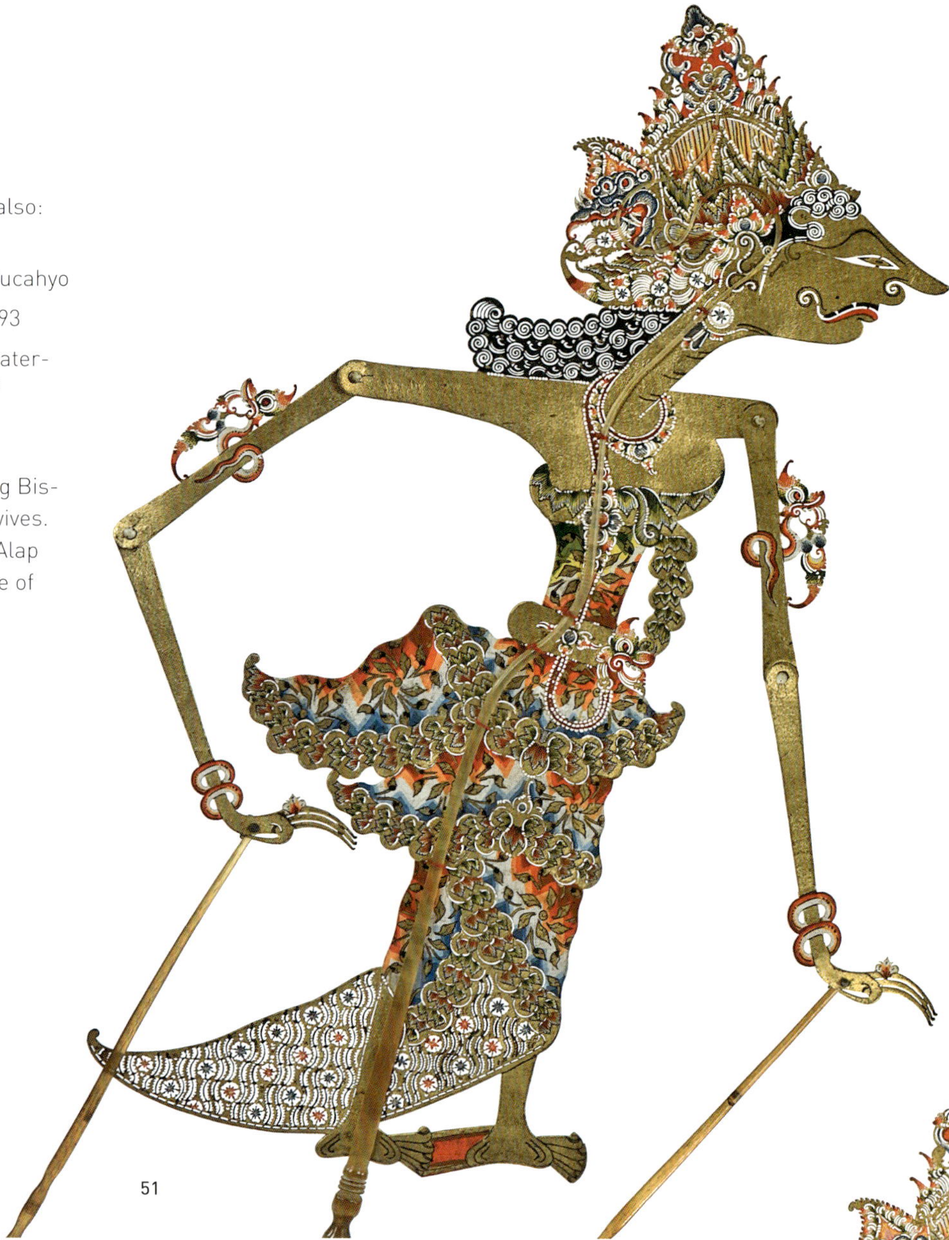

51

52. **Déwi Setyaboma**

FA.2007.40.48

Performer: Ki Purbo Asmoro; also: Ki Sudarsono

Artists: Wisnu and Bambang Sucahyo

Place and Date Made: Solo, 1993

Water buffalo hide and horn, water-based paint, *ancur*, bronze leaf

H: 69, W: 24 (cm)

Setyaboma is one of Kresna's wives and the daughter of King Setyajid and Déwi Wresini. Her brother is the noble warrior, Harya Setyaki. Setyaboma's main role is in the *lakon*, "Alap-Alapan Setyaboma" [The Marriage of Setyaboma], of the *Mahabharata*.

52

53. **Déwi Kunthi**

FA.2007.40.49

Performer: Ki Purbo Asmoro; also: Ki Sudarsono

Artists: Wisnu and Bambang Sucahyo

Place and Date Made: Solo, 1993

Water buffalo hide and horn, water-based paint, *ancur*, bronze leaf

H: 62, W: 20 (cm)

Kunthi is the daughter of King Basukunthi of Mandura; her brother is Basudéwa (Kresna's father, which makes her Kresna's paternal aunt).

In her youth, she studies with Druwasa, a noble priest at her father's court. Druwasa gives Kunthi an amulet, called *Aji Pepanggil*. The amulet allows her to call upon the gods and bring them to her as she wishes. Kunthi tries the amulet by calling upon Surya, the sun god. This results in an immaculate conception. Because she is not yet married, and with the help of the gods, the pregnancy and birth are kept a secret. Kunthi bears a son named Karna through her ear, but she abandons the boy in the forest. Karna was found and raised by foster parents, and he eventually joins forces with the Kurawas.

Meanwhile, Kunthi's hand is won in a contest by Pandhu Déwanata, King of Hastina. Pandhu is unable to have children, so Kunthi uses her amulet to ask the gods to for help. According to the Javanese version of the story, Kunthi and Pandu have three children (Puntadéwa, Bima, and Arjuna) with the help of Bathara Dharma (the god of justice), Bathara Bayu (the god of the wind), and Bathara Indra (the god of the sky and storms), respectively. Déwi Kunthi raises the five sons of Pandhu (including twin stepsons, Nakula and Sadéwa), and is referred to as the mother of the five Pandhawas.

Kunthi belongs to the *Mahabharata* cycle of stories. She stars in *lakon* such as "Lahiré Kunthi" [The Birth of Kunthi], "Kunthi Pilih" [Kunthi Makes a Choice], "Kunthi Dhuta" [Kunthi Serves as Arbitraitor], "Sudamala" [Disease and Despair Reduced or The Cleansing of Impurities], and "Kunthi Muksa" [Kunthi's Spirit Rises Up to the Heavens].

54. **Déwi Sumbadra** (*wanda*: Lentreng)
FA.2007.40.50

Performer: Ki Purbo Asmoro;
also: Ki Sudarsono

Artists: Wisnu and Bambang Sucahyo

Place and Date Made: Solo, 1993

Water buffalo hide and horn, water-based paint, *ancur*, bronze leaf

H: 61, W: 24 (cm)

Born as Rara Ireng, Sumbadra is the daughter of Déwi Badrahini and King Basudéwa of Mandura. She is the sister of Baladéwa and Kresna. Sumbadra is Arjuna's first, or primary, wife and is known and appreciated for her gentle and loving nature. She is the mother of Abimanyu.

Wanda Lentreng, refers to Sumbadra's subdued, quiet nature. Sumbadra appears in *lakon* such as "Sumbadra Larung" [Sumbadra is Sent Downstream], "Kresna Gugah" [Kresna Wakes from his Meditation], and "Sidalamong" [Gone Off the Deep End]" of the *Mahabharata* cycle.

54. detail

54

55. **Déwi Srikandhi**
FA.2007.40.51

Performer: Ki Purbo Asmoro;
also:Ki Sudarsono

Artists: Wisnu and Bambang Sucahyo

Place and Date Made: Solo, 1993

Water buffalo hide and horn, water-based paint, *ancur*, bronze leaf

H: 61, W: 24 (cm)

Srikandhi is one of Arjuna's wives and is the daughter of Drupada (King of Pancala) and Déwi Gandawati. Her older sister is Drupadi (Puntadéwa's wife).

Srikandhi falls in love with Arjuna (an unequalled archer), becomes his student, and an excellent archer in her own right. Arjuna returns her love and they eventually marry. Holding her own on the battlefield, Srikandhi kills Bisma, who is one of the main advisors to the Kurawas (and also a teacher to the Pandhawas). She is therefore murdered in her sleep by Aswatama.

Although female wayang characters are ideally modest, tender, and dutiful, Srikandhi is famous for her confidence, fierce independence, self-sufficiency, and extraordinary skills as a warrior. The physical form of this puppet holds its head high, a sign of Srikandhi's personality. Srikandhi appears in several *Mahabharata* episodes, including "Srikandhi Meguru Manah" [Srikandhi Studies Archery].

55

56. **Déwi Sinta, also known as Sita**

FA.2007.38.6

Performer and Designer: Ki Enthus Susmono

Artist: Rasimin

Place and Date Made: Surakarta, 2005

Water buffalo hide and horn, water-based paint and dyes, *ancur*, gold leaf

H: 61, W: 23 (cm)

Sinta is the heroine of *Ramayana*. An incarnation of a goddess, she possesses ideal feminine qualities; she is humble, gentle, and a faithful wife. In the Javanese version of *Ramayana*, Sinta is the daughter of Rahwana, the Demon-King of Alengka, who is despised for his greed, insatiable lust, and vicious disposition. When she is born, Rahwana's more kindly brother, Wibisana, hides Sinta in an effort to give her a better life. Sinta is found in a field and raised by a virtuous king.[3]

Sinta is married to Rama, Prince of Ayodya, and follows her husband and her brother-in-law, Laksmana, into exile when they were banished from the kingdom. Rahwana spies her and captures her through trickery—neither of the two knowing that they are father and daughter. During Sinta's captivity, Rahwana tries to seduce her, but he is unsuccessful. After many trials, Sinta is rescued and reunited with Rama. When Rama becomes King, Sinta must prove her fidelity by walking through fire. Sinta passes the test but, in some interpretations of the story, she is still banished because Rama could not allay public suspicion that she may have been unfaithful with Rahwana. Sinta's fate varies greatly in the different versions of the *Ramayana* that are found in South and Southeast Asia.

3. David Irvine, *Leather Gods and Wooden Heros: Java's Classical Wayang*. (Singapore: Marshall Cavendish International (Asia) Private Limited, 2005), 274. Dr. Sumarsam notes that most audiences are rarely familiar with this aspect of the story. Phone communication, August 27, 2009.

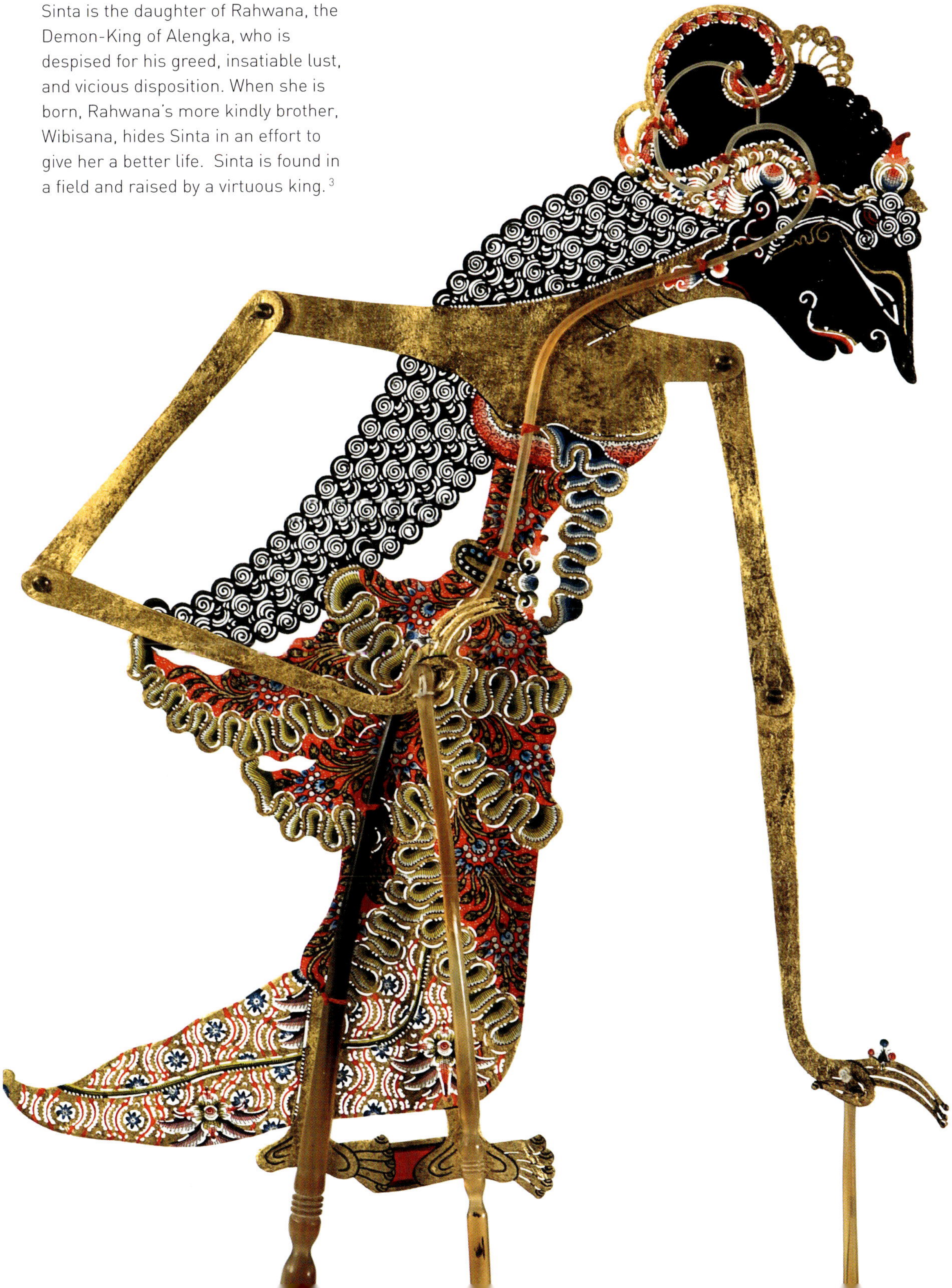

57. **Déwi Trijatha**

FA.2007.40.52

Performer: Ki Purbo Asmoro;
also: Ki Sudarsono

Artists: Wisnu and Bambang Sucahyo

Place and Date Made: Solo, 1993

Water buffalo hide and horn, water-based paint, *ancur*, bronze leaf

H: 62.5, W: 22 (cm)

Déwi Trijatha is Wibisana's daughter (and Rahwana's niece), who is assigned as Sinta's lady-in-waiting while Sinta is held captive by Rahwana. She shows great loyalty to Sinta, and for this Déwi Trijatha is eventually cursed by her uncle.

Déwi Trijatha marries the monkey priest Jembawan, and together they have a daughter, Jembowati, who marries Kresna (in the *Mahabharata*).

Trijatha appears in *lakon* such as "Anoman Dhuta" [Anoman Serves as Messenger] in the *Ramayana* cycle.

57

58. **Déwi Rara Ireng, also known as Lara Ireng** (*wanda*: Lenceng)

FA.2007.40.53

Performer: Ki Purbo Asmoro;
also: Ki Sudarsono

Artists: Wisnu and Bambang Sucahyo

Place and Date Made: Solo, 1993

Water buffalo hide and horn, water-based paint, *ancur*, bronze leaf

H: 63, W:21(cm)

Lenceng means "straightforward and down to earth." This is Sumbadra depicted in her youth. This wayang kulit figure appears in the *lakon*, "Kangsa Léna" [The Death of Kangsa], "Kresna Kembang" [Kresna Marries Rukmini], and "Parta Krama" [Arjuna's Wedding] from the *Mahabharata*.

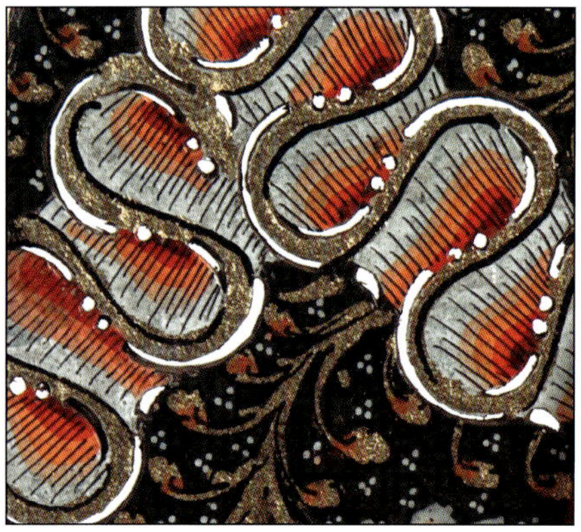

58. detail

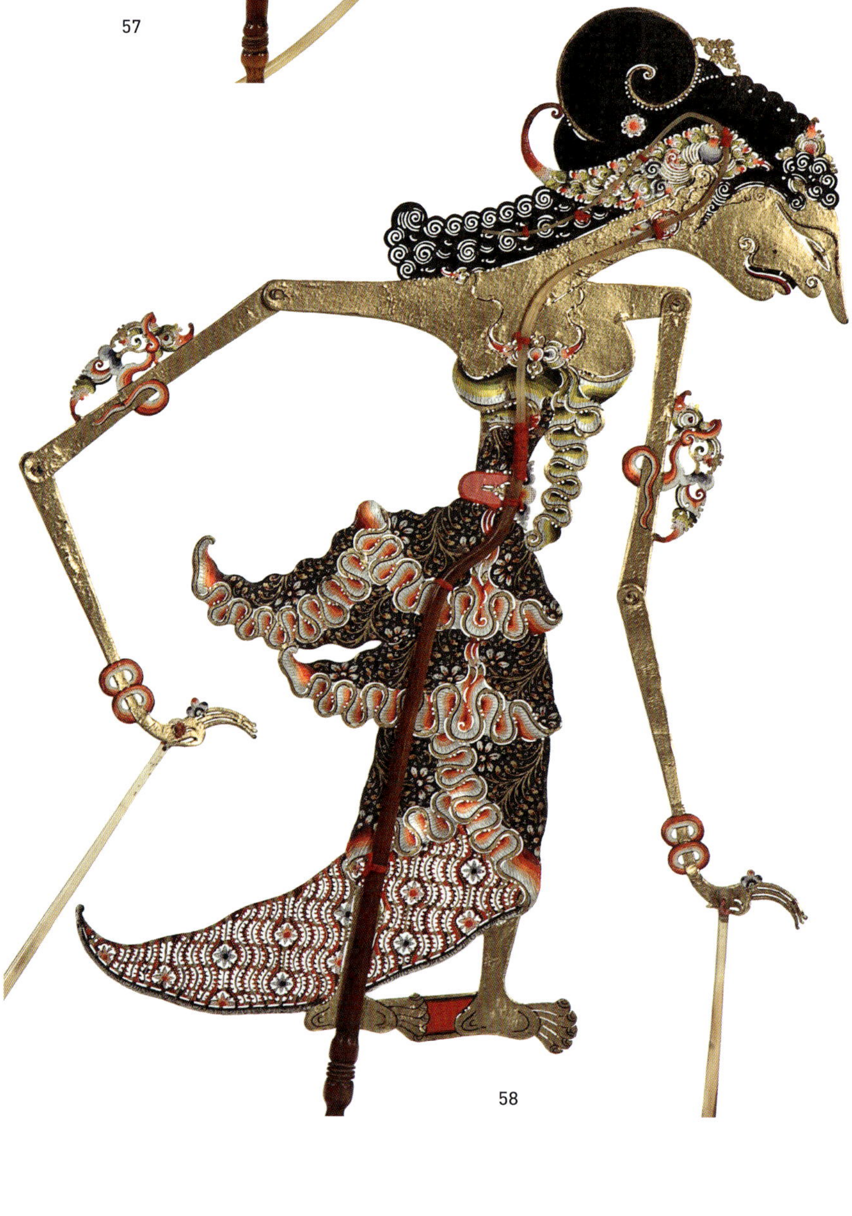

58

Putren are the women. These figures are used by the dhalang for female characters as needed—they are like a "wildcard" for female characters. Particular figures that exhibit a certain posture or hairstyle, and wear certain jewelry or clothing may be an option for specific wayang characters.

59

59. **Putren**

FA.2007.40.54

Ki Purbo Asmoro Collection

Performers: Ki Purbo Asmoro

Artists: unknown

Place and Date Made: unknown

Water buffalo hide and horn, water-based paint, *ancur*, metal leaf (gold or bronze)

H: 61.5, W: 21.5 (cm)

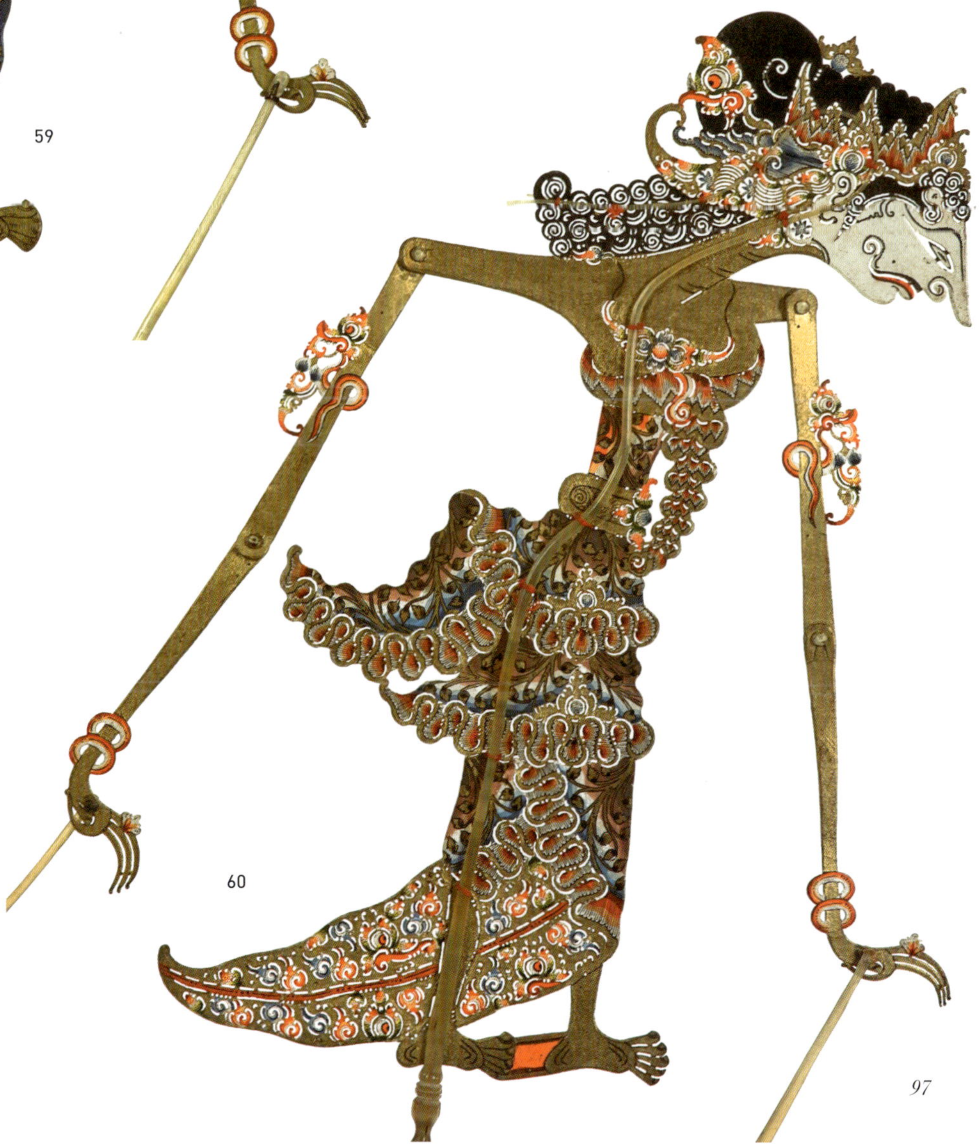

60

60. **Putren**

FA.2007.40.55

Ki Purbo Asmoro Collection

Performers: Ki Purbo Asmoro

Artists: unknown

Place and Date Made: unknown

Water buffalo hide and horn, water-based paint, *ancur*, metal leaf (gold or bronze)

H: 59, W: 20 (cm)

61. **Putren**

FA.2007.40.56

Performer: Ki Purbo Asmoro

Artists: unknown

Place and Date Made: unknown

Water buffalo hide and horn, water-based paint, *ancur*, metal leaf (gold or bronze)

H: 53, W: 20 (cm)

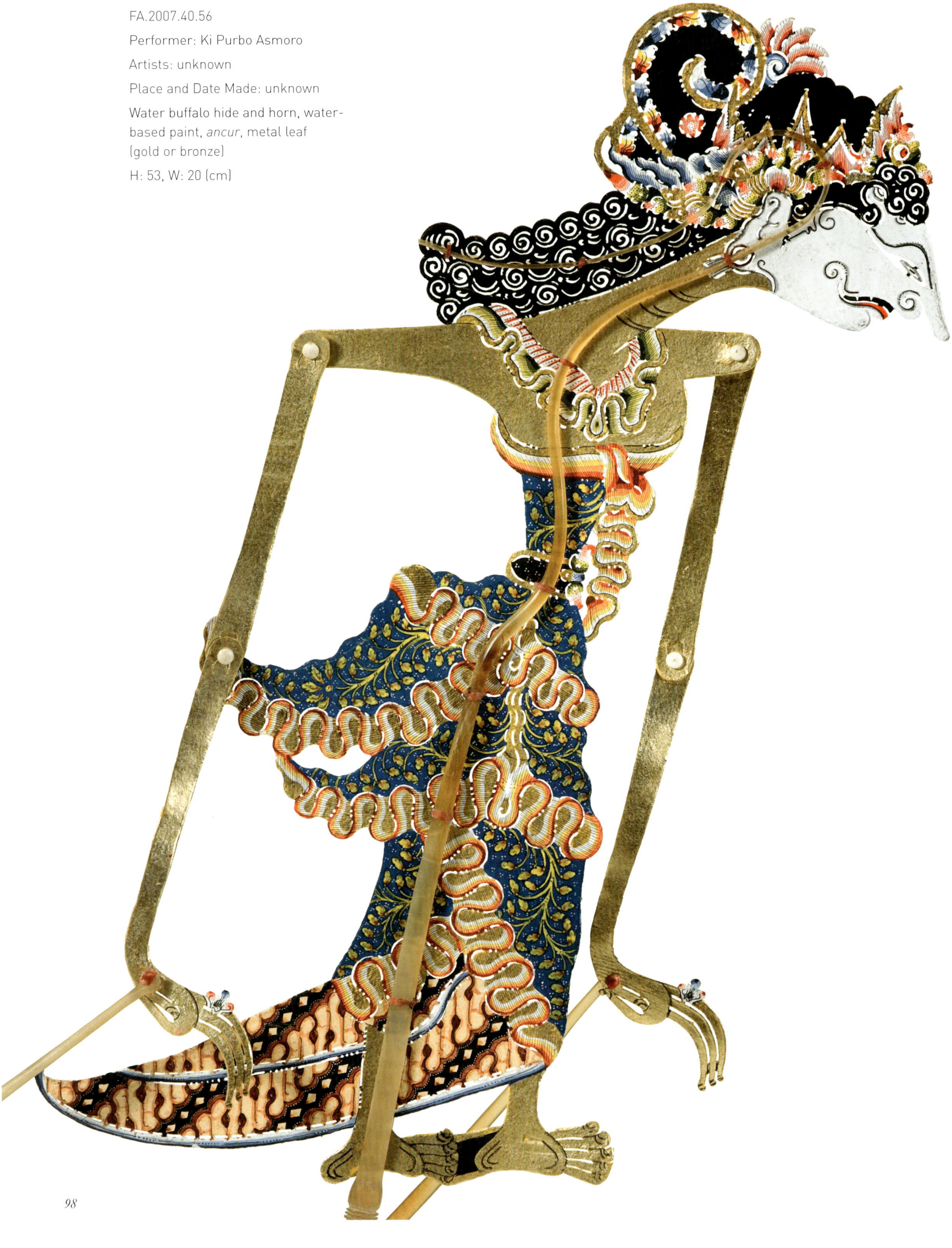

62

62. **Putren**

FA.2007.40.57

Performer: Ki Purbo Asmoro

Artists: unknown

Place and Date Made: unknown

Water buffalo hide and horn, water-based paint, *ancur*, metal leaf (gold or bronze)

H: 59, W: 20 (cm)

63. **Putren**

FA.2007.40.58

Performer: Ki Purbo Asmoro

Artists: unknown

Place and Date Made: unknown

Water buffalo hide and horn, water-based paint, *ancur*, metal leaf (gold or bronze)

H: 59.5, W: 20 (cm)

63

64. **Sang Hyang Wenang**

FA.2007.40.59

Performer: Ki Purbo Asmoro

Artists: Wisnu and Bambang Sucahyo

Place and Date Made: Solo, 1993

Water buffalo hide and horn, water-based paint, *ancur*, bronze leaf

H: 48, W: 18 (cm)

Sang Hyang Wenang is a high god who has power over all gods. He lives in Ondhar Andhir Bahwana ("The World in the Sky"), a special place in the abode of the gods. Sang Hyang Wenang appears in the *lakon*, "Bima Suci," (Bima as Priest) and other plays.

65. **Déwa Ruci**

FA.2007.40.60

Performer: Ki Purbo Asmoro

Artists: Wisnu and Bambang Sucahyo

Place and Date Made: Solo, 2006

Water buffalo hide and horn, water-based paint, *ancur*, bronze leaf

H: 49, W: 21 (cm)

Déwa Ruci is a god whose has a face that resembles Bima, but who has the body of a miniature person; he is the size of a pinky. Déwa Ruci is Bima's teacher and the star of the *Mahabharata* episode "Déwa Ruci" (Ruci: The Inner Spirit), the only *lakon* in which he appears. In this deeply philosophical episode, Bima journeys through the depths of the ocean where he meets Déwa Ruci. Bima enters the body of Déwa Ruci through his ear in order to see the world through the god's eyes. Déwa Ruci bestows upon Bima an understanding of the meaning of life and the secrets of the universe.

64

65

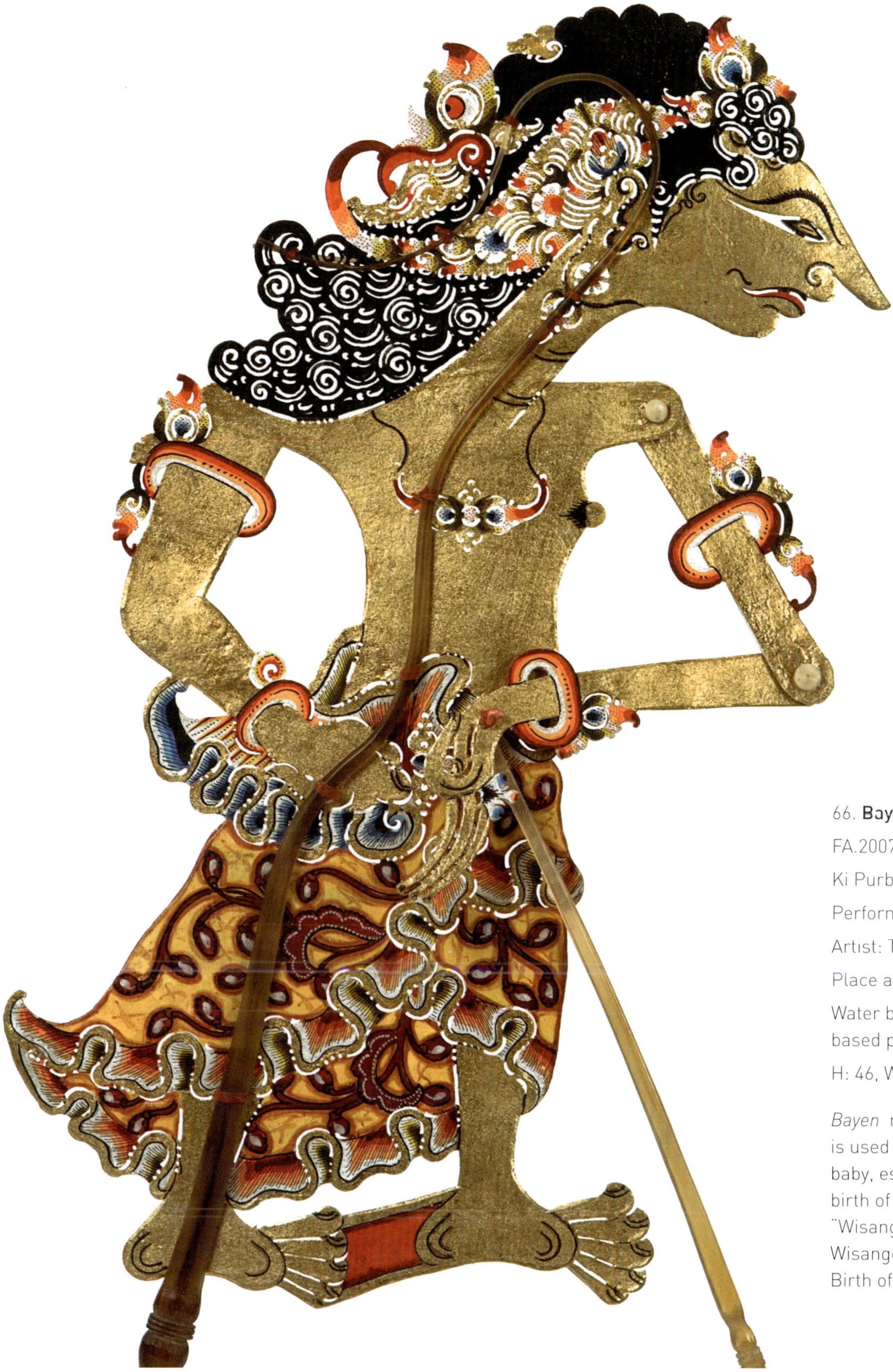

66. **Bayen**

FA.2007.40.61

Ki Purbo Asmoro Collection

Performer: Ki Purbo Asmoro

Artist: Tanto

Place and Date Made: Wonogiri, 2006

Water buffalo hide and horn, water-based paint, *ancur*, bronze leaf

H: 46, W: 20 (cm)

Bayen means "baby," and this wayang is used in any *lakon* that requires a baby, especially scenes showing the birth of a character, such as "Wisanggeni Lahir" [The Birth of Wisanggeni], or "Abimanyu Lahir" [The Birth of Abimanyu].

This section presents wayang kulit that would be displayed on a banana log base to the dhalang's left, as he sits facing the screen, during a performance. The figures are listed in order, beginning with the figure farthest from the dhalang's left (the largest), and ending with the shadow puppet closest to the dhalang's left (the smallest). Set up on the log, these figures all face left.

Simpingan Kiri

1. **Brahala Ireng**

FA.2007.39.1

Performer and Designer: Ki Enthus Susmono

Artist: Rasimin

Place and Date Made: Solo, 1992

Water buffalo hide and horn, water-based paint and dyes, *ancur*, gold leaf, wood

H: 126, W: 70 (cm)

Brahala Ireng (Very Large Black Giant) is the black-blooded Kresna, an incarnation of the god Wisnu. Kresna has the ability be transformed into this furious giant through intense meditation or is forced into the transformation due to intense anger. Kresna's special weapon, his *Cakra Baskara*, is tucked into his fiery hair.

Brahala Ireng is calmed and returned to his usual (non-violent and logical) self with the help of his cousin and friend, Puntadéwa. Puntadéwa, the eldest Pandhawa brother, transforms himself into Brahala Putih in order to spiritually connect and communicate with Brahala Ireng (see plate 1, Simpingan Kanan).

Brahala Ireng and Brahala Putih originated from the Yogyakarta tradition. Today, they are popularly used by many Solo-style dhalang who enjoy them either for display on the banana log or for use in performances.

Brahala Ireng may be found in *Mahabharata* episodes such as "Déwa Amral" (The Story of Déwa Amral: Puntadéwa Transformed into an Ogre) and "Pandhawa Pitu" (Sumbadra and Srikandhi: The Seven Pandhawas).

2. **Niwata Kawaca**

FA.2007.40.62

Performer: Ki Purbo Asmoro;
also: Ki Tristuti

Artists: Wiji Sutikno and Murtiyonta

Place and Date Made: Sukoharjo, 1994

Water buffalo hide and horn, water-based paint, *ancur*, gold leaf, wood

H: 120, W: 56 (cm)

Niwata Kawaca, who is usually depicted with a blue face, is the Ogre King of Hima Himantaka. He meets his death at the hands of Arjuna, who shoots Niwata Kawaca with an arrow through his open mouth (the arrow pierces the roof of his mouth, the only vulnerable part of his body). Niwata Kawaca only appears in one *lakon*: "Ciptoning" (Arjuna's Deep Meditation), of the *Mahabharata*.

3. **Kumbakarna**

FA.2007.38.3

Performer and Designer: Ki Enthus Susmono

Artist: Rasimin

Place and Date Made: Solo, 1992

Water buffalo hide and horn, water-based paint and dyes, *ancur*, gold leaf

H: 91.4, W: 48.3 (cm)

The rather tragic character, Kumbakarna, is the ogre brother of Wibisana and Rahwana, the Demon-King of Alengka.

Kumbakarna disagrees with many of Rahwana's actions (such as kidnapping Sinta and attempting to burn Anoman at the stake); and Kumbakarna even leaves his brother's kingdom for a time. Despite his outward appearance, at his core, Kumbakarna is ethical and noble. However, he succumbs to the pressures of familial loyalty and to perceptions of patriotic duty. In the end he fights with Rahwana against Rama's army.

His devotion to his vicious brother has serious consequences, and Kumbakarna lives with a great burden of guilt for supporting Rahwana's harshness and cruelty. Kumbakarna dies in battle at the hands of Laksmana—who learns of Kumbakarna's vulnerability from Wibisana, Kumbakarna's own brother. That vulnerability is his throat; the rest of Kumbakarna's body is invincible. Kumbakarna is a major character in *Ramayana*, and stars in the *lakon*, "Kumbakarna Gugur" (The Death of Kumbakarna).

Most **Buta Raton** (ogre-giant) figures can be used interchangeably, in any story, whenever a generic buta character is needed. In the *wanda* listed below, *macan* means "tiger," and these pieces have been used by Ki Purbo Asmoro to portray ogre characters in *lakon* such as "Kumbakarna Gugur" [The Death of Kumbakarna], "Rama Tambak" [Rama Bridges the Way], and "Wahyu Makutharama" [Makutharama: A Boon from the Gods].

4. **Buta Raton** (*wanda*: Macan)

FA.2007.40.63

Performer: Ki Purbo Asmoro

Artist: unknown

Place and Date Made: Klaten, date unknown; acquired by Ki Purbo Asmoro in Klaten, 1993

Water buffalo hide and horn, water-based paint, *ancur*, gold leaf

H: 96.5, W: 53 (cm)

This particular buta raton giant is larger than normal in size.

5. **Buta Raton** (*wanda*: Macan)

FA.2007.40.64

Performer: Ki Purbo Asmoro; also: Ki Sukasdi

Artist: Ki Sukasdi (Painter)

Place and Date Made: Sukoharjo, date unknown; acquired by Ki Purbo Asmoro in 2004

Water buffalo hide and horn, water-based paint, *ancur*, imitation gold leaf

H: 124, W: 59 (cm)

This generic buta raton figure can be used to portray a Giant King or the figure Kumbakarna.

4

5

6

6. **Buta Raton** (*wanda*: Macan)

FA.2007.40.65

Performer: Ki Purbo Asmoro;
also: Ki Sukarno

Artist: Ki Sukarno

Place and Date Made: unknown; acquired by Ki Purbo Asmoro in Karang Anyar, 1990

Water buffalo hide and horn, water-based paint, *ancur*, gold leaf

H: 114, W: 48 (cm)

7

7. **Prahasta**

FA.2007.40.66

Performer: Ki Purbo Asmoro;
also: Ki Suryanta; Ki Ramta

Artist: Joko Metengan (leather carver)

Place and Date Made: Klaten, date unknown; acquired by Ki Purbo Amoro in Boyolali, 2000

Water buffalo hide and horn, water-based paint, *ancur*, bronze leaf, wood

H: 119, W: 52 (cm)

Prahastha is the son of King Sumali of Alengka. Sumali's nephew, Rahwana, succeeds Sumali as King. Prahastha becomes Rahwana's loyal prime minister, but he disagrees with a number of Rahwana's harsh deeds. Prahastha is eventually killed by the monkey soldier, Anila. He appears in *Ramayana* episodes like "Prahastha Gugur" [The Death of Prahastha] and "Kembang Déwa Retna" [The Déwa Retna Flower].

8

8. **Brajadenta**

FA.2007.40.67

Performer: Ki Purbo Asmoro

Artist: Wiji Sutikno

Place and Date Made: Sukoharjo, 1989

Water buffalo hide and horn, water-based paint, *ancur*, gold leaf, wood

H: 115, W: 53 (cm)

Brajadenta is the son of Trembaka. His siblings include Arimba, Arimbi (Bima's wife), Brajamusti, Brajamikalpa, Brajalamatan, and Kala Bendana. He plays a major role in the *lakon* "Brajadenta Mbaléla" [Brajadenta Revolts] of the *Mahabharata*.

9. **Buta Patih**

FA.2007.40.68

Performer: Ki Purbo Asmoro; also: Sri Joko Raharjo

Artists: Wiji Sutikno (leather carver), Murdiyonto (painter)

Place and Date Made: Sukoharjo, 2000

Water buffalo hide and horn, water-based paint, *ancur*, gold leaf, wood

H: 111, W: 55 (cm)

This generic ogre figure can be used in an antagonist army in any wayang play.

9

Maésasura is a King with a buffalo-head who attacks the heavens when his love for an angel is thwarted. The gods call upon the brothers Subali and Sugriwa for help and they kill Maésasura and his chief minister, **Lembusura**. (Lembusura is depicted with a strong build and a cow's head.) Ki Purbo Asmoro commissioned these wayang figures, which display clothing patterns requested by Ki Purbo. These characters belong to the story of Maésasura in the *lakon* "Subali-Sugriwa" [The Story of Subali and Sugriwa] of the *Ramayana*.

10. **Lembusura**

FA.2007.40.69

Performer: Ki Purbo Asmoro; also:Ki Tristuti; Ki Toto Atmojo

Artists: Wiji Sutikno (leather carver), Murdiyonto (painter); Designer: Ki Mulyanta

Place and Date Made: Sukoharjo, 1997

Water buffalo hide and horn, water-based paint, *ancur*, gold leaf, wood

H: 111.5, W: 56 (cm)

11. **Maésasura**

FA.2007.40.70

Performer: Ki Purbo Asmoro; also:Ki Tristuti; Ki Toto Atmojo

Artists: Wiji Sutikno (leather carver), Murdiyonto (painter); Designer: Ki Mulyanta

Place and Date Made: Sukoharjo, 1997

Water buffalo hide and horn, water-based paint, *ancur*, gold leaf, wood

H: 106, W: 49 (cm)

Although Maésasura is normally depicted with a crown, this wayang figure does not wear one.

10. detail

10

11

12. **Rajamala**

FA.2007.40.71

Performer: Ki Purbo Asmoro; also: Ki Puntana

Artists: Sutar (leather carver), Murdiyonto (painter); Designer: Ki Mulyanta

Place and Date Made: Sukoharjo, 2005

Water buffalo hide and horn, water-based paint, *ancur*, bronze leaf, wood

H: 111, W: 54.5 (cm)

Rajamala is the commander-in-chief of the country, Wirata. He is killed by Jagal Bilawa. His primary *lakon* is "Adon-Adon Rajamala" [Rajamala Enters the Ring] from the *Mahabharata*. Elements such as the *keris* (a special Indonesian knife often believed to be magically charged) and the style of trousers worn by this wayang figure are traditional Indonesian elements that appear as influences from *wayang gedhog* (the third generation of wayang stories, originating around the sixteenth century).

Rahwana, the chief villain in *Ramayana,* is also known as Dasamuka, or a "ten-faced" demon. He is a power-hungry ogre, who is despised for his greed, insatiable lust, and vicious disposition. He succeeds his father, King Wisrawa of Alengka to the throne. His siblings are Wibisana (who was born in human form) and the ogres Kumbakarna and Sarpanaka.

Rahwana's malignant actions begin in the era of Arjuna Sasrabahu (which take place in early episodes of the *Ramayana* cycle of stories). The story of Arjuna Sasrabahu sets the stage for the *Ramayana* by telling important sub-stories: one of these stories is about Rahwana's unrequited love for Kusalya (a woman who later marries King Dasarata of Ayodya, and gives birth to Prince Rama).[1]

In the *Ramayana*, Rahwana revenges himself on Kusalya and King Dasarata by pursuing Rama and his wife, Sinta, while they are in exile, and by abducting Sinta through trickery. While Rahwana holds Sinta in captivity, he unsuccessfully attempts to seduce her. (In fact, Rahwana and Sinta are father and daughter—a fact that is unknown to both.[2]) Rama and his brother Laksmana set out to rescue Sinta, and during the quest, the two brothers are aided by faithful allies, like Anoman and his monkey army. After many great battles, Rama decapitates Rahwana. The head is buried under a mountain by Anoman, thus ensuring that Rahwana will never come back to life.

1. David Irvine, *Leather Gods and Wooden Heros: Java's Classical Wayang*. (Singapore: Marshall Cavendish International [Asia] Private Limited, 2005), 257.

2. Dr. Sumarsam notes that most audiences are rarely familiar with this aspect of the story. Phone communication, August 27, 2009.

13. **Rahwana, also known as Dasamuka** (*wanda*: Iblis)

FA.2007.40.72

Performer: Ki Purbo Asmoro; also: Ki Ary Bodro

Artists: Joko (leather carver), Murdiyonto (painter); Designer: Marsana

Place and Date Made: Sukoharjo, date unknown; acquired by Ki Purbo Asmoro in Sragen, 2000

Water buffalo hide and horn, water-based paint, *ancur*, gold leaf, wood

H: 105.5, W: 47 (cm)

Wanda Iblis means "devil".

14. **Rahwana, also known as Dasamuka** (*wanda*: Bengis)

FA.2007.40.73

Performer: Ki Purbo Asmoro; also: Ki Manta; Ki Bowo; Ki Pathut

Artists: Wiji Sutikno (leather carver), Pardi (painter)

Place and Date Made: Sukoharjo, date unknown; acquired by Ki Purbo Asmoro in Sragen, 2000

Water buffalo hide and horn, water-based paint, *ancur*, gold leaf, wood

H: 100, W: 43.5 (cm)

The term bengis means "cruel and harsh."

14

15

15. **Burisrawa**

FA.2007.40.74

Performer: Ki Purbo Asmoro

Artist: unknown

Place and Date Made: Sukoharjo, date unknown; acquired by Ki Purbo Asmoro in Sukoharjo, 2005

Water buffalo hide and horn, water-based paint, *ancur*, imitation gold leaf, wood

H: 85.5, W: 44 (cm)

Burisrawa is a son of King Salya of Mandraka. His siblings include Erawati, Surtikanti, and Banowati. In the *Mahabharata* cycle, this character is killed in the great war of Bharatayuda by Setyaki and Arjuna, under the guidance of Kresna.

He appears in *lakon* such as "Kresna Dhuta" [Kresna Serves as an Arbitrator], "Parta Krama" [Arjuna's Wedding], "Timpalan" [The Violent Deaths of Jayadrata and Burisrawa], and "Bharatayuda" [The Great War of Bharatayuda].

16. **Sugriwa**

FA.2007.40.75

Performer: Ki Purbo Asmoro

Artists: Sriyadi (leather carver), Yatna (painter)

Place and Date Made: Wonogiri, 2006

Water buffalo hide and horn, water-based paint, *ancur,* imitation gold leaf, wood

H: 98, W: 41 (cm)

This crowned wayang figure depicts Sugriwa as King of Kiskenda. Sugriwa helps Rama defeat Rahwana in the *Ramayana*. This is an elder version of Sugriwa than the piece presented in the Simpingan Kanan section (see plate 21).

17. **Subali**

FA.2007.40.76

Performer: Ki Purbo Asmoro

Artist: Tugimin (leather carver); Designer: Ki Purbo Asmoro

Place and Date Made: Sukoharjo, 2000

Water buffalo hide and horn, water-based paint, *ancur,* bronze leaf, wood

H: 92, W: 40 (cm)

In this version of the *Ramayana* character, Subali has grown older. (see plate 22, Simpingan Kanan for a more youthful version of the character) Here, Subali wears a *praba* (headdress) and *selendang* (shoulder cloth).

16

17

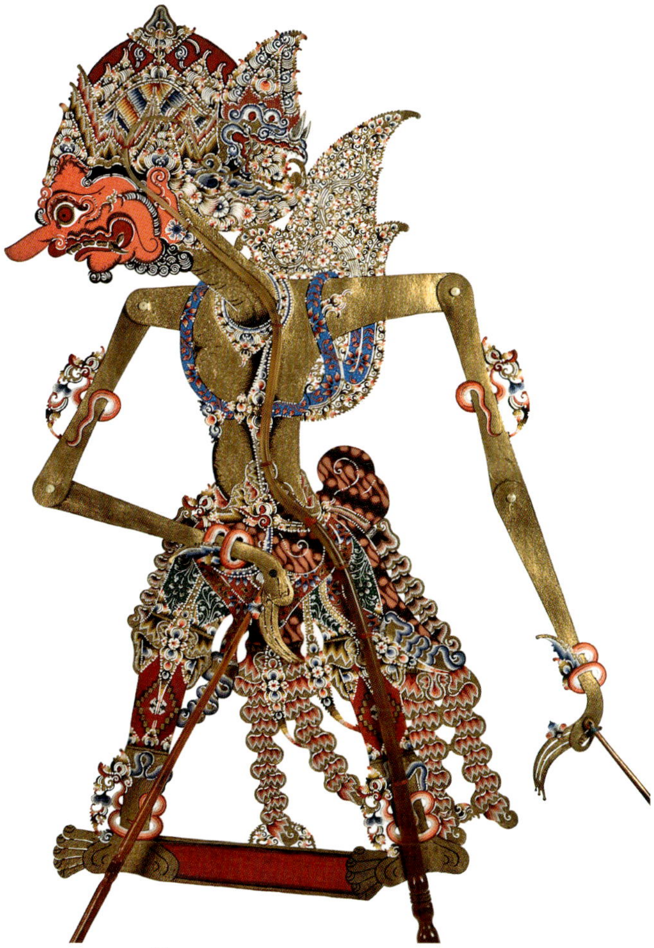

18

18. **Trikaya**

FA.2007.40.77

Performer: Ki Purbo Asmoro; also: Ki Tristuti

Artists: Tugimin (leather carver), Murdiyonto (painter)

Place and Date Made: Sukoharjo, 2000

Water buffalo hide and horn, water-based paint, *ancur,* gold leaf, wood

H: 97, W: 38 (cm)

Trikaya is Rahwana's son in the *Ramayana.*

19. **Supala**

FA.2007.40.78

Performer: Ki Purbo Asmoro; also: Ki Puntana; Ki Heri Sutrisno

Artists: unknown

Place and Date Made: Sukoharjo, date unknown; acquired by Ki Purbo Asmoro in Klaten, 1997

Water buffalo hide and horn, water-based paint, *ancur,* bronze leaf, wood

H: 95, W: 42 (cm)

Supala is the King of Cedhi, who is killed by Kresna for violating an oath and fighting against Kresna in the *lakon*, "Sesaji Raja Suya" [The Grand Offering of the Kings], of the *Mahabharata.*[3]

3. Dr. Suyanto S.Kar., MA, E-mail communication, August 19, 2009

19

Wayang figures of **Bomo** can be used to represent an antagonist king in any *lakon*. "Encik" connotes an Arabian-like face; it is a wanda that developed in Klaten puppetry.

22

22. **Bomo**

FA.2007.40.81

Performer: Ki Purbo Asmoro;
also: Ki Sunarna; Ki Tristuti

Artists: Wiji Sutikno (leather carver), Murdiyonto (painter)

Place and Date Made: Sukoharjo, 1994

Water buffalo hide and horn, water-based paint, *ancur*, gold leaf

H: 100, W: 35 (cm)

This Bomo figure with long hair, a *keris*, and short pants is a unique dipiction.

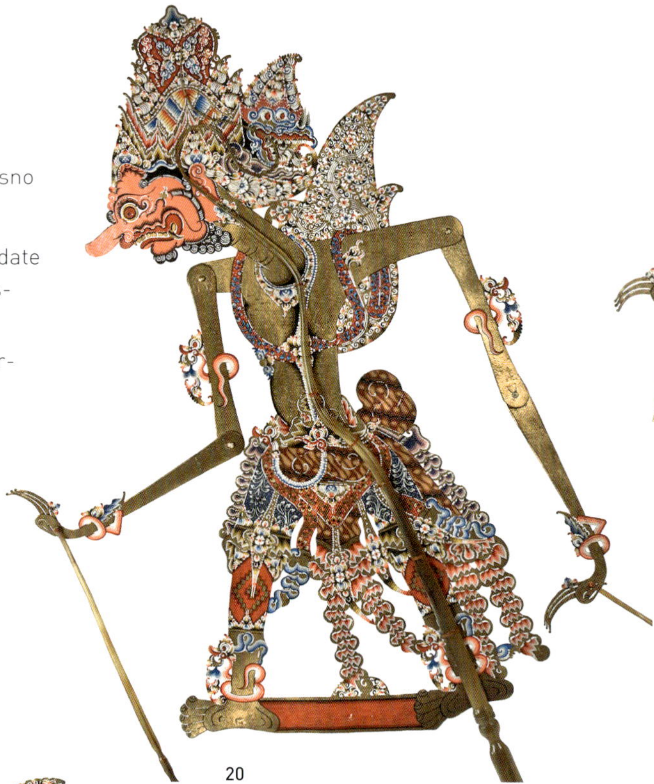

20

20. **Bomo** (*wanda:* Encik)

FA.2007.40.79

Performer: Ki Purbo Asmoro;
also: Ki Wiji Santoso; Ki Heri Sutrisno

Artists: unknown

Place and Date Made: Sukoharjo, date unknown; acquired by Ki Purbo Asmoro in Klaten, 1997

Water buffalo hide and horn, water-based paint, *ancur*, bronze leaf

H: 93, W: 42 (cm)

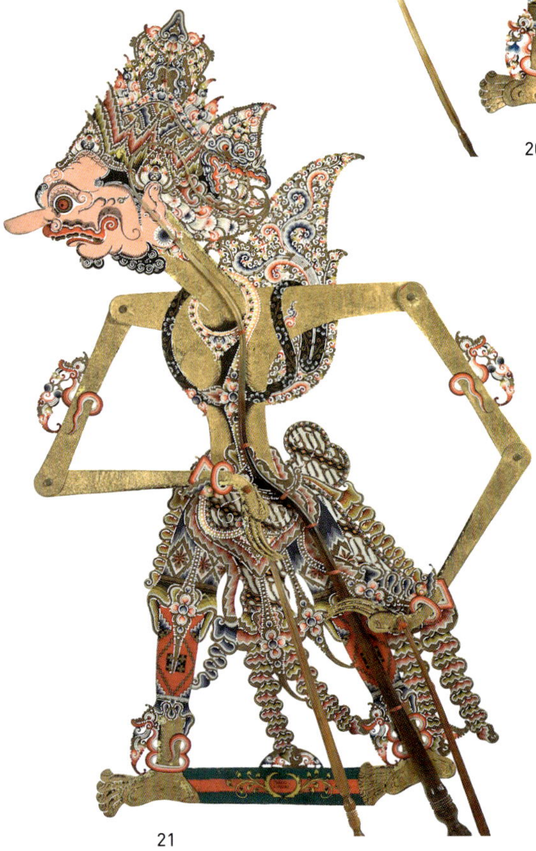

21

21. **Bomo** (*wanda:* Encik)

FA.2007.40.80

Performer: Ki Purbo Asmoro

Artists: unknown

Place and Date Made: unknown

Water buffalo hide and horn, water-based paint, *ancur*, metal leaf (gold or bronze), wood

H: 98.5, W: 39 (cm)

23

23. **Kangsa**

FA.2007.40.82

Performer: Ki Purbo Asmoro; also: Ki Sajali

Artists: Jono (leather carver), Slamet (painter); Designer: Pringgo Satota

Place and Date Made: Wonogiri and Sukoharjo, 1994

Water buffalo hide and horn, water-based paint, *ancur,* bronze leaf

H: 91.5, W: 36 (cm)

Kangsa is the son of Gorowongsa and Dewi Maerah. Kangsa is killed by Kakrasana and Narayana (as Baladéwa and Kresna were known in their youth). When Kangsa sought to destroy them and their kingdom, the two heroes defend themselves. This character's *lakon* include "Kangsa Léna" [The Death of Kangsa] and "Joko Maruta" [The Story of Joko Maruta] of the *Mahabharata*.

24

24. **Trisirah**

FA.2007.40.83

Performer: Ki Purbo Asmoro

Artist: unknown

Place and Date Made: Wonogiri, date unknown; acquired by Ki Purbo Asmoro in Wonogiri, 1994

Water buffalo hide and horn, water-based paint, *ancur*, gold leaf, wood

H: 93, W: 41 (cm)

Trisirah is a child of Rahwana, who appears in the *lakon*, "Rama Tambak" [Rama Bridges the Way] of the *Ramayana*.

25. **Sutejo**

FA.2007.40.84

Performer: Ki Purbo Asmoro

Artist: unknown

Place and Date Made: Wonogiri, date unknown

Water buffalo hide and horn, water-based paint, *ancur*, bronze leaf

H: 98, W: 37 (cm)

Sutejo, the King of Trajutrisna, appears in *lakon* such as "Kikis Tunggorono" [The Border Dispute at Tunggorono] and "Samba Juwing" [Samba is Viciously Killed] of the *Mahabharata*.

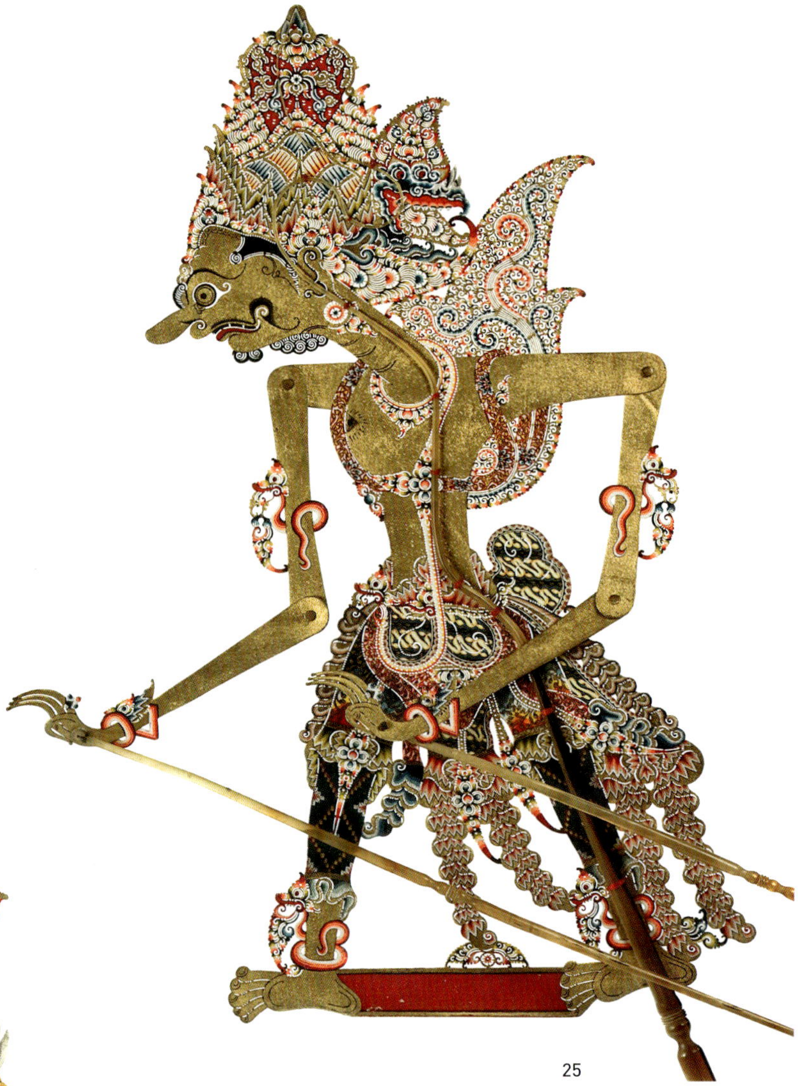

25

26

26. **Kurupati**

FA.2007.40.85

Performer: Ki Purbo Asmoro

Artist: unknown

Place and Date Made: Sukoharjo, date unknown; acquired by Ki Purbo Asmoro in Sukoharjo, 2005

Water buffalo hide and horn, water-based paint, *ancur*, bronze leaf

H: 98, W: 39 (cm)

Kurupati is the name of the youthful Duryudana character. He appears in *lakon* such as "Kurupati Rabi" [Kurupati's Wedding] and "Babad Wanamarta" [The Clearing of the Amarta Forest] of the *Mahabharata*.

Known as Kakrasana in his youth, **Baladéwa** succeeds his father, Basudéwa as the King of Mandura. Baladéwa is the brother of the great Kresna and Sumbadra (Arjuna's wife). Although Baladéwa has admirable traits, his loyalty lies with the Kurawas because of his marriage to King Salya's daughter, Dewi Erawati. To keep his brother safe, Kresna dupes Baladéwa into staying out of the final great war, known as the Bharatayuda. In the end, when Baladéwa learns that the Kurawas are defeated, he is reunited with his family, and the virtuous Pandhawas.

All four of these versions of Baladéwa may be used in battle scenes and appear in *Mahabharata* episodes like "Kresna Gugah" [Kresna Wakes from his Meditation], "Gandamana Sayembara" [Gandamana Designs a Competition], "Parta Krama" [Arjuna's Wedding], "Sesaji Raja Suya" [The Grand Offering of the Kings], and "Baladéwa Jago" [Baladéwa Steps Forth as Champion].

27. **Baladéwa** (*wanda*: Gègèr)

FA.2007.40.86

Performer: Ki Purbo Asmoro;
also: Ki Pringgo Darsana

Arist: Pardi; Designer: Marsana

Place and Date Made: Sragen, date unknown; acquired by Ki Purbo Asmoro in Sragen, 2003

Water buffalo hide and horn, water-based paint, *ancur*, gold leaf, wood

H: 100, W: 41 (cm)

The term *Gègèr* means "noisy" and refers to a noisy situation when someone gets angry.

28. **Baladéwa** (*wanda*: Paripeksa)

FA.2007.40.87

Performer: Ki Purbo Asmoro;
also: Ki Suyono

Artists: Indratmi (leather carver),
Ki Suyono (painter)

Place and Date Made: Klaten, date unknown; acquired by Ki Purbo Asmoro in Sukoharjo, 2000

Water buffalo hide and horn, water-based and oil paints, *ancur*, imitation gold leaf

H: 93, W: 38 (cm)

In the *wanda* Paripeksa, Baladéwa is in an insistent mood. *Wanda* Paripeksa and Pideksa (plate 29) are used interchangeably, depending on the situation and the dhalang's preference. Both are used for the common role of Baladéwa as a guest, and both are used to portray Baladéwa in battle scenes.[4]

4. Interview with Ki Purbo Asmoro, Surakarta, June 25, 2009.

27

28

29. **Baladéwa** (*wanda*: Pideksa)

FA.2007.40.89

Performer: Ki Purbo Asmoro

Artists: Indratmi (leather carver), Suyono (painter)

Place and Date Made: Klaten, date unknown, acquired by Ki Purbo Asmoro in Sukoharjo, 2000

Water buffalo hide and horn, water-based paint, *ancur*, imitation gold leaf

H: 93, W: 37 (cm)

The term *Pideksa* refers to Baladéwa's tall stature.

29

30

30. **Baladéwa** (*wanda*: Jago)

FA.2007.40.88

Performer: Ki Purbo Asmoro; also: Ki Mulyana

Artists: Ki Mulyana (leather carver), Murdiyanta (painter)

Place and Date Made: Semarang, 1997

Water buffalo hide and horn, water-based paint, *ancur*, gold leaf

H: 97, W: 38 (cm)

Jago means "rooster," and implies a small, thin, and cruel figure. Many dhalang prefer this figure for battle scenes, probably because the size makes it somewhat easier to use in these active scenes.[5]

5. Interview with Ki Purbo Asmoro, Surakarta, June 25, 2009.

31

31. **Kakrasana**

FA.2007.40.90

Performer: Ki Purbo Asmoro;
also: Ki Tristuti

Artists: Wiji Sutikno and Murtiyanta;
Designer: Marsana

Place and Date Made: Sukoharjo, 1997; acquired by Ki Purbo Asmoro in Sragen, 1999

Water buffalo hide and horn, water-based paint, *ancur*, gold leaf

H: 90.5, W: 36 (cm)

In his youth, Baladéwa is known as Kakrasana. Notice the youthful character's full hairline. Kakrasana appears in *lakon* such as "Jaladara Rabi" [Jaladara's Wedding] and "Kangsa Léna" [The Death of Kangsa] of the *Mahabharata*.

32. **Kincaka**

FA.2007.40.91

Performer: Ki Purbo Asmoro;
also: Ki Toto Atmojo

Artists: Yatna Tentrem (leather carver), Beny (painter)

Place and Date Made: Klaten, date unknown; acquired by Ki Purbo Asmoro in Klaten, 1995

Water buffalo hide and horn, water-based paint, *ancur*, bronze leaf

H: 83, W: 36 (cm)

In the *Mahabharata* episode, "Adon-Adon Rajamala" [Rajamala Enters the Ring], Kincaka is the older brother of Rupakinca. A government official of the country Wirata, Kincaka is killed by Jagal Abilawa (Bima disguised as a butcher) when he tries to seduce Drupadi (who, at the time, is disguised as a handmaiden to the queen).

32

33. **Rupakinca**

FA.2007.40.92

Performer: Ki Purbo Asmoro; also: Ki Toto Atmojo

Artists: Yatna Tentrem (leather carver), Beny (painter)

Place and Date Made: Klaten, date unknown; acquired by Ki Purbo Asmoro in Klaten, 1995

Water buffalo hide and horn, water-based paint, *ancur*, bronze leaf

H: 86.5, W: 34 (cm)

In the *Mahabharata* episode, "Adon-Adon Rajamala" [Rajamala Enters the Ring], Rupakinca is the younger brother of Kincaka. Rupakinca has a fuller hairline than Kincaka.

33

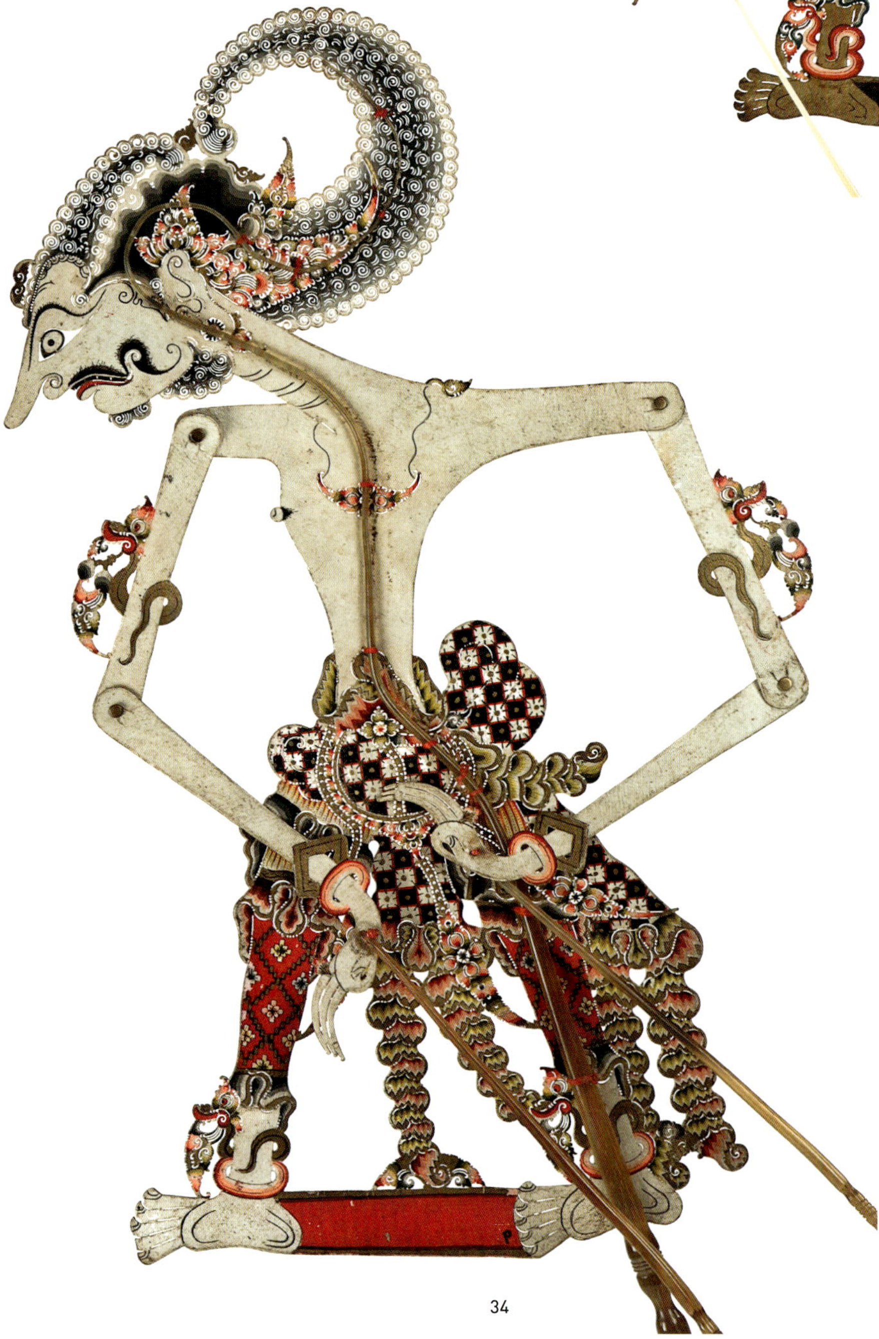

34

34. **Séta**

FA.2007.40.93

Performer: Ki Purbo Asmoro; also: Ki Puntana; Ki Heri Sutrisno; Ki Joko; Ki Riyanta

Artists: Supena (leather carver), Ngatimin (painter)

Place and Date Made: Solo, 1990

Water buffalo hide and horn, water-based paint, *ancur*, bronze leaf

H: 88.5, W: 96 (cm)

Séta (a warrior-priest who is well studied in religious philosophy) is the son of Matswapati, King of Wirata. His siblings include Utara, Wratsangka, and Utari. He commands the Pandhawa army and is aided by his brother, Utara, in the great war known as the Bharatayuda. Séta is quickly killed by Bisma, who commands the Kurawa army.

Séta appears in *lakon* such as "Wiratha Parwa" [The Story of the Kingdom Wiratha], "Séta Jambak" [The Death of Séta], and "Bisma Gugur" [The Death of Bisma] in the *Mahabharata*. Séta's name means "white" (he is an albino). The color of this figure is usually gold—this white-painted figure is an innovation of Ki Purbo Asmoro.

Utara and **Wratsangka** are the younger brothers of Séta and appear in the *lakon*, "Wiratha Parwa" [The Story of the Kingdom Wiratha], of *Mahabharata*.

35. **Utara**

FA.2007.40.94

Performer: Ki Purbo Asmoro;
also: Ki Tristuti

Artist: Diman (painter)

Place and Date Made: Klaten, date unknown; acquired by Ki Purbo Asmoro in Klaten, 1994

Water buffalo hide and horn, water-based paint, *ancur,* gold leaf

H: 84, W: 32 (cm)

36. **Wratsangka**

FA.2007.40.95

Performer: Ki Purbo Asmoro;
also: Ki Tristuti

Artist: Diman (painter)

Place and Date Made: Klaten, date unknown; acquired by Ki Purbo Asmoro in Klaten, 1994

Water buffalo hide and horn, water-based paint, *ancur,* gold leaf

H: 74, W: 33 (cm)

36

35

37

37. **Sucitra**

FA.2007.40.96

Performer: Ki Purbo Asmoro

Artists: unknown

Place and Date Made: Klaten, date unknown; acquired by Ki Purbo Asmoro in Klaten, 1994

Water buffalo hide and horn, water-based paint, *ancur,* bronze leaf

H: 82, W: 32 (cm)

When he was young, Drudapa went by the name Sucitra. Sucitra and Pandhu (father of the Pandhawa brothers) were great friends and both entered a contest for Dewi Gandawati's hand in marriage. With Pandhu's help, Sucitra won the maiden's hand. Sucitra subsequently became King and took the name Drupada. Sucitra plays one of his most important roles in the *Mahabharata* episode, "Kumbayana Meguru" [Kumbayana Takes on a Teacher].

38

38. **Ugrasena**

FA.2007.40.97

Performer: Ki Purbo Asmoro

Artists: Diyarman (leather carver), Kuwat (painter)

Place and Date Made: Sukoharjo, 1984

Water buffalo hide and horn, water-based paint, *ancur,* bronze leaf

H: 80, W: 32.5 (cm)

This figure appears in *lakon* such as "Kangsa Léna" [The Death of Kangsa] and "Kunthi Pilih" [Kunthi Makes a Choice] from the *Mahabharata*. Ugrasena is the son of Kunthiboja, the king of Mandura, and among his siblings are Basudéwa and Kunthi. Later in life, Ugrasena becomes the King of Lesanpura and takes the name Setyajid. He fights with the Pandhawas in the great war known as the Bharatayuda.

Setyaki is used in the performance of a number of *lakon* from the *Mahabharata* cycle, such as "Kresna Dhuta" [Kresna Serves as Arbitrator], "Bharatayuda" [The Great Bharatayuda War], "Sesaji Raja Suya" [The Grand Offering of the Kings], and "Alap Alapan Setyoboma" [The Marriage of Setyaboma]. Setyaki is the son of Setyajid, the King of Lesanpura. His older sister is Setyaboma, who becomes one of Kresna's wives. A supreme example of a *satria* (noble knight), Setyaki chooses to serve King Kresna in Dwarawati instead of ascending the throne himself after his father's death.

39

39. **Setyaki** (*wanda*: Akik)

FA.2007.40.98

Performer: Ki Purbo Asmoro; also: Ki Joko Riyanto

Artist: Indratmi

Place and Date Made: Klaten, date unknown; acquired by Ki Purbo Asmoro in Sukoharjo, 2000

Water buffalo hide and horn, water-based paint, *ancur,* imitation gold leaf, wood

H: 81, W: 32 (cm)

Akik means "carnelian," (an agate) and this *wanda* connotes a "stone-eyed" glare.

40

40. **Setyaki** (*wanda*: Wisuna)

FA.2007.40.99

Performer: Ki Purbo Asmoro; also: Ki Randyo

Artist: unknown

Place and Date Made: Wonogiri, date unknown; acquired by Ki Purbo Asmoro in Solo, 1997

Water buffalo hide and horn, water-based paint, *ancur,* bronze leaf, wood

H: 79, W: 30 (cm)

Wisuna refers to a dialogue or debate about some topic or a comprehensive discussion with another person. In this version, Setyaki is in a calmer mood than the previous example.

Basudéwa is the King of Mandura. His father is Kunthiboja and his sister is Dewi Kunthi. He has two sons with Dewi Mahindra: Kakrasana (Baladéwa) who succeeds him as king, and Narayana (Kresna) who becomes King of Dwarawati. "Kangsa Léna" [The Death of Kangsa] of the *Mahabharata* is one of the *lakon* in which this character appears.

41. **Basudéwa**

FA.2007.40.100

Performer: Ki Purbo Asmoro

Artists: Yatna Tentrem (leather carver), Beny (painter)

Place and Date Made: Klaten, date unknown; acquired by Ki Purbo Asmoro in Klaten, 1996

Water buffalo hide and horn, water-based paint, *ancur,* bronze leaf, wood

H: 84 W:31 (cm)

This wayang kulit version of Basudéwa is depicted with a face that is a deeper shade of red than the following example, indicating the character is angry, perhaps engaged in battle.

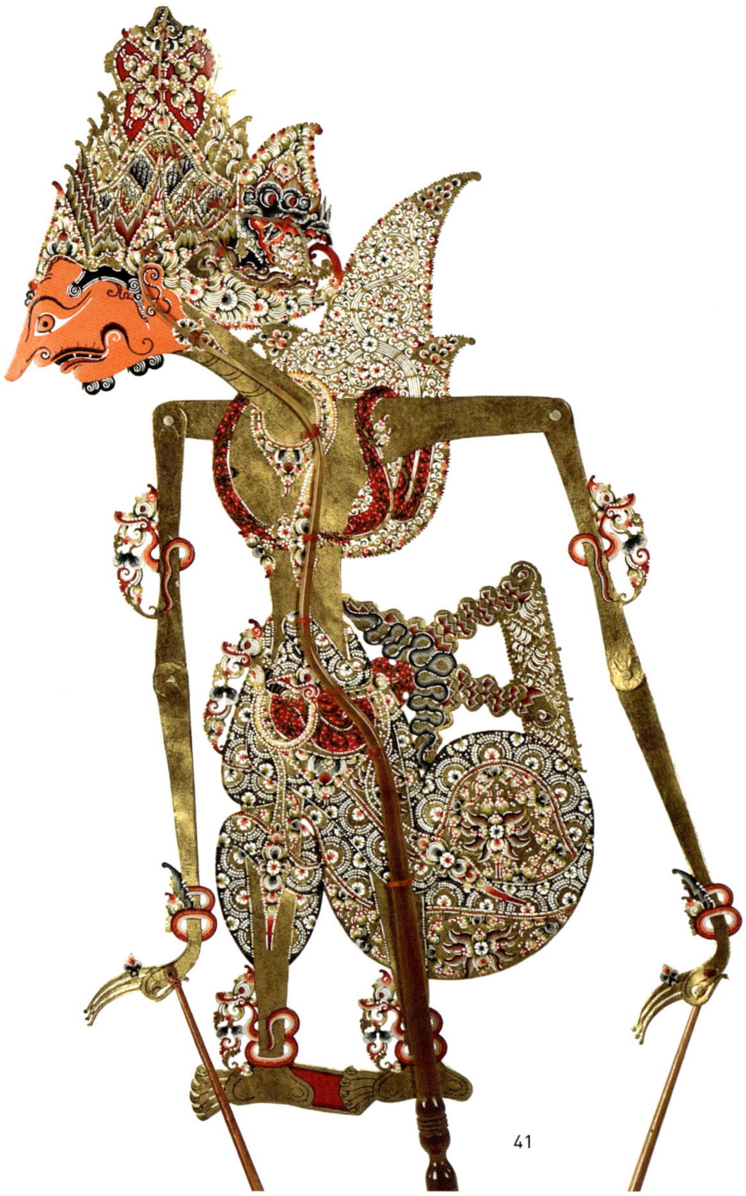

41

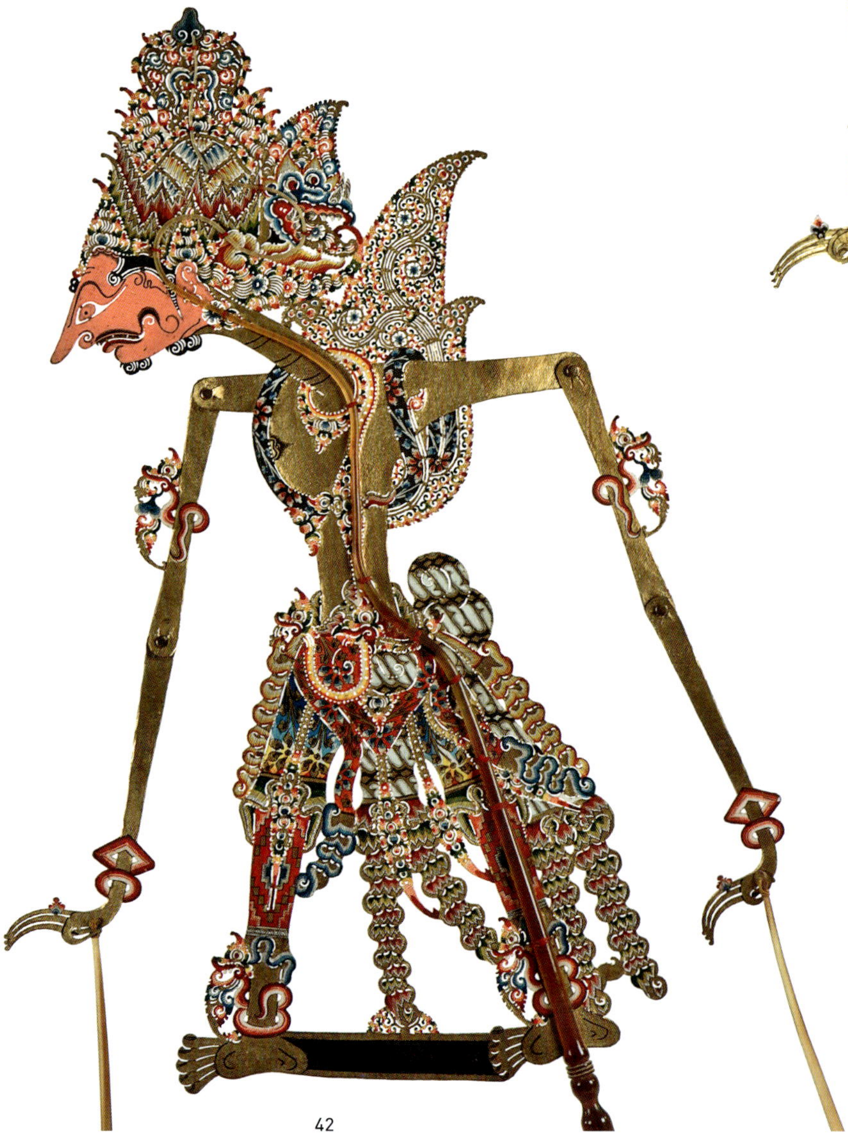

42

42. **Basudéwa**

FA.2007.40.101

Performer: Ki Purbo Asmoro; also: Ki Mulyanto

Artist: Sadipon (leather carver)

Place and Date Made: Sukoharjo, 1996

Water buffalo hide and horn, water-based paint, *ancur,* imitation gold leaf

H: 77, W: 29 (cm)

43. Setyajid

FA.2007.40.102

Performer: Ki Purbo Asmoro

Artists: Wiji Sutikno (leather carver), Murdiyonto (painter)

Place and Date Made: Sukoharjo, date unknown; acquired by Ki Purbo Asmoro in Sragen, 2004

Water buffalo hide and horn, water-based paint, *ancur,* gold leaf, wood

H: 75, W: 29 (cm)

Setyajid was known as Ugrasena when he was young; he took the name Setyajid when he was older and became King of Lesanpura. He is the son of Kunthiboja, and his children are Setyaki and Setyaboma (who marries Kresna). One of the stories in which this figure appears is "Alap Alapan Setyaboma" [The Marriage of Setyaboma] of the *Mahabharata*.

44. Salya

FA.2007.40.103

Performer: Ki Purbo Asmoro; also:Ki Sajali; Ki Rusni

Artists: Yatma (leather carver), Diman (painter)

Place and Date Made: Klaten, date unknown; acquired by Ki Purbo Asmoro in Klaten, 2000

Water buffalo hide and horn, water-based paint, *ancur,* bronze leaf

H: 79, W: 27 (cm)

Salya is known in his youth as Narasoma; he took the name Salya when he became king of Mandraka after his father Mandrapati. His sister is Dewi Madrim. He marries Satyawati, and their daughters are Dewi Erawati (who married King Baladéwa), Dewi Surtikanthi (who married Karna), Dewi Banowati (who married Duryudana), and their sons are Burisrawa and Rukmarata. King Salya does not completely agree with Duryudana's grounds for fighting the Pandhawas, but, because of Salya's relationship with the family and their allies, he nevertheless helps lead Kurawa armies. King Salya is eventually killed on the battlefield by Puntadéwa, whose body at the time is possessed by Salya's father-in-law, Bagaspati (who Salya murdered years ago).[6]

Salya's *lakon* include "Suryatmaja Maling" [The Thief Suryatmaja] and "Salya Gugur" [The Death of Salya] from the *Mahabharata*.

6. Irvine, *Leather Gods and Wooden Heros,* 264-266.

43

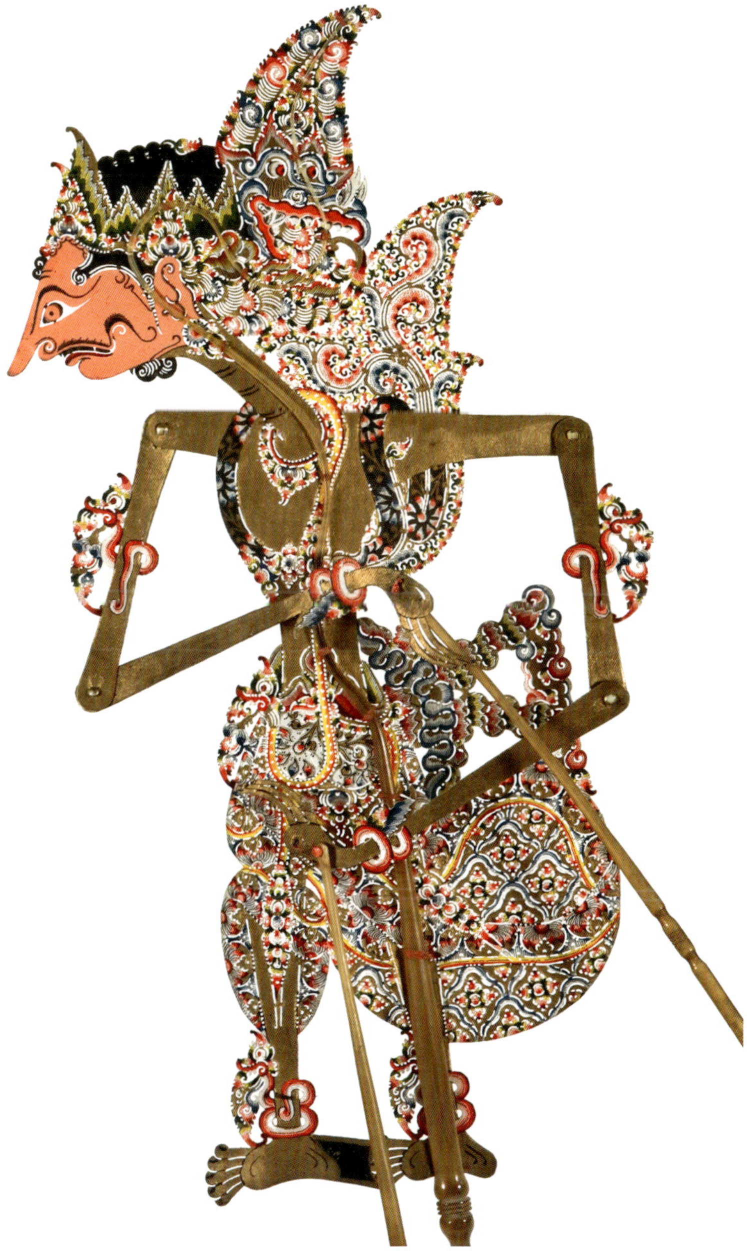

44

45. **Bismaka**

FA.2007.40.104

Performer: Ki Purbo Asmoro

Artists: Tugimin (leather carver), Murdiyonto (painter)

Place and Date Made: Sukoharjo, date unknown; acquired by Ki Purbo Asmoro in 2000

Water buffalo hide and horn, water-based paint, *ancur,* bronze leaf, wood

H: 81, W: 26 (cm)

Bismaka, King of Kumbina, is the son of Kunthiboja. Bismaka's daughter, Dewi Rukmini, is abducted by Kresna and later marries him. Bismaka appears in *lakon* such as "Kresna Kembang" [Kresna Marries Rukmini] in the *Mahabharata*.

45

46. **Matswapati**

FA.2007.40.105

Performer: Ki Purbo Asmoro;
also: Ki Sajali; Ki Toto Atmojo

Artists: unknown

Place and Date Made: Klaten, date unknown; acquired by Ki Purbo Asmoro in Klaten, 2000

Water buffalo hide and horn, water-based paint, *ancur,* bronze leaf, wood

H: 81, W: 28 (cm)

Matswapati is the king of Wirata. It was in King Matswapati's court that the Pandhawas took refuge when they lost the Amarta Kingdom to the Kurawas.

Matswapati has four children with Dewi Rekathawati (Palasara's daughter and Abiyasa's sister) and they are: Séta, Utara, Wratsangka, and Utari. Dewi Utari married Arjuna's son, Abimanyu, and their son, Parikesit, was eventually crowned King of Hastina when Puntadéwa relinquishes the throne.

Matswapati appears in the *Mahabharata* episodes "Wiratha Parwa" [The Story of the Kingdom Wiratha] and "Sesaji Raja Suya" [The Grand Offering of the Kings].

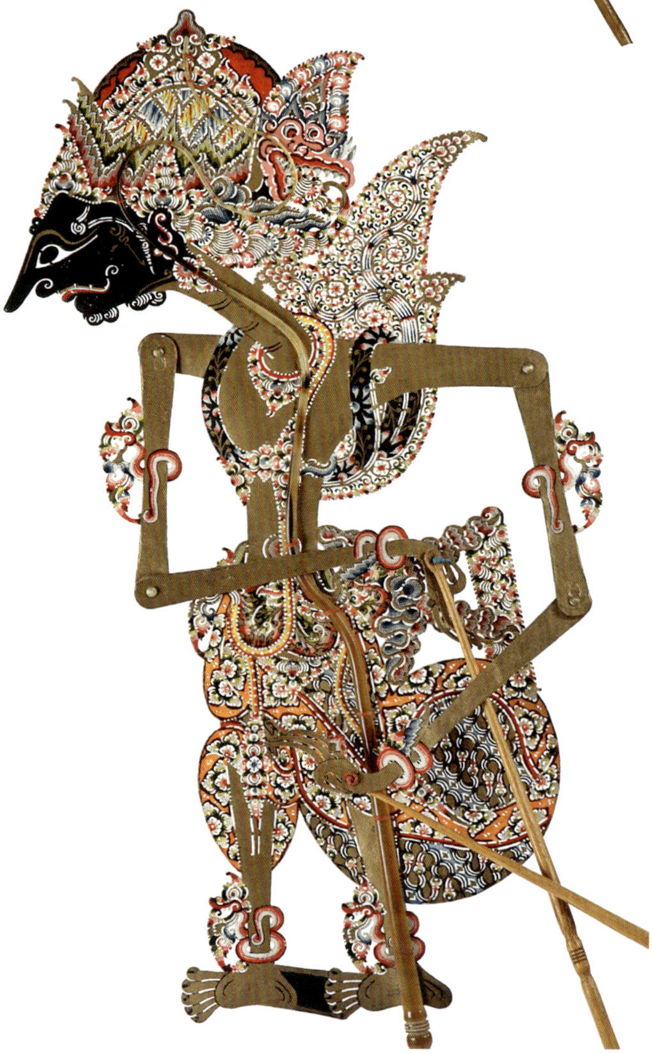

46

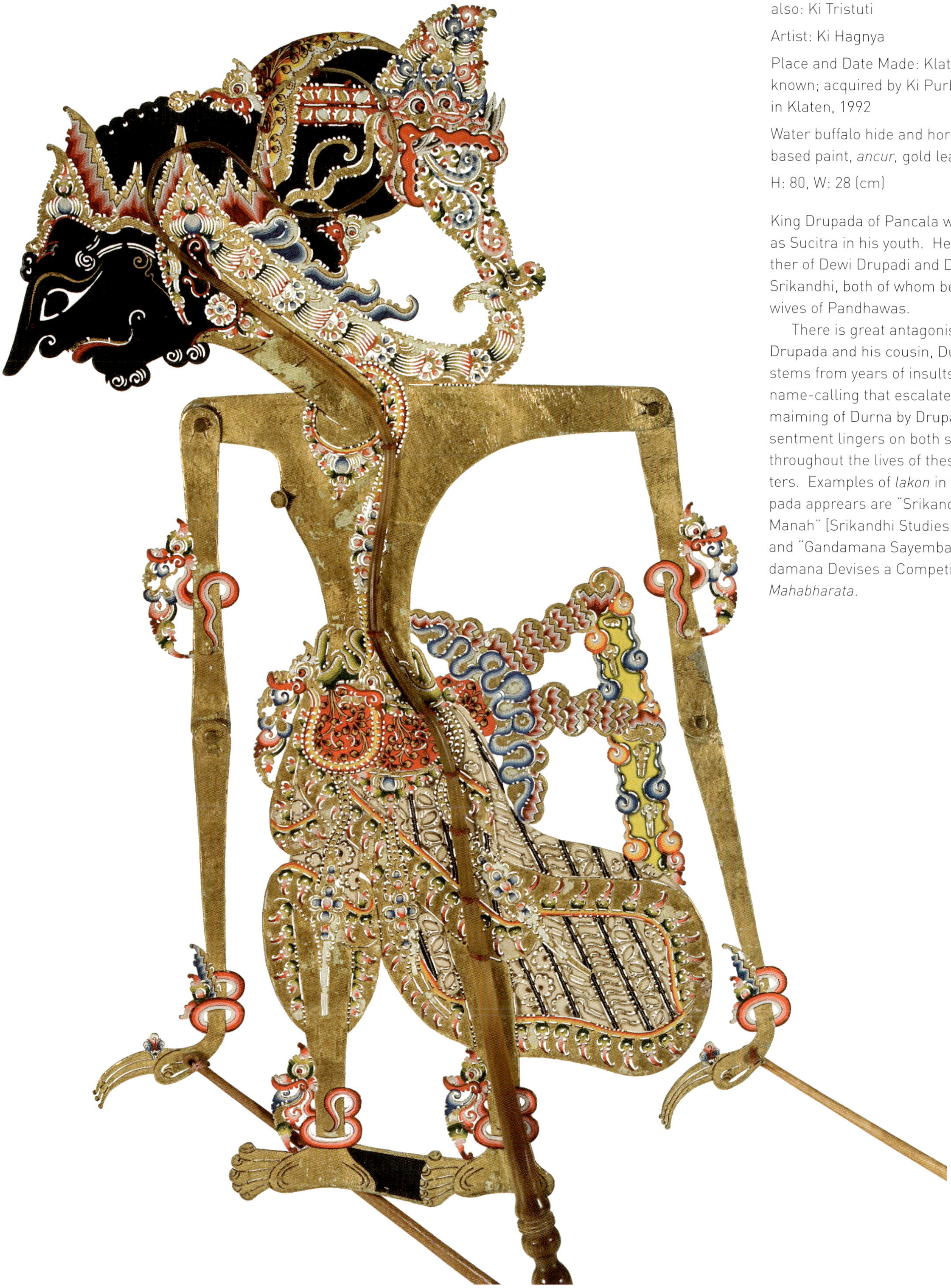

47. **Drupada**

FA.2007.40.106

Performer: Ki Purbo Asmoro; also: Ki Tristuti

Artist: Ki Hagnya

Place and Date Made: Klaten, date unknown; acquired by Ki Purbo Asmoro in Klaten, 1992

Water buffalo hide and horn, water-based paint, *ancur,* gold leaf, wood

H: 80, W: 28 (cm)

King Drupada of Pancala was known as Sucitra in his youth. He is the father of Dewi Drupadi and Dewi Srikandhi, both of whom become wives of Pandhawas.

There is great antagonism between Drupada and his cousin, Durna, which stems from years of insults and name-calling that escalate into the maiming of Durna by Drupada. Resentment lingers on both sides throughout the lives of these characters. Examples of *lakon* in which Drupada apprears are "Srikandhi Meguru Manah" [Srikandhi Studies Archery] and "Gandamana Sayembara" [Gandamana Devises a Competition] from *Mahabharata.*

Karna is the first born child of Dewi Kunthi. Kunthi conceives Karna by miraculous means, before she is married to Pandhu Déwanata. She gives birth to the baby boy through her ear, and with the help of the gods, Kunthi's pregnancy and the birth are kept secret. She then abandons the child, who is raised by a foster family. Karna learns the code of the *satria* (noble knight) and becomes a skilled warrior. Karna is banned from an archery contest organized by the Pandhawas because they believe Karna to be of a low caste (and thus not an appropriate competitor for archers of their own status). The Kurawas, however, recognize Karna's talents, and Duryudana (the oldest brother and leader of Kurawas) makes him a regent. Karna pledges his loyalty to Duryudana's side in gratitude for the Kurawas' acceptance and support.

Karna learns of his true heritage during a battle against his blood-brothers, the Pandhawas. However, he continues fighting against them—on the side of the Kurawas. He does so because he took an oath to support the Kurawas, but also because he rationalizes that if he refused to fight, there would be no war. If there were no war, the Pandhawas would not win control over the Hastina kingdom, which is the will of the gods. Ultimately, his duty is to fulfill the gods' will that the Pandhawas should regain the Hastina. So, Karna fights long and hard and is finally decapitated by his own brother, Arjuna. In the end, the Pandhawas win the war and win control over Hastina. Karna appears in "Karna Tanding" [Karna Faces His Opponent], "Wahyu Makutharama" [Makutharama: A Boon from the Gods] and many other *Mahabharata* episodes.

48. **Karna** (*wanda*: Lonthang)

FA.2007.40.107

Performer: Ki Purbo Asmoro; also: Ki Tristuti; Ki Mulyono

Arists: Kuncung (leather carver), Slamet (painter)

Place and Date Made: Sragen (carved) and Sukoharjo (painted), 1993; acquired by Ki Purbo Asmoro in Sragen, 1994

Water buffalo hide and horn, water-based paint, *ancur*, gold leaf, wood

H: 80, W: 30 (cm)

This wayang kulit figure has a gold face, which is considered rare and unusual. Ki Purbo chose this piece for his collection because he found it visually compelling.[7]

The *Wanda* Lonthang refers to Karna as he walks along, without carrying anything.

7. Interview with Ki Purbo Asmoro, Surakarta. June 25, 2009.

49. **Karna** (*wanda*: Bèdru)

FA.2007.40.108

Performer: Ki Purbo Asmoro; also: Ki Maryono; Ki Suryanto

Artist: Pardi

Place and Date Made: Sukoharjo, date unknown; acquired by Ki Purbo Asmoro in Sragen, 2000

Water buffalo hide and horn, water-based paint, *ancur*, gold leaf, wood

H: 81, W: 30 (cm)

Bèdru means "misunderstanding." The shape of the Karna's face (in this wanda Bèdru) is said to resemble that of Kresna (*wanda* Botoh).[8] (See plate 32 in the Simpingan Kanan Section)

8. Dr. Suyanto, S.Kar., MA, E-mail communication, August 19, 2009.

49

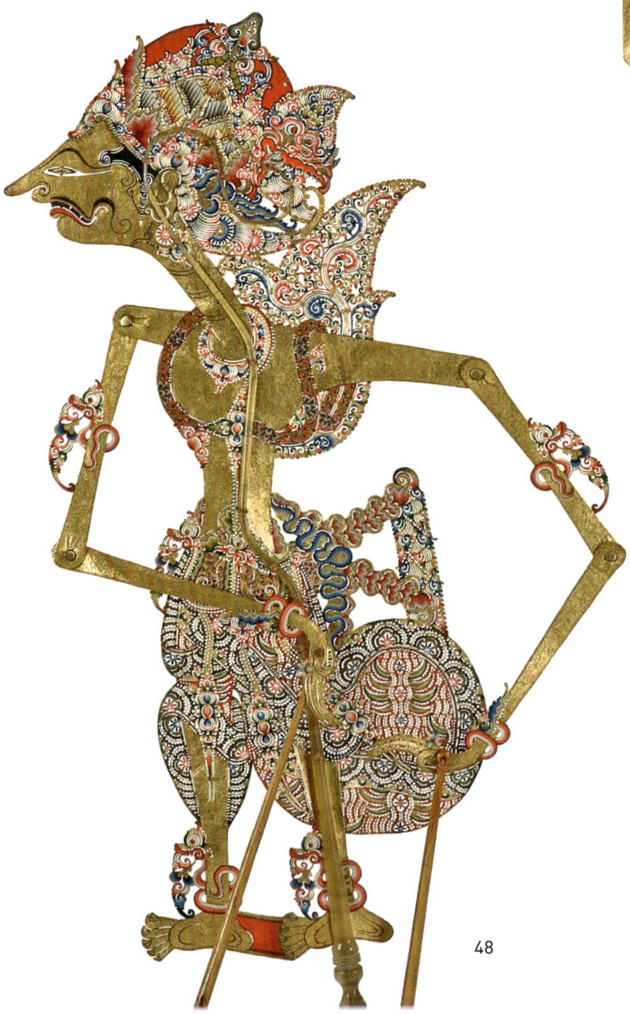

48

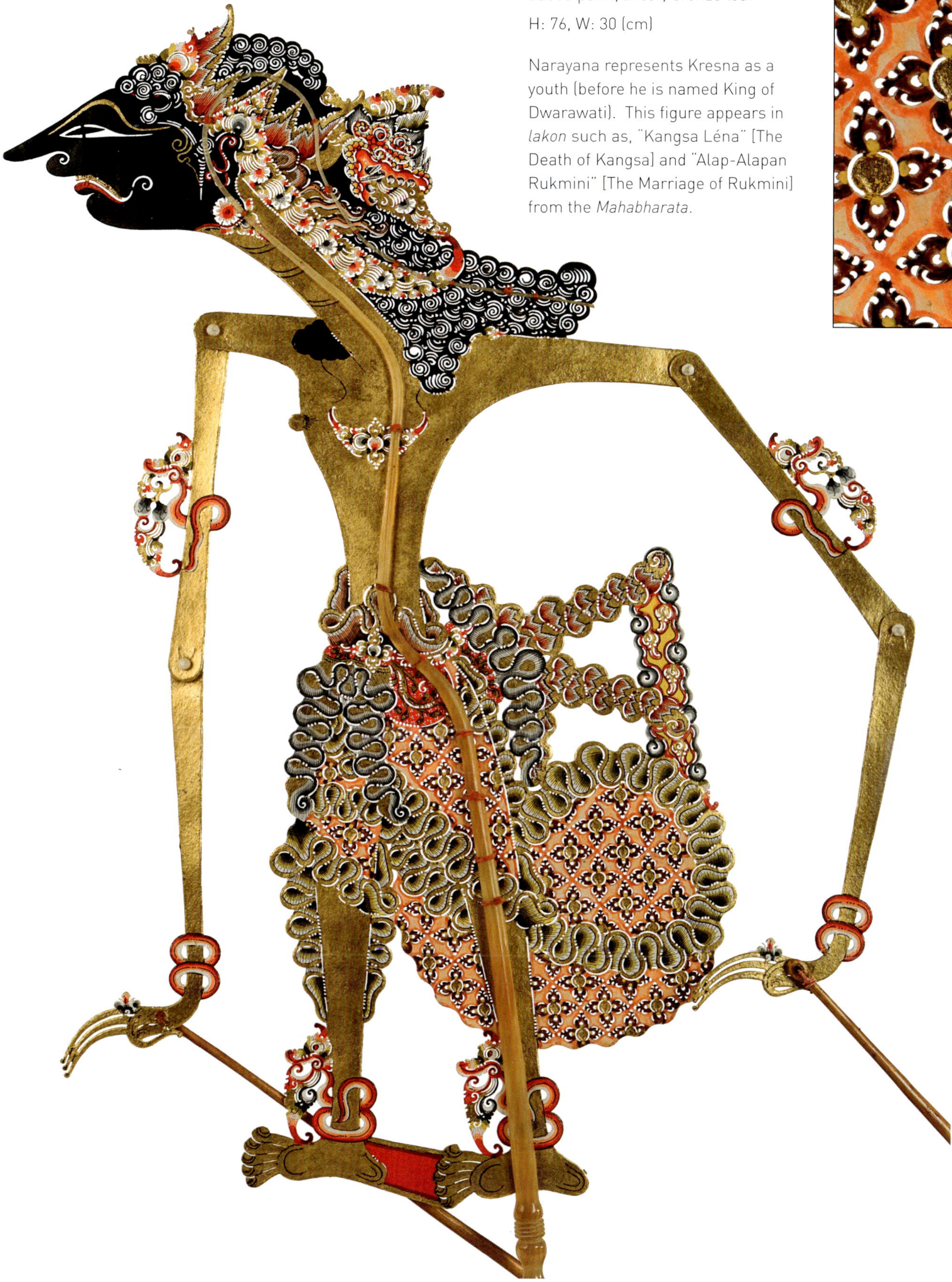

50. **Narayana**

FA.2007.40.109

Performer: Ki Purbo Asmoro;
also: Ki Tristuti

Artists: Wiji Sutikno (leather carver)

Place and Date Made: Sukoharjo, date unknown; acquired by Ki Purbo Asmoro in Sukoharjo, 1998

Water buffalo hide and horn, water-based paint, *ancur*, bronze leaf

H: 76, W: 30 (cm)

Narayana represents Kresna as a youth (before he is named King of Dwarawati). This figure appears in *lakon* such as, "Kangsa Léna" [The Death of Kangsa] and "Alap-Alapan Rukmini" [The Marriage of Rukmini] from the *Mahabharata*.

51. **Drestarastra**

FA.2007.40.110

Performer: Ki Purbo Asmoro;
also: Ki Sajali; Ki Kasim

Artists: unknown

Place and Date Made: Klaten, date unknown; acquired by Ki Purbo Asmoro in Klaten, 2000

Water buffalo hide and horn, water-based paint, *ancur*, bronze leaf

H: 80, W: 29 (cm)

Drestarastra is the blind son of Abiyasa and is Pandhu Déwanata's brother. With his cunning wife, Déwi Gendari (also known as Anggendari), Drestarastra has one hundred children, known as the Kurawas. Though Drestarastra himself is virtuous and honest, he is a weak ruler, so blinded by his love for his sons that he does not recognize their malicious behavior. Drestarastra's physical blindess is depicted in this shadow puppet by his closed eye.

Because of Drestarastra's disability, his brother Pandhu (father of the Pandhawas) takes the throne of Hastina after Abiyasa resigns. But when Pandhu himself dies, Drestarastra is called upon to serve as an interim ruler—until the next generation comes of age.

When the Pandhawa-Kurawa cousins reach adulthood, it is not clear if the next ruler will come from Pandhu's or Drestarastra's lineage. Although Abiyasa decreed that the next king should be Puntadéwa (the eldest Pandhawa), Gendari and her sinister brother, Sengkuni, manipulate Drestarastra and convince him to name Duryudana (the eldest Kurawa) as King of Hastina. From this action, the tensions between the cousins reached its tipping point and their hostilities grew into outright battles and wars, which lasted another several generations.

This character appears in lakon from the *Mahabharata* such as "Babad Wanamarta" [The Clearing of the Amarta Forest], and "Bima Bungkus" [Bima Encased in a Bundle].

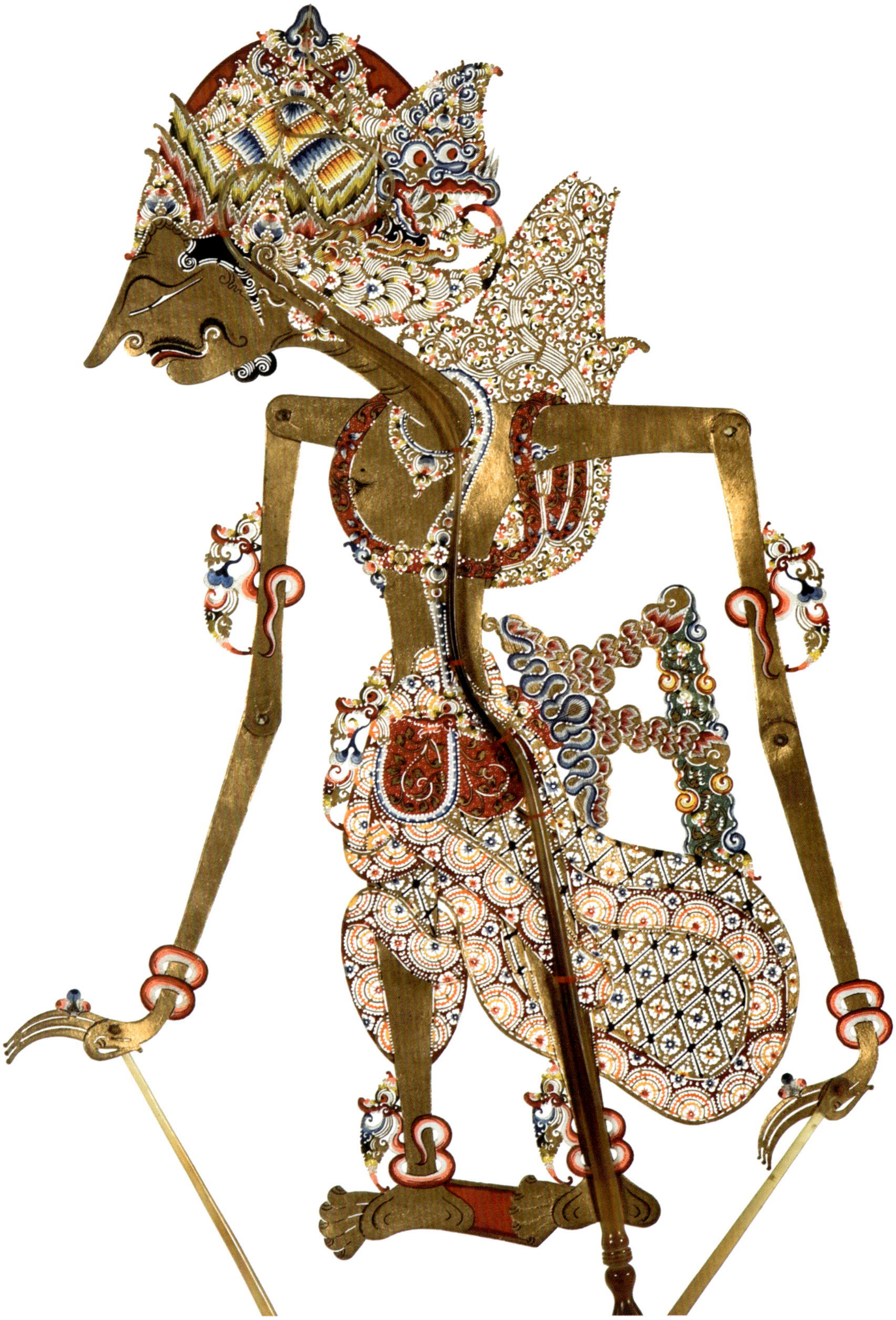

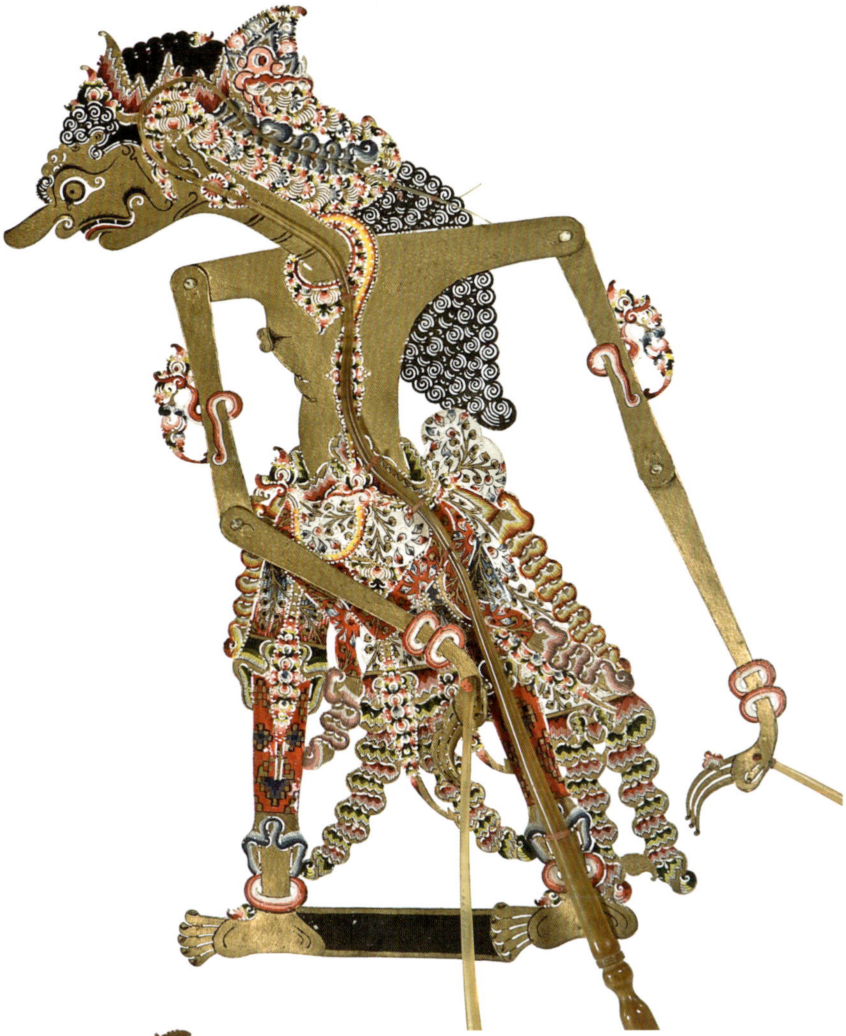

52

52. **Lesmana Mandrakumata**

FA.2007.40.111

Performer: Ki Purbo Asmoro

Artists: Yatna Tentrem (leather carver), Diman (painter)

Place and Date Made: Klaten, date unknown; acquired by Ki Purbo Asmoro in Klaten, 1992

Water buffalo hide and horn, water-based paint, *ancur,* bronze leaf

H: 76, W: 29 (cm)

Lesmana Mandrakumara is Duryudana's son with Banowati and expected to become heir to Duryudana's throne in Hastina. He is depicted as a foolish glutton and a lecher with few talents and little understanding of virtue and nobility.[9] He meets his death in the great war, known as the Bharatayuda, at the hands of Abimanyu.

This wayang figure has appeared in *Mahabharata* episodes like "Cakraningrat" [Cakraningrat: A Boon From the Gods], "Pregiwa Pregiwati" [The Story of Pregiwa and Pregiwati], and "Abimanyu Ranjab" [Abimanyu is Pierced to Death], which is also known as "Abimanyu Gugur" [The Death of Abimanyu].

9. Benedict Anderson, *Mythology and the Tolerance of the Javanese*. Ithaca, N.Y.: Modern Indonesia Project; Southeast Asia Program, Department of Asian Studies, Cornell University, 1965, 37.

53

53. **Bisawarna**

FA.2007.40.112

Performer: Ki Purbo Asmoro

Artists: Joko (leather carver), Murdiyonto (painter)

Place and Date Made: Sukoharjo, date unknown; acquired by Ki Purbo Asmoro in Sragen, 2001

Water buffalo hide and horn, water-based paint, *ancur,* gold leaf

H: 81, W: 27 (cm)

Bisawarna is Wibisana's son and he appears in the *lakon*, "Wahyu Makutharama" [Makuthrama: A Boon From the Gods] of the *Ramayana*.

54. **Sumantri**

FA.2007.40.113

Performer: Ki Purbo Asmoro; also: Ki Agus Pramana; Ki Ary Bodro

Artists: Joko (leather carver), Murdiyonto (painter)

Place and Date Made: Sukoharjo, date unknown; acquired by Ki Purbo Asmoro in Sragen, 2000

Water buffalo hide and horn, water-based paint, *ancur*, gold leaf

H: 74.5, W: 26 (cm)

Sumantri is the son of the wise priest, Suwandageni. Sumantri betrays Arjuna Sasrabahu, to whom he is bound by an oath; but later Sumantri attempts to make amends. Sumantri appears in the *lakon*, "Sumantri Ngèngèr" [Sumantri as Apprentice] and "Sumantri Gugur" [The Death of Sumantri] in the epic, the *Ramayana*.

55. **Narasoma**

FA.2007.40.114

Performer: Ki Purbo Asmoro

Artists: Joko (leather carver), Murdiyonto (painter)

Place and Date Made: Sragen, 2000

Water buffalo hide and horn, water-based paint, *ancur*, gold leaf, wood

H: 76.5, W: 27 (cm)

The character, King Salya, is known as Narasoma in his youth. He appears in *lakon* such as "Narasoma" [The Story of Narasoma] and "Kunthi Pilih" [Kunthi Makes a Choice] from the *Mahabharata*.

The youthful Narasoma enters a contest to win the hand of Dewi Kunthi in marriage. However, Narasoma loses to Pandhu, who also takes Narasoma's sister, Dewi Madrim, as a second wife.

Narasoma's own wife, Satyawati, is the daughter of the good-hearted ogre-priest named Begawan Bagaspati. Narasoma is afraid that having an ugly ogre as his father-in-law will reflect poorly on his own high status. After much discussion with Satyawati (and with Bagaspati himself) Narasoma kills Bagaspati. Narasoma's father commits suicide because he is ashamed of his son's actions.[10] Narasoma succeeds his father as King of Mandraka and takes the name Salya.

10. David Irvine, *Leather Gods and Wooden Heros*, 264-265..

54

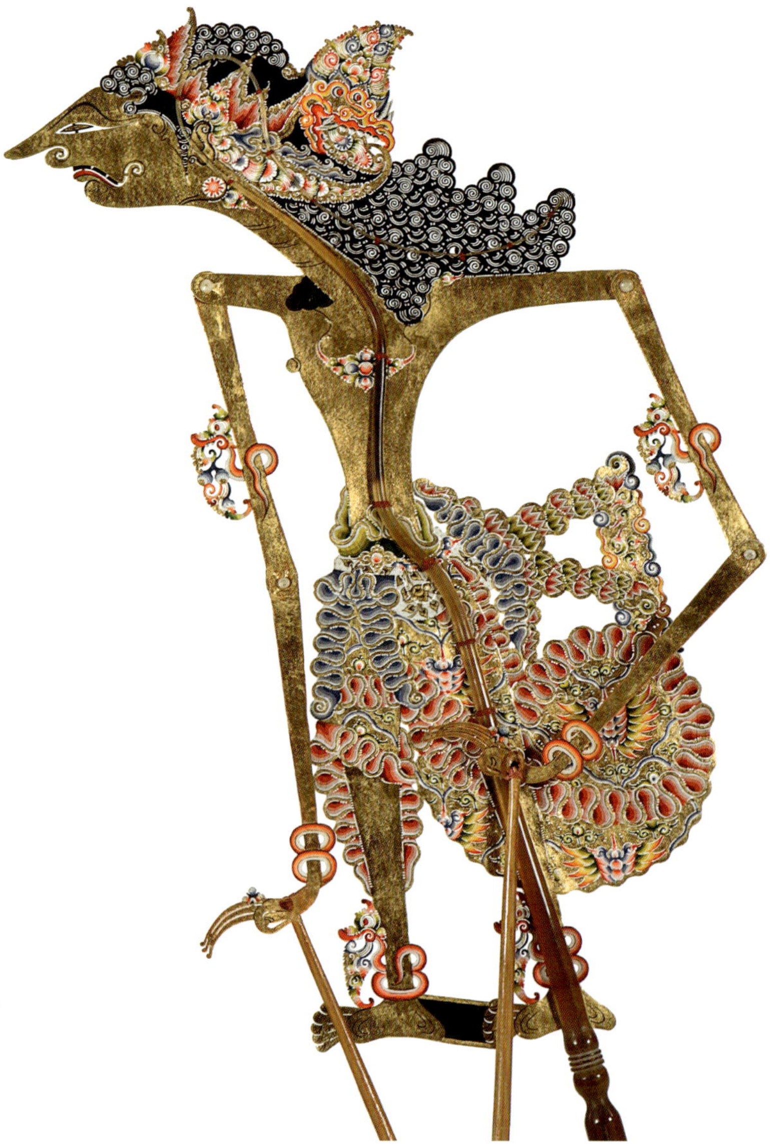

55

56. **Suman**

FA.2007.40.115

Performer: Ki Purbo Asmoro

Artists: Jono (leather carver), Murdiyonto (painter); Designer: Ki Purbo Asmoro

Place and Date Made: Wonogiri, 1997

Water buffalo hide and horn, water-based paint, *ancur*, gold leaf, wood

H: 73.5, W: 29 (cm)

Suman is the name of Sengkuni in his youth. He appears in *lakon* such as "Gandamana Luweng" [Gandamana is Buried Alive] and "Bima Bungkus" [Bima Encased in a Bundle] from the *Mahabharata*. This rarely made wayang figure is a special design by Ki Purbo Asmoro and is rarely seen in classic sets of wayang kulit.

57

Trusthajumena

FA.2007.40.116

Performer: Ki Purbo Asmoro; also: Ki Sajali

Artists: Diyo (leather carver), Ki Sajali (painter)

Place and Date Made: Klaten, date unknown; acquired by Ki Purbo Asmoro in Klaten, 2000

Water buffalo hide and horn, water-based paint, *ancur*, bronze leaf

H: 72.5, W: 28 (cm)

Trusthajumena is the son of King Drupada of Pancala. Trusthajumena decapitates Durna, King Drupada's rival and cousin—an act which causes deep grief among both the Kurawas and Pandhawas, all of whom studied with Durna as children. Trusthajumena is ultimately killed by Durna's son, Aswatama.

This character is found in *lakon* such as "Bharatayuda" (The Great Bharatayuda War) and "Srikandhi Meguru Manah" (Srikandhi Studies Archery) from the *Mahabharata*.

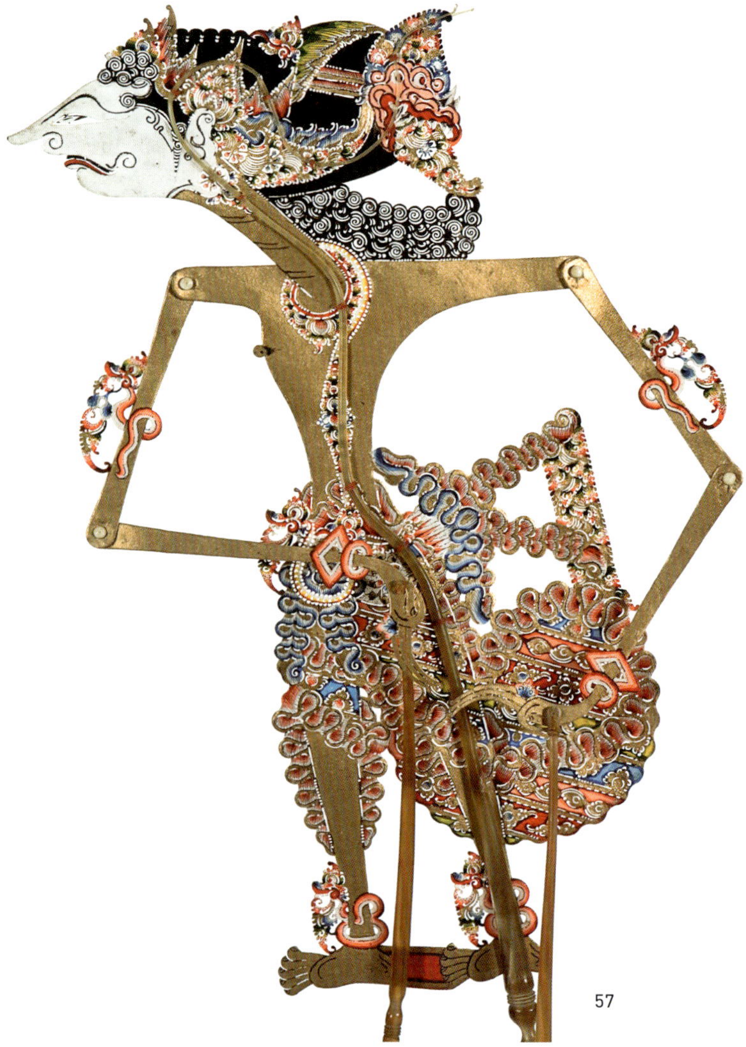

57

58. **Samba**

FA.2007.40.117

Performer: Ki Purbo Asmoro; also: Ki Pringgo Darsono

Artists: Joko (leather carver), Murdiyonto (painter)

Place and Date Made: Sukoharjo, 1994

Water buffalo hide and horn, water-based paint, *ancur*, gold leaf, wood

H: 74, W: 28 (cm)

Samba is Kresna's son with Dewi Jembawati. Though very handsome, noble, and full of good intentions, he can also be a bit arrogant. At times, he is somewhat of a disappointment to his parents.[11] The character appears in *lakon* such as "Samba Juwing" (Samba Is Viciously Killed) and "Cakraningrat" (Cakraningrat: A Boon From the Gods) from the *Mahabharata*.

11. Dr. Suyanto S.Kar., MA, Email communication, August 19, 2009.

58

59

59. **Setyaka**

FA.2007.40.118

Performer: Ki Purbo Asmoro;
also: Ki Puntono

Artists: Mulyono and Murdiyonto (painter)

Place and Date Made: Semarang, 1996

Water buffalo hide and horn, water-based paint, *ancur,* gold leaf

H: 73, W: 28 (cm)

Setyaka is Kresna's son with Dewi Setyaboma. His *lakon* include, "Kresna Gugah" [Kresna Wakes From His Meditation] and "Gendrèh Kemasan" [Arjuna Disguised as Gendrèh Kemasan] of the epic, the *Mahabharata*.

60. **Wisanggeni**

FA.2007.40.119

Performer: Ki Purbo Asmoro

Artists: Tugimin and Murdiyanto

Place and Date Made: Sukoharjo, 2003

Water buffalo hide and horn, water-based paint, *ancur,* gold leaf, wood

H: 70.5, W: 25 (cm)

Arjuna spends several years in Heaven where he has a son with Dewi Dresanala (Bathara Brahma's daughter). This boy, Wisanggeni, is Arjuna's son and Brama's grandson. The *lakon* "Wisanggeni Lahir" [The Birth of Wisanggeni] and "Wisanggeni Krama" [Wisanggeni's Wedding], from the *Mahabharata* epic, recount the events of Wisangqeni's birth and his earthly adventures as he searches for Arjuna.

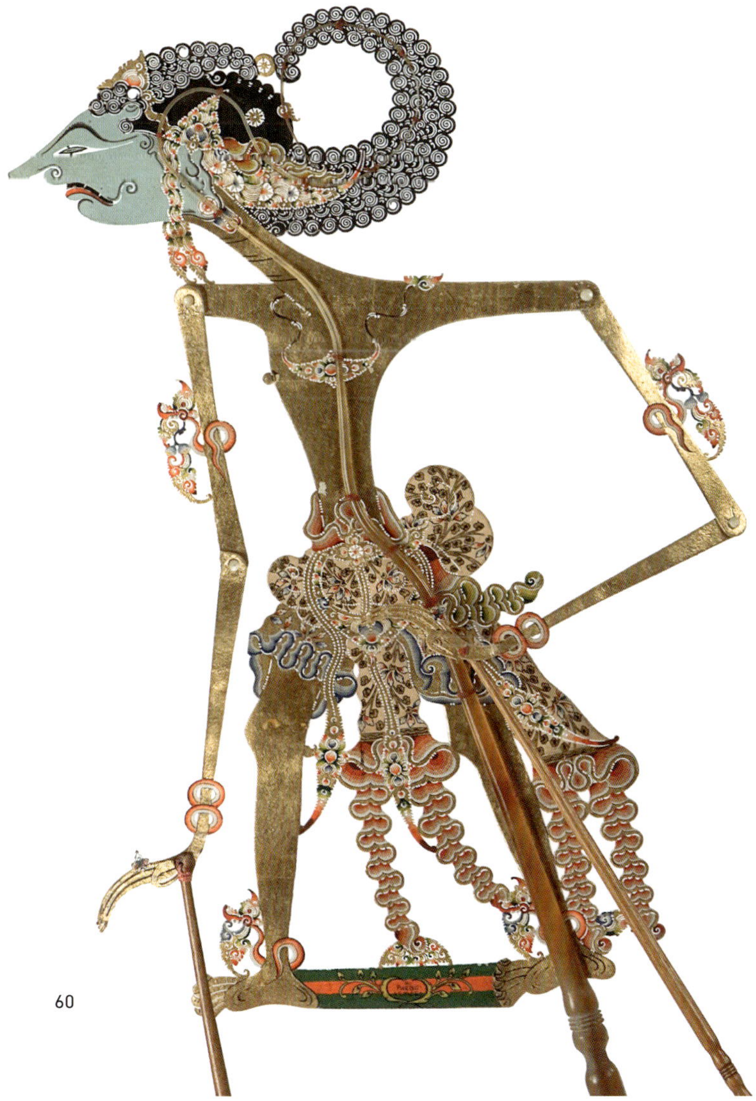

60

Nakula and **Sadéwa** are the fourth and fifth Pandhawa brothers (twins) who are born to Pandhu Déwanata and Dewi Madrim. Nakula and Sadéwa are raised by Kunthi after Madrim commits suttee upon Pandhu's death. The twins fight in the great war, the Bharatayuda, where their major contribution is their discovery of King Salya's vulnerabilities, a discovery that helps Puntadéwa to win the war. The two figures appear in *lakon* involving the Pandhawa brothers, and are also noted for their role in "Sesaji Raja Suya" [The Grand Offering of the Kings] of the *Mahabharata*.

61. **Nakula**

FA.2007.40.120

Performers: Ki Purbo Asmoro; also: Ki Sajali; Ki Kesdik; Ki Ga'ib

Artists unknown

Place and Date Made: Klaten, date unknown; acquired by Ki Purbo Asmoro in Klaten, 2000

Water buffalo hide and horn, water-based paint, *ancur*, bronze leaf

H: 65, W: 24 (cm)

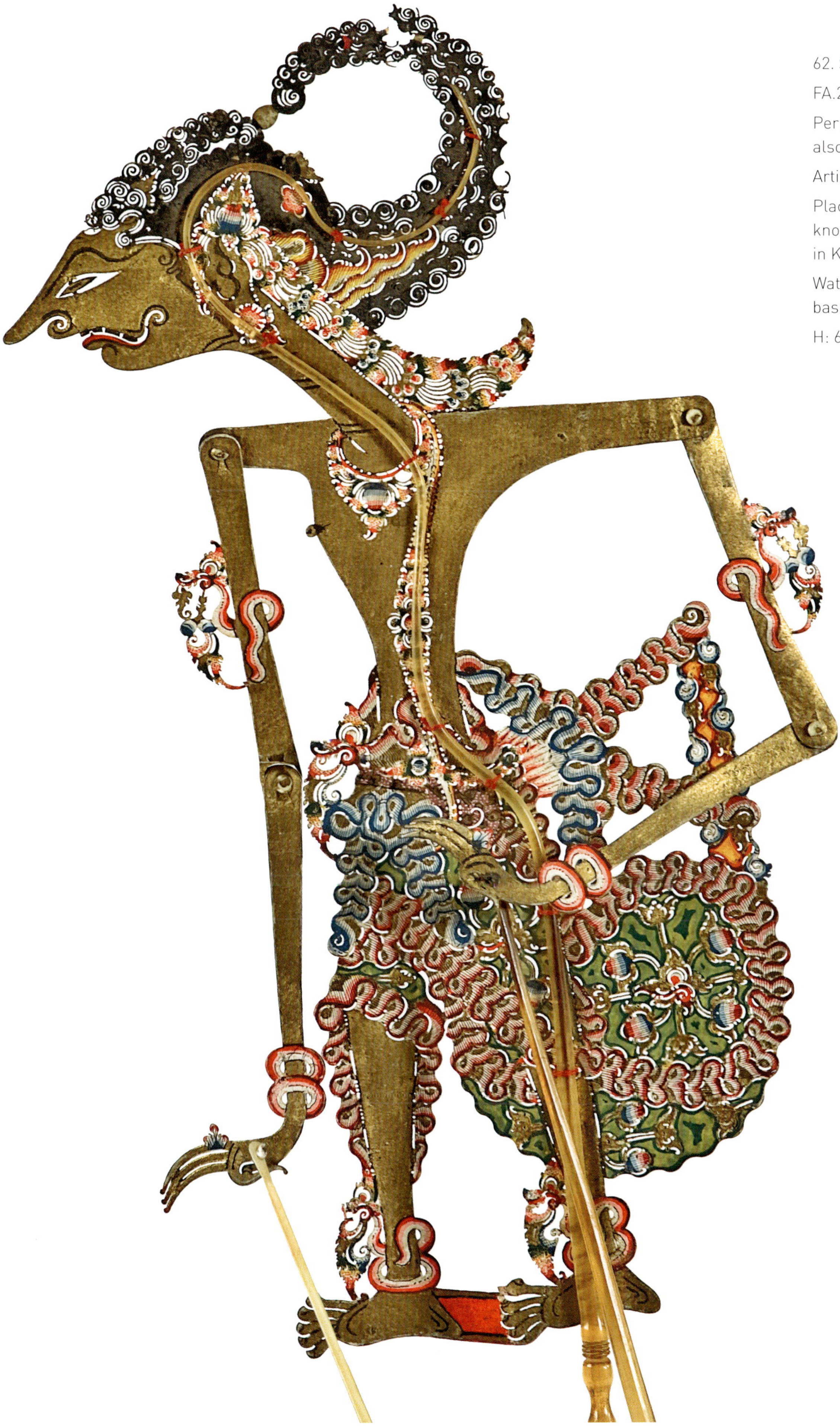

62. **Sadéwa**

FA.2007.40.121

Performers: Ki Purbo Asmoro; also: Ki Sajali; Ki Kesdik; Ki Ga'ib

Artists unknown

Place and Date Made: Klaten, date unknown; acquired by Ki Purbo Asmoro in Klaten, 2000

Water buffalo hide and horn, water-based paint, *ancur*, bronze leaf

H: 67, W: 24 (cm)

Dhudhahan Group

A third group of puppets is kept apart by the dhalang: this is the *dhudhahan* group. Unlike the puppets of the *simpingan kanan* and *simpingan kiri* groups, the dhudhahan puppets are not placed on the *gedebog* (the banana log used as a base for the wayang in front of the screen). The dhudhahan group includes wayang figures that either do not fit the aesthetics of the right-left display, or figures that might be used in the evening's performance. Those used in the performance are kept nearby, either on top of the box to the dhalang's left as he faces the screen or on top of the box lid to the dhalang's right.

Generally, characters in the dhudhahan group may vary by the episode that is performed.

DHUDHAHAN I

This group includes puppets that represent members of the Kurawa family (Mahabharata), advisors to the Kurawas, Butas (ogres), Punakawan (clown servant characters), Parekan (ladies-in-waiting), and miscellaneous and "generic" types of wayang characters.

1. **Dursasana** (*wanda*: Robyong)

FA.2007.40.122

Performer: Ki Purbo Asmoro; also: Ki Bowo; Ki Manto

Artist: Supardi

Place and Date Made: Sragen, date unknown; acquired by Ki Purbo Asmoro in Sragen, 2000

Water buffalo hide and horn, water-based paint, *ancur,* gold leaf, wood

H: 100, W: 46 (cm)

Dursasana, the second-eldest of the Kurawa brothers, is the son of Drestarastra and Dewi Gendari (also known as Anggendari). Dursasana is considered by his family to be devoted and loyal, particularly to Duryudana's cause. Nevertheless, Dursasana commits heinous acts, particularly against the Pandhawas (who make his death a high priority). In the end, Dursasana's body is torn to pieces by Bima in the great Bharatayuda War.

Robyong means "noisy" and refers to the various clanking weapons that the ostentatious Dursasana wears, which make a lot of noise.[1] Dursasana appears in most *lakon* involving the Kurawas, but is particularly noted for his roles in "Dursasana Gugur" [The Death of Dursasana], "Wahyu Makutharama" [Makutharama: A Boon from the Gods], and "Aji Narantaka" [The Narantaka Amulet].

1. Interview with Dr. Suyanto, S.Kar., MA, Surakarta, June 24, 2009.

2. **Durmagati**

FA.2007.40.123

Performer: Ki Purbo Asmoro; also: Ki Bowo

Artist: Supardi

Place and Date Made: Sragen, date unknown

Water buffalo hide and horn, water-based paint, *ancur,* gold leaf, wood

H: 82, W: 36 (cm)

Durmagati is one of the Kurawa brothers; the son of Drestarastra and Dewi Gendari. Durmagati is noted for being one of the most ill-natured of the Kurawa brothers. This figure is used in most *Mahabharata* episodes that involve the Kurawas.

3. **Sengkuni**

FA.2007.40.125

Performer: Ki Purbo Asmoro; also: Ki Bowo; Ki Puthut

Artists: Wiji Sutikno (leather carver), Murdiyonto (painter)

Place and Date Made: Sragen, date unknown; acquired by Ki Purbo Asmoro in Sragen, 2000

Water buffalo hide and horn, water-based paint, *ancur*, imitation gold leaf, wood

H: 79, W: 28 (cm)

Sengkuni is the Kurawas' uncle and one of the most sinister characters in the *Mahabharata*.

Sengkuni's father is King Gendara (from Plasajenar) and his sister is Gendari (also known as Anggendari). Gendari initially wants to marry Pandhu Déwanata, but is instead given in marriage to his brother, the blind Drestarastra (Gendari and Drestarastra are the parents of the Kurawas). She thus swears vengeance against Pandhu and his children (the Pandhawas). Sengkuni, a loyal brother, is always behind Gendari in her efforts to thwart the Pandhawas.

Together with his sister, Sengkuni exerts a strong influence over his blind brother-in-law, Drestarastra, who becomes King of Hastina after Pandhu's death. The Pandhawa – Kurawa cousins grew up together in Hastina. Their mentors include Durna and Bisma (both noble characters who eventually sided with the Kurawas), and Sengkuni. When they were young boys, Sengkuni enjoyed pitting the cousins against each other, setting obstacles for the Pandhawas in all their endeavors. When the cousins come of age, Sengkuni and Gendari manipulate Drestarastra into naming Duryudana the king (the eldest Kurawa child), instead of rightfully giving the crown to Puntadéwa (the eldest Pandhawa child). Sengkuni becomes Duryudana's prime minister and chief advisor and feeds Duryudana malicious ideas and supports the horrendous acts he commits against his cousins.

Some of Sengkuni's most important roles are in *lakon* such as "Sengkuni Gugur" [The Death of Sangkuni] and "Bima Suci" [Bima as Priest] of the *Mahabharata*.

4. **Durna**

FA.2007.40.124

Performer: Ki Purbo Asmoro; also: Ibu Suharni

Artists: Munaji (leather carver), Mentong (painter)

Place and Date Made: Sragen, date unknown; acquired by Ki Purbo Asmoro in Sragen, 1996

Water buffalo hide and horn, water-based paint, *ancur,* gold leaf, wood

H: 75.5, W: 28.5 (cm)

The noble priest Durna is a teacher of the young Pandhawa and Kurawa cousins. His wife is Dewi Wilutama and their son is Aswatama. Although Durna knows right from wrong, he is, nevertheless, a rather devious character. Durna does not always agree with Duryudana's cause, but because Durna's loyalty is to the Kurawas, he continues to support their side. In the end, Durna is tricked by Pandhawa allies into believing his son, Aswatama, has died. The Pandhawa allies take advantage of Durna's grief and vulnerability, and kill him.

As a young man, Durna was severely beaten and maimed on the orders of his cousin, King Drupada, after a perceived insult. In this wayang figure, Durna's disfigured arm is articulated at the wrist, not at the elbow, which shows his handicap.

Durna appears in numerous *lakon*, and this figure was used by Ki Purbo Asmoro in *Mahabharata* episodes such as "Kumbayana" [The Story of Kumbayana] and "Durna Gugur" [The Death of Durna].

5. **Kartamarma**

FA.2007.40.126

Performer: Ki Purbo Asmoro;
also: Ki Sayoko; Ki Tristuti

Artists: Wiji Sutikno, and Slamet Rabarjo

Place and Date Made: Sukoharjo, 1993

Water buffalo hide and horn, water-based paint, *ancur*, gold leaf, wood

H: 87, W: 37 (cm)

Kartamarma is one of the Kurawa brothers, the son of Drestarastra and Gendari, who features prominently in numerous *Mahabharata lakon* about the Kurawas. He aids Aswatama in killing Dewi Banowati (Duryudana's wife) who is in love with Arjuna. Kartamarma is eventually killed by Bima.

5

6

6. **Aswatama**

FA.2007.40.127

Performer: Ki Purbo Asmoro;
also: Ki Sayoko; Ki Tristuti

Artists: Wiji Sutikno, and Slamet Rabarjo

Place and Date Made: Sukoharjo, 1993

Water buffalo hide and horn, water-based paint, *ancur*, gold leaf

H: 84, W: 36 (cm)

Aswatama is Durna's son. His mother is Dewi Kahyangan, a goddess. Although there is no specific story regarding Aswatama's marriage, he does have a son. This boy (Dahyang Suwela) is himself a god, and he appears rather suddenly (and with no previous introduction) after the great war, known as The Bharatayuda.[2]

Aswatama fights for the Kurawas. He is a stalwart fighter and he avenges his father's death by killing Drupada's son Trusthajumena; he avenges Bisma's death by killing Srikandhi; and he avenges the dishonor he believes Banowati has brought Duryudana by killing her in her sleep. Finally, Aswatama attempts to avenge the defeat of friends, family, and Kurawa allies by killing Arjuna's grandson, Parikesit. However, Arjuna's magic weapon kills Aswatama instead.

Aswatama appears in *Mahabharata* episodes involving the Kurawas, particularly those with the character Durna. One of his biggest roles is in the *lakon*, "Aswatama Nglandak" [Aswatama Digs a Tunnel].

2. Interview with Dr. Suyanto, S.Kar, MA, Surakarta, June 24, 2009

7. **Citraksi**

FA.2007.40.128

Performer: Ki Purbo Asmoro; also: Ki Tristuti

Artists: Tugimin (leather carver), Murdiyonto (painter)

Place and Date Made: Sukoharjo, 1999

Water buffalo hide and horn, water-based paint, *ancur*, imitation gold leaf

H: 80.5, W: 31 (cm)

Citraksi is one of the Kurawa brothers, the son of Drestarastra and Gendari. He appears in numerous *lakon* involving the Kurawas.

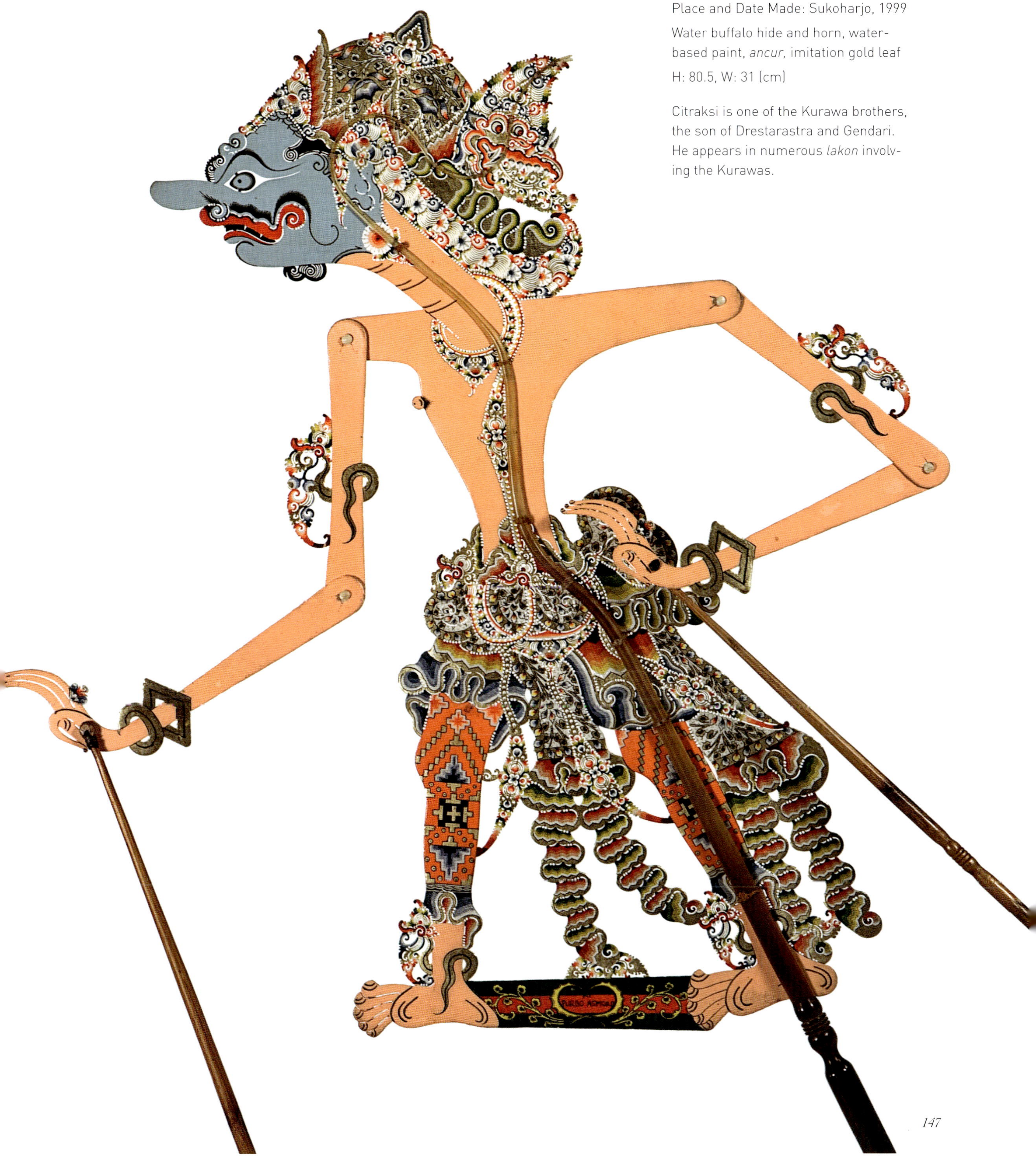

8. **Jayadrata**

FA.2007.40.129

Performer: Ki Purbo Asmoro;
also: Ki Tristuti; Ki Puntono

Artist: Sukarno

Place and Date Made: Karanganyar, date unkown; acquired by Ki Purbo Asmoro in Sukoharjo, 2000

Water buffalo hide and horn, water-based paint, *ancur,* bronze leaf, wood

H: 90, W: 39 (cm)

Jayadrata is one of the Kurawa brothers, the son of Drestarastra and Gendari. When Bima is born, his amniotic sac is thrown away and is found by a noble ascetic who meditates deeply and transforms the sac into the boy Jayadrata.[3] Jayadrata therefore closely resembles Bima and shares Bima's great strength. Jayadrata is raised to be loyal and noble and is trained to be an adept fighter—a true *satria* warrior. Sengkuni lures Jayadrata into joining the Kurawas and into marrying Duryudana's sister, which binds Jayadrata to the Kurawas.

Jayadrata kills Abimanyu in battle and, in turn, is killed by Abimanyu's father, the great Arjuna.

This wayang kulit figure makes appearances in *lakon* about the Pandhawas and Kurawas, and has a special role in "Jayadrata Gugur" [The Death of Jayadrata] of the *Mahabharata*.

3. David Irvine, *Leather Gods and Wooden Heros: Java's Classical Wayang*. (Singapore: Marshall Cavendish International [Asia] Private Limited, 2005), 226-227.

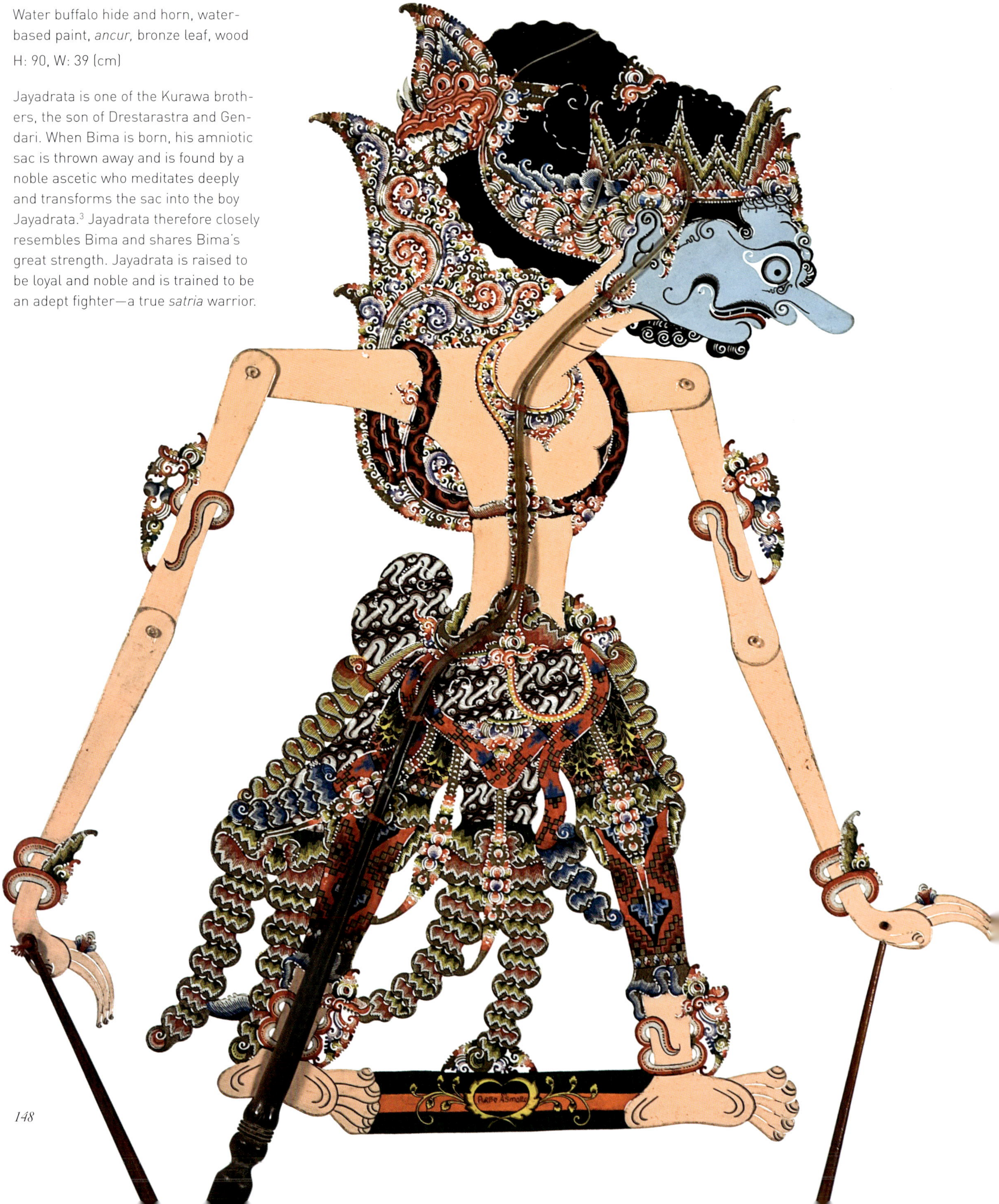

9

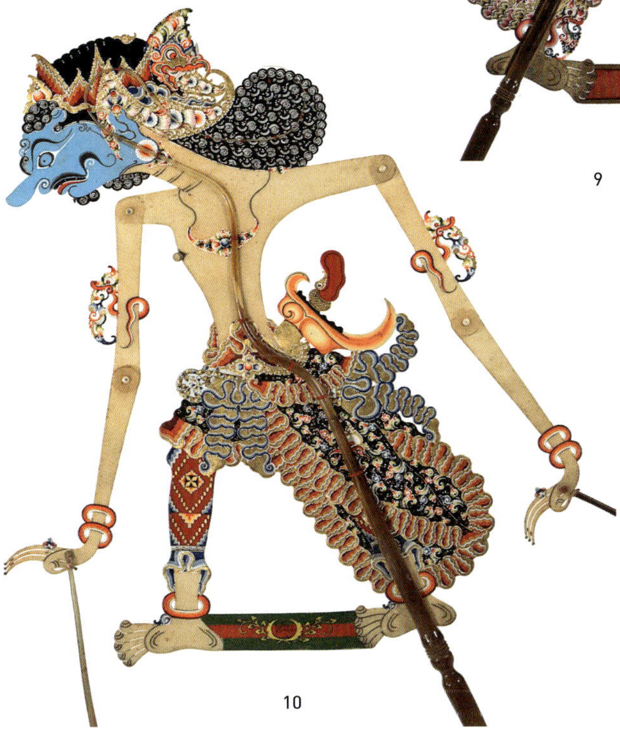

10

9. **Udawa** (*wanda*: Jaran)

FA.2007.40.130

Performer: Ki Purbo Asmoro

Artist: unknown

Place and Date Made: unknown

Water buffalo hide and horn, water-based paint, *ancur,* bronze leaf, wood

H: 83, W: 38 (cm)

Udawa is a noble knight from Widarakandang, and the foster son of Antyagopa and Ken Sagupi (or Ken Yasuda, as she is also known). He grows up with Narayana (Kresna), Kakrasena (Baladéwa), and Rara Ireng (Sumbadra). Udawa becomes the chief minister of the Kingdom of Dwarawati, and serves Kresna when he becomes King.

Jaran means "horse," and refers to the size and strength of this character. This figure makes appearances in the *lakon* "Udawa Waris" [The Inheritance of Udawa], "Kresna Kembang" [Kresna Marries Rukmini], and "Udawa Sayembara" [Udawa Designs a Competition] from the *Mahabharata*.

10. **Tambak Ganggeng**

FA.2007.40.131

Performer: Ki Purbo Asmoro;
also: Ki Heri Sutrisno

Artists: Wiji Sutikno (leather carver), Murdiyonto (painter)

Place and Date Made: Sukoharjo, 1994

Water buffalo hide and horn, water-based paint, *ancur,* gold leaf.

H: 87, W: 38 (cm)

Tambak Ganggeng (Antyagopa's son) becomes a chief minister to Puntadéwa. He appears in the *lakon*, "Sesaji Raja Suya" [The Grand Offering of the Kings] of the *Mahabharata*.

11. **Nirbita**

FA.2007.36.132

Performer: Ki Purbo Asmoro;
also: Sri Joko Raharjo

Artists: Yatna Tentrem (leather carver), Diman (painter)

Place and Date Made: Klaten, date unknown; acquired by Ki Purbo Asmoro in Klaten, 1992

Water buffalo hide and horn, water-based paint, *ancur,* bronze leaf, wood

H: 85, W: 34.5 (cm)

Nirbita is chief minister to King Matswapati of Wirata, and is allied with the Pandhawa brothers. He is killed in the great war known as the Bharatayudha. Nirbita makes his appearance in the *lakon*, "Wiratha Parwa" [The Story of the Kingdom of Wiratha] from the *Mahabharata*.

11

A **Patih Sabrang** figure is a foreign minister; and wayang kulit that are labeled "Patih Sabrang" can be used generically as foreign soldiers that fight for an antagonist king (sabrang means "overseas" or "foreign").

12. **Patih Sabrang**

FA.2007.40.133

Performer: Ki Purbo Asmoro

Artists: Wasono (leather carver), Murdiyanto (painter)

Place and Date Made: Sukoharjo, 2000

Water buffalo hide and horn, water-based paint, *ancur,* gold leaf, wood

H: 92, W: 41 (cm)

12

13

13. **Patih Sabrang**

FA.2007.40.134

Performer: Ki Purbo Asmoro

Artist: unknown

Place and Date Made: Wonogiri, date unknown; acquired by Ki Purbo Asmoro in Wonogiri, 1992

Water buffalo hide and horn, water-based paint, *ancur,* gold leaf, wood

H: 93, W: 41 (cm)

14. **Patih Sabrang**

FA.2007.40.135

Performer: Ki Purbo Asmoro; also: Ki Jono; Ki Sukadi

Artist: unknown

Place and Date Made: Wonogiri, date unknown; acquired by Ki Purbo Asmoro in Wonogiri, 1999

Water buffalo hide and horn, water-based paint, *ancur,* imitation gold leaf, wood

H: 90, W: 39.5 (cm)

14

15

15. **Jaya Lodhong, also known as Genthong Lodhong**

FA.2007.40.136

Performer: Ki Purbo Asmoro

Artist: Beny (painter)

Place and Date Made: unknown; acquired by Ki Purbo Asmoro in Klaten, 1992

Water buffalo hide and horn, water-based paint, *ancur,* bronze leaf, wood

H: 83, W: 43 (cm)

Joyo Londong is a human soldier in the army of a *raksasa* (demon-giant) king. He appears in many *lakon* that present raksasa armies onstage, especially scenes where raksasa troops fight armies of *bacingah* (characters that are half human, half animal, such as Maésasura and Lembusura; see plates 10 and 11 in the Simpingan Kiri section).[4]

4. Kathryn Emerson, on behalf of Ki Purbo Asmoro. Email communication, January 26, 2009.

Some wayang experts describe **Pragota** and **Prabawa** as brothers, although others describe the two as friends.[5] Pragota becomes the chief minister to King Baladéwa of Mandura, and Prabawa becomes a court official.

They appear in *Mahabharata* episodes like "Abimanyu Gendhong" [Abimanyu is Cradled], "Gendrèh Kemasan" [Arjuna Disguised as Gendrèh Kemasan], and other stories involving Baladéwa.

5. Interview with Dr. Suyanto, S.Kar., MA., Surakarta, June 24, 2009; Ki Purbo Asmoro describes the two as friends.

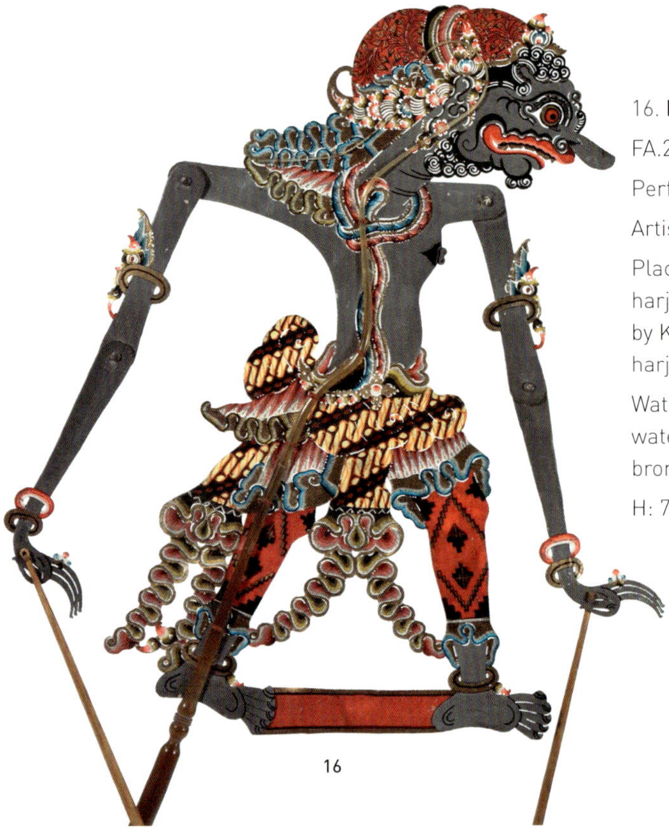

16

16. **Prabawa**

FA.2007.40.138

Performer: Ki Purbo Asmoro

Artists: unknown

Place and Date Made: Sukoharjo, date unknown; acquired by Ki Purbo Asmoro in Sukoharjo, 2000

Water buffalo hide and horn, water-based paint, *ancur*, bronze leaf, wood

H: 79, W: 30 (cm)

18

18. **Arimbi**

FA.2007.40.140

Performer: Ki Purbo Asmoro; also: Ki Puntono

Artist: Yatna Tentrem

Place and Date Made: Klaten, date unknown; acquired by Ki Purbo Asmoro in Klaten, 1992

Water buffalo hide and horn, water-based paint, *ancur*, bronze leaf, wood

H: 78, W: 29 (cm)

Arimbi is a *raseksi* (female giant) who is a princess of Pringgadani. She falls in love with Bima (the second of five Pandhawa brothers). Her inner beauty is rewarded and she is transformed into a beautiful woman. Arimbi marries Bima, and they become the parents of Gathutkaca.

17

17. **Pragota** (*wanda*: Pocol)

FA.2007.40.137

Performer: Ki Purbo Asmoro

Artists: unknown

Place and Date Made: Sukoharjo, date unknown; acquired by Ki Purbo Asmoro in Sukoharjo, 2000

Water buffalo hide and horn, water-based paint, *ancur*, bronze leaf, wood

H: 87, W: 42 (cm)

Pocol means "smashed out" and characters of this *wanda* strive to be superior.

Buta is a general term for "ogre." Some buta characters play very specific roles, but others are used interchangeably (in scenes when any ogre puppet will do). Buta Babrah characters are generally used as soldiers in the *raksasa* (demon-giants) armies. They are usually thought of as enemies from "overseas" and inevitably obstruct the heroes' actions.

19. **Buta Kenthus**

FA.2007.40.139

Performer: Ki Purbo Asmoro; also: Ki Puntono; Ki Sudarman

Artists: Munaji and Murdiyanto; Designer: Joko Langgeng

Place and Date Made: Sragen and Sukoharjo, 1993; acquired by Ki Purbo Asmoro in Sragen, 1994

Water buffalo hide and horn, water-based paint, *ancur,* bronze leaf, wood

H: 94, W: 51 (cm)

Buta Kenthus is a *raksasa* soldier. This particular wayang figure was specially designed by Joko Langgeng for Ki Sudarman (the dhalang who originally commissioned the piece).

20. **Kenyawandu**

FA.2007.40.141

Performer: Ki Purbo Asmoro

Artist: Yatna Tentrem

Place and Date Made: Klaten, date unknown; acquired by Ki Purbo Asmoro in Klaten, 1992

Water buffalo hide and horn, water-based paint, *ancur,* bronze leaf

H: 82, W: 36 (cm)

This shadow puppet may be used by dhalang when a female *buta* (ogre) is needed, but the Kenyawandu character is actually a male ogre transvestite dressed as a woman. Kenyawandu is a servant to an ogre king and she has special powers, such as the ability to fly. Kenyawandu also steals for her king: for example she might steal away a princess or a special, magical weapon.[6]

This figure has been used by Ki Purbo Asmoro in *lakon* such as "Kresna Kembang" [Kresna Marries Rukmini] and "Bima Bumbu" [Bima Served Up as a Side Dish] of the *Mahabharata*.

6. Interview with Dr. Suyanto, S.Kar., MA, Surakarta, June 24, 2009.

20

21. **Buta Baya, also known as Wil Kataksini**

FA.2007.40.142

Performer: Ki Purbo Asmoro; also: Ki Arif

Artist unknown; Designer: Ki Gondo Sudarman

Place and Date Made: Wonogiri, date unknown; acquired by Ki Purbo Asmoro in 1996

Water buffalo hide and horn, water-based paint, *ancur,* imitation gold leaf

H: 68.6, W: 48.3 (cm)

Buta Baya is a "Crocodile Ogre." This ogre puppet is used as a particular soldier in Rahwana's army, named Wil Kataksini, who is killed by the great monkey warrior Anoman. He appears only in one *lakon*, "Anoman Dhuta" [Anoman Serves as Messenger] of the *Ramayana* cycle.

21

22. **Buta Cakil** (*wanda*: Bathang)

FA.2007.40.148

Performer: Ki Purbo Asmoro

Artists: Tugimin (leather carver), Murdiyonto (painter)

Place and Date Made: Sukoharjo, 2005

Water buffalo hide and horn, water-based paint, *ancur*, wood, imitation gold leaf

H: 83.5, W: 38 (cm)

Buta Cakil is a stereotypical ogre who is offensive, aggressive, and crude. He is typically put onstage to fight the hero in the famous battle scene, the *perang kembang* (the "flower battle" also known as the *cakilan*). Cakil appears in almost every performance, regardless of the *lakon*, and is followed by his entourage, Buta Térong and Buta Pragalba. Together the three form a sort of mafia, or gang, and often, other buta characters join in their cause. Cakil is inevitably killed by the hero in each performance, but reemerges with every new performance.

Cakil represents one of four human desires that people must abandon when they leave this earth. He represents desire for worldly possessions and privileged life conditions, such as personal happiness or physical beauty (*supiyah*).[7]

Cakil means "prognathous". *Bathang* means "corpse" and this personifies Cakil, who looks like a dead man walking and is described as pale and unhealthy.

7. Kathryn Emerson, on behalf of Ki Purbo Asmoro. Email communication, January 26, 2009

23. **Buta Térong**

FA.2007.38.7

Performer and Designer: Ki Enthus Susmono

Artists: Kemo (leather carver), Paidi (painter)

Place and Date Made: Surakarta, 2005

Water buffalo hide and horn, water-based paint, *ancur*, wood, gold leaf

H: 82, W: 54 (cm)

This *buta* (ogre) character is named for his eggplant-shaped nose (*térong* means "eggplant" in Indonesian). The size and shape of his nose have an impact on the character's voice, which is recognized by its nasal quality. Because of this speech impediment, Térong's appearance and mannerisms are often viewed by the audience as humorous.

Térong is in Buta Cakil's gang, along with Buta Pragalba. The three usually appear together as regulars in almost every *lakon*. They have a noteworthy appearance in the famous battle scene, the *perang kembang* (the "flower battle" also known as the *cakilan*) where they put the heroes to a test. Térong represents one of four human desires that that people must abandon when they leave this earth. He represents the desire for food and drink (*aluamah*).[8]

8. Kathryn Emerson, on behalf of Ki Purbo Asmoro. Email communication, January 26, 2009.

24

24. **Buta Pragalba, also known generically as Buta Babrah**

FA.2007.40.143

Performer: Ki Purbo Asmoro

Artists: Tugimin (leather carver), Murdiyonto (painter)

Place and Date Made: Sukoharjo, 2005

Water buffalo hide and horn, water-based paint, *ancur,* imitation gold leaf, wood

H: 89, W: 39 (cm)

Buta Pragalba is an ogre in Cakil's gang; Buta Pragalba and Buta Térong usually appear with Buta Cakil in the *perang kembang* (the "flower battle" also referred to as the *cakilan*). This *buta* is oafish, vulgar, rude, and loud. His role is to thwart the heroes as they set out on their mission.

Pragalba represents one of four human desires that people must abandon when they leave this earth. He represents desire for power and success (*amarah*).[9]

9. Kathryn Emerson, on behalf of Ki Purbo Asmoro. Email communication, January 26, 2009.

25

25. **Buta Rambutgeni, also known generically as Buta Babrah**

FA.2007.40.144

Performer: Ki Purbo Asmoro; also: Ki Toto Atmojo

Artists: unknown

Place and Date Made: Sukoharjo, date unknown; acquired by Ki Purbo Asmoro in Sukoharjo, 2000

Water buffalo hide and horn, water-based paint, *ancur,* bronze leaf, wood

H: 88, W: 40 (cm)

Rambutgeni means "hair of fire," referring to this *buta's* hair. The character is vulgar and rude, and may appear with Buta Cakil and his ogre-entourage in the *perang kembang*. His role, like that of other buta characters, is to thwart the heroes as they set out on their mission. Rambutgeni represents one of four human desires that people must abandon when they leave this earth. He represents desire for love and sensual engagement (*mutmainah*).[10]

10. Kathryn Emerson, on behalf of Ki Purbo Asmoro. Email communication, January 26, 2009.

26. **Buta Babrah**

FA.2007.40.145

Performer: Ki Purbo Asmoro; also: Ki Mulyono

Artist: Pardi

Place and Date Made: Sukoharjo, date unknown; acquired by Ki Purbo Asmoro in Sragen, 2000

Water buffalo hide and horn, water-based paint, *ancur*, gold leaf

H: 78, W: 41 (cm)

26

27

27. **Buta Punuk, also known generically as Buta Babrah**

FA.2007.40.146

Performer: Ki Purbo Asmoro; also: Ki Toto Atmojo; Ki Tristuti; Ki Pringgo Darsono

Artist: Diman (leather carver)

Place and Date Made: Klaten, date unknown; acquired by Ki Purbo Asmoro in Klaten, 1992

Water buffalo hide and horn, water-based paint, *ancur*, bronze leaf, wood

H: 77, W: 42 (cm)

Buta Punuk is a particularly rough and uncouth *buta* (ogre) character.[11] Punuk means "humpback;" this wayang figure has a bump on the back of his neck.

11. Kathryn Emerson, on behalf of Ki Purbo Asmoro. Email communication, January 26, 2009.

28

28. **Buta Glundhung, also known as Buta Punuk**

FA.2007.38.8

Performer and Designer: Ki Enthus Susmono

Artists: Kemo (leather carver), Paidi (painter);

Place and Date Made: Surakarta, 2005

Water buffalo hide and horn, water-based paint and dyes, oil treatment, *ancur*, wood, gold leaf

H: 80.5, W: 39 (cm)

Glundhung means "rolled or curled up in a ball" and is another name for Buta Punuk.[12]

12. Kathryn Emerson, on behalf of Ki Purbo Asmoro. Email communication, January 26, 2009.

29

29. **Buta Galiyuk**

FA.2007.40.147

Performer: Ki Purbo Asmoro

Artists: unknown

Place and Date Made: Sukoharjo, date unknown; acquired by Ki Purbo Asmoro in Sukoharjo, 2000

Water buffalo hide and horn, water-based paint, *ancur*, wood, bronze leaf

H: 76, W: 36 (cm)

Galiyuk is a humorous ogre character who appears in the scenes of the *raksasa* (demon-giants) armies.

The **punakawan** play a special role in wayang kulit performances. They are servants to the gods and to royalty and add comic relief to an otherwise profoundly serious performance.

In today's performances, these characters are best known for their own special scene (the *gara-gara*) that is typically separate from the main storyline. During this interlude the dhalang may present his personal point of view, a political message, social service information—or the scene may serve simply as a humorous break.

30. **Bilung**

FA.2007.40.150

Permormer: Ki Purbo Asmoro;
also: Ki Tristuti

Artist: Ki Kuwat

Place and Date Made: Karanganyar, 1990

Water buffalo hide and horn, water-based paint, *ancur*, wood, bronze leaf

H: 68, W: 26 (cm)

Bilung is Togog's companion, and together, they serve the antagonist king. Bilung is a foreigner, known to be a sycophant.[13]

13. Interview with Dr. Suyanto, S.Kar., MA, Surakarta, June 24, 2009.

31. **Togog**

FA.2007.40.149

Performer: Ki Purbo Asmoro;
also: Ki Tristuti; Ki Pringgo

Artist: Ki Kuwat

Place and Date Made: Karanganyar, 1990

Water buffalo hide and horn, water-based paint, *ancur*, wood, bronze leaf

H: 71, W: 33 (cm)

Togog and his companion Bilung are servants and advisors to the antagonist king and are friendly with their counterparts, Semar and his sons (who serve the protagonists). Togog is believed to be Semar's brother, and though he is an ethical character, he is not as wise as Semar and tends to be swayed by material wealth. Nevertheless, he is sometimes successful in keeping his overlords (the enemy forces) from overreacting and directing them towards the Right Path.

In this set of wayang, the design of Togog and Bilung follows the Banyumas tradition.

32. **Semar** (*wanda*: Ginuk)

FA.2007.40.151

Performer: Ki Purbo Asmoro;
also: Ki Sumarno

Artists: Ki Wiji Sutikno and Murdiyonto

Place and Date Made: Sukoharjo, 1994

Water buffalo hide and horn, water-based paint, *ancur*, wood, bronze leaf

H: 74, W: 36 (cm)

Semar and his three sons (Gareng, Petruk, and Bagong) serve and advise the protagonist king.[14] Semar is noted for his infamous burping and farting, his round build, and his comedic wit. However, more importantly, he is loved for his good-hearted nature, sagacity, and optimism. Semar is an audience favorite and is also favored by the other wayang characters. Even the high gods come to Semar for advice—for Semar is himself the high god, Sang Hyang Ismaya, and is the father of a number of gods who reside in heaven. In wayang plays, Semar materializes as this servant character. Semar's personal history (how he comes to earth and his relationship with his sons) may be interpreted differently by individual dhalang. Nevertheless, Semar is one of the most beloved, widely recognized, and revered of all the wayang characters.

Ginuk means "very fat."

14. Some accounts describe Gareng and Petruk as adopted sons. And although certain regional styles include only Gareng and Petruk (not Bagong) among Semar's followers, other regions only include Bagong (considered Semar's Shadow). In today's performance, in the Solo tradition, all three figures (Gareng, Petruk, and Bagong) are generally accepted as Semar's sons. There are also variations to how the *gara-gara* scene is presented; sometimes only Gareng and Petruk enter the *gara-gara* scene. Interview with Dr. Suyanto S.Kar., MA, June 24, 2009.

These comedic characters and the *gara-gara* scene are commonly audience favorites, and the characters usually evoke uproarious laughter from the audience. Appearing in every performance, the *punakawan* characters are Javanese in origin and do not exist in the Indian version of the epics.

33. **Gareng** (*wanda*: Wregul)

FA.2007.40.152

Performer: Ki Purbo Asmoro;
also: Ki Sumarno

Artists: Ki Wiji Sutikno and Murdiyonto

Place and Date Made: Sukoharjo, 1994

Water buffalo hide and horn, water-based paint, *ancur,* wood, bronze leaf

H: 74, W: 23 (cm)

Semar's eldest son, Gareng, is polio-stricken, club-footed, cross-eyed, and pessimistic. The wayang figure's arms and foot are misshapen, illustrating his disabilities. Gareng's humor is one of silly joking, comedic allusions, and clever one-liners.

In *gara-gara* scenes, Gareng and Petruk engage in slapstick skirmishes between their discussions of social service programs, politics, or other current events. These *gara-gara* scenes are distinct digressions from the serious story that is being told. Within the storyline, the brothers may accompany the heroes on their journeys, cheering them up, or making them laugh when they need it along their way.

Wregul means "fat."

34. **Petruk** (wanda: Jlegong)

FA.2007.40.153

Performer: Ki Purbo Asmoro;
also: Ki Sumarno

Artists: Ki Wiji Sutikno and Murdiyonto

Place and Date Made: Sukoharjo, 1994

Water buffalo hide and horn, water-based paint, *ancur,* wood, bronze leaf

H: 89, W: 27 (cm)

Petruk is generally accepted as Semar's second son. Like Semar, he is optimistic, but he is best known as a sardonic prankster, with Gareng as his usual victim.

Wanda Jlegong refers to a tendency Petruk has to get his foot stuck in a hole when he is walking; in this portrayal, the figure is leaning back.

35. **Bagong** (*wanda*: Gilut)

FA.2007.40.154

Performer: Ki Purbo Asmoro;
also: Ki Sumarno

Artists: Ki Wiji Sutikno and Murdiyonto

Place and Date Made: Sukoharjo, 2006

Water buffalo hide and horn, water-based paint, *ancur,* wood, imitation gold leaf

H: 60, W: 25 (cm)

Bagong is a rather obtuse character, something that causes numerous misunderstandings with his superiors and companions.[15] Bagong is literally Semar's shadow; when Semar came to live on earth, the gods gave him a companion that materialized from his own shadow. Bagong is generally accepted as Semar's last son in today's performances.

Gilut means "approaching or following something like a shadow."

15. Benedict Anderson, *Mythology and the Tolerance of the Javanese.* Ithaca, N.Y.: Modern Indonesia Project; Southeast Asia Program, Department of Asian Studies, Cornell University, 1965, 44.

30 31

34
32
33
35

The **parekan** are ladies-in-waiting to the protagonist king and appear in every performance. *Parekan buta* hold the same position, but serve the antagonist king (parekan buta are not always used by dhalang and are not always included in classical sets).

At the opening of a performance, the parekan appear after the *kayon/gunungan* (tree of life/cosmic mountain puppet) and before the *jejer* scene (where the king is met by his officials in the main audience hall of the palace). The appearance of the parekan signals that the king is ready to meet with his officials. This follows royal protocol in the *kraton* (royal palace): chief ministers and other officials wait in the *pagelaran* (the front hall of the palace; a waiting area) until the king is ready meet with his audience. The king takes his place on his seat of honor in the royal audience hall. The parekan then signal to the guests that the king is ready to see them. The word *parek* means "near," and refers to the parekan's role in allowing people to be near to the king.[16]

16. Interview with Dr. Suyanto, S.Kar., MA., Surakarta, June 24, 2009.

36. **Parekan**

FA.2007.40.155; FA.2007.40.156

Performer: Ki Purbo Asmoro

Artists: unknown

Place and Date Made: unknown; acquired by Ki Purbo Asmoro in Sukoharjo, 2000

Water buffalo hide and horn, water-based paint, *ancur*, bronze-leaf

H: 62, W: 20 (cm)

37. **Parekan Buta**

FA.2007.38.9x

Performer and Designer: Ki Enthus Susmono

Artists: Kemo (leather carver), Paidi (painter)

Place and Date Made: Tegal, 1997

Water buffalo hide and horn, water-based paint, *ancur*, wood, gold leaf

H: 68, W: 25 (cm)

Parekan buta are not standard characters in classical sets, but some dhalang, such as Ki Enthus Susmono, include them and enjoy using them in performances.

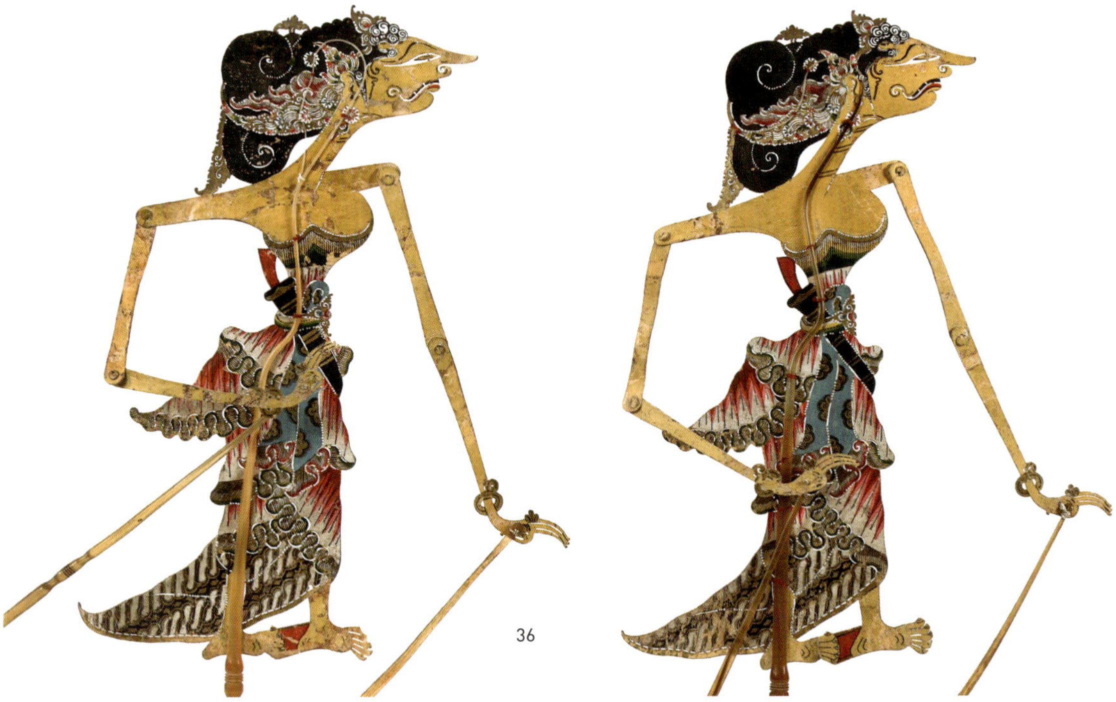

36

37

In almost every performance today, **Limbuk** and **Cangik** appear in a special scene known as the *limbukan*, which usually introduces the audience to the musicians, singers, and sponsors of the event—and also notes the occasion for which the performance was commissioned (for example, a wedding). The *limbukan* is a popular scene and draws much laughter from the audience.

38. **Limbuk**

FA.2007.40.157

Performer: Ki Purbo Asmoro; also: Ki Sudarsono

Artists: unknown

Place and Date Made: Sukoharjo, date unknown; acquired by Ki Purbo Asmoro in Sukoharjo, 2000

Water buffalo hide and horn, water-based paint, *ancur,* wood, bronze leaf

H: 88, W: 34 (cm)

Limbuk and her mother, Cangik, are serving women to a queen. Although Limbuk is no great beauty, she is rather vain. Limbuk is traditionally represented holding a comb or a fan. This version of Limbuk holds a clove cigarette (*kretek*). Smoking is considered unfeminine, and in the past was taboo for women, so this depiction illustrates Limbuk's unruly behavior.

39. **Cangik**

FA.2007.40.158

Performer: Ki Purbo Asmoro; also: Ki Sudarsono

Artists: unknown

Place and Date Made: Sukoharjo, date unknown; acquired by Ki Purbo Asmoro in Sukoharjo, 2000

Water buffalo hide and horn, water-based paint, *ancur,* wood, bronze leaf

H: 67, W: 19 (cm)

Cangik is Limbuk's old and drooping mother, who also serves the queen. She is portrayed with a comb, which shows her own vanity, but which may also be used to comb the queen's hair or her daughter's hair.

38

39

40. **Sukrasana**

FA.2007.40.159

Performer: Ki Purbo Asmoro

Artists: Wiji Sutikno and Murdiyonto; Designer: Ki Gondo Darman

Place and Date Made: Sukoharjo, 1994

Water buffalo hide and horn, water-based paint, *ancur*, wood, gold leaf

H: 54, W: 20 (cm)

Sukrasana is Sumantri's brother. Sukrasana's physical form has taken the shape of an ogre-dwarf. Ki Purbo Asmoro considers this particular figure to be a "new creation." The figure has been used by Ki Purbo in *lakon* such as "Lahir Sumantri" [The Birth of Sumantri], "Sumantri Ngèngèr" [Sumantri as Apprentice], and "Sumantri Gugur" [The Death of Sumantri] from the *Ramayana*. These episodes belong to Arjuna Sasrabahu's era.

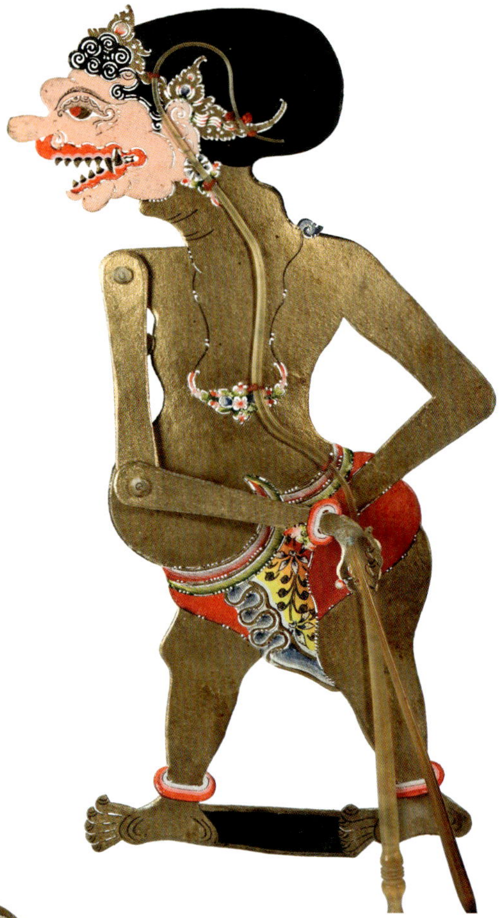

40

41. **Abiyasa**

FA.2007.40.160

Performer: Ki Purbo Asmoro; also: Sri Joko Raharjo

Artists: Sadi Pon and Murdiyonto; Designer: Karno Diharja

Place and Date Made: Sukoharjo, 1999

Water buffalo hide and horn, water-based paint, *ancur*, wood, bronze leaf

H: 77, W: 29 (cm)

In the *Mahabharata* cycle, Abiyasa is the common grandfather of the feuding cousins (the five Pandhawa brothers and the hundred Kurawas).

Abiyasa is an ascetic priest of noble origin. Growing up, he lives in the forests of Saptaarga with his father, Palasara, who has retreated there to meditate after his divorce from Durgandini. Abiyasa is called away from the forest to rule the Kingdom of Hastina. He does not want to be king but must have children to ensure a royal heir. Abiyasa accepts the crown out of a sense of duty and becomes a sucessful ruler. As king, he keeps peace in the land and has three sons: Pandhu Déwanata (father of Pandhawas); Drestarastra (father of the Kurawas); and Widura. After fulfilling his responsibility to have children, Abiyasa resigns as King.

Because Drestarastra is blind and Widura is lame, Pandhu is named heir to the throne. When Pandhu dies young, Abiyasa allows Drestarastra to rule only until Pandhu's eldest son (Puntadéwa) is mature enough to become king. That plan, however is thwarted by the Kurawas. Later in Life Abiyasa counsels the Pandhawas during the great Bharatayuda war.

Abiyasa plays a major role in the *lakon*, "Abiyasa Muksa" [The Spirit of Abiyasa Rises Up to the Heavens], and other *Mahabharata* episodes.

41

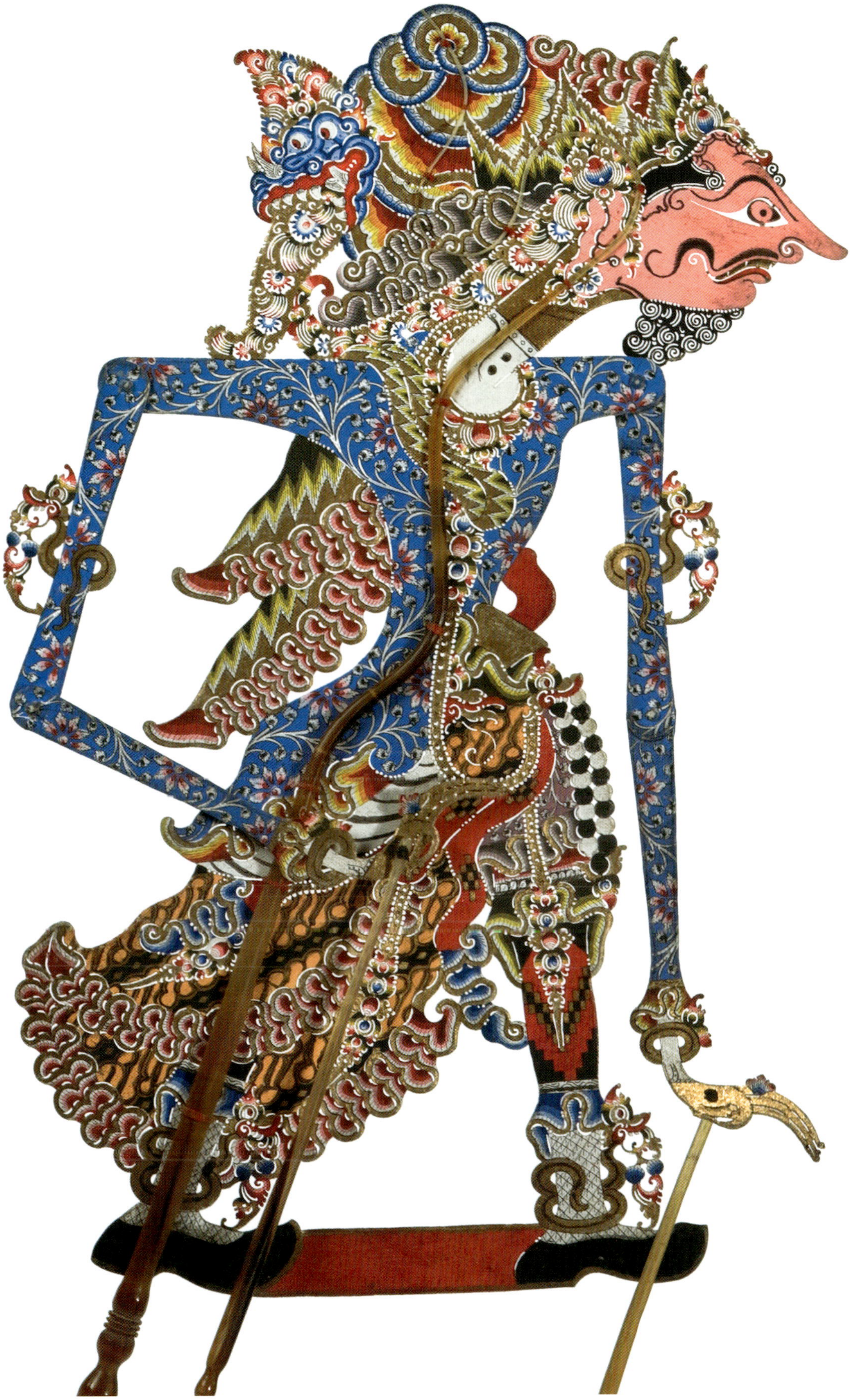

42. **Bisma, also known as Déwa Brata**

FA.2007.40.161

Performer: Ki Purbo Asmoro; also: Ki Sajali

Artists: Diyo (leather carver) and Ki Sajali (painter)

Place and Date Made: Klaten, date unknown; acquired by Ki Purbo Asmoro in Klaten, 2001

Water buffalo hide and horn, water-based paint, *ancur*, bronze leaf

H: 79.5, W: 33 cm

The mystic priest, Bisma, is mentor to both the Pandhawa and Kurawa cousins during their childhood. He is himself one of the greatest *satria* (noble knights), and he has been trained by the gods. The son of Sentanu, he is from Pertapan Talkanda.

Bisma is a truly noble character, who always remains faithful to his oath to support the Kingdom of Hastina. However, this obligation means that he must support the Kurawas, and must fight against the Pandhawas when Hastina is ruled by Duryudana. Bisma unsuccessfully attempts to convince Duryudana to relinquish the crown to the rightful heir, Puntadéwa. Because of his obligations to his oath, Bisma must kill armies of soldiers that he loves and must fight for a cause in which he does not believe.

Bisma's god-given gift allows him to choose the moment of his own death: this comes when he feels hopeless and depressed from considering the futility of war. When Bisma dies in battle, at the hands of Srikandhi (Arjuna's wife), both armies cease fighting and the cousins come together to mourn the loss of their beloved teacher.

He appears in many *Mahabharata* episodes such as "Babad Wanamarta" [The Clearing of the Amarta Forest] and "Wiratha Parwa" [The Story of the Kingdom Wiratha], but he is a central figure in other *lakon* such as "Bisma Gugur" [The Death of Bisma].

43. **Pandhita Tua**

FA.2007.40.162

Performer: Ki Purbo Asmoro;
also: Ki Tristuti

Artists: Sadi Pon and Murdiyonto

Place and Date Made: Sukoharjo, 2000

Water buffalo hide and horn, water-based paint, *ancur*, bronze leaf

H: 78, W: 23 (cm)

Used in the *lakon*, "Wahyu Dharma" [The Gift of Great Responsibility] from the *Mahabharata*, this wayang is used as a *srambahan* figure, a type of puppet that can be used to portray a number of characters of a similar type. That is, this figure can be used to portray any *pandhita tua* figure (*pandhita tua* means "old religious ascetic" or "person who teaches religious philosophy").

43

44. **Antyagopa**

FA.2007.40.163

Performer: Ki Purbo Asmoro;
also: Ki Tristuti

Artists: Sadi Pon and Murdiyonto

Place and Date Made: Sukoharjo, 2000

Water buffalo hide and horn, water-based paint, *ancur*, wood, bronze leaf

H: 71, W: 19.5 cm

Antyagopa is a Lurah (the head of a village, who is elected by popular vote). Antyagopa raises Basudéwa's children: Narayana (who later becomes Kresna, King of Dwarawati); Kakrasena (who later becomes Baladéwa, King of Mandura), and Rara Ireng (who later becomes Sumbadra, the wife of Arjuna). When Basudéwa's kingdom is under attack by Kangsa, he sends his children to live with Antyagopa, where they remain safe. Antyagopa appears in the *lakon*, "Kangsa Adu Jago" [Kangsa Puts Forth An Opponent] from the *Mahabharata*.

44

45

45. **Walakas**

FA.2007.40.164

Performer: Ki Purbo Asmoro;
also: Ki Puntono; Ki Heri Sutrisno

Artists: unknown

Place and Date Made: Sukoharjo, date unknown; acquired by Ki Purbo Asmoro in Sukoharjo, 2000

Water buffalo hide and horn, water-based paint, *ancur*, bronze leaf

H: 72, W: 29 cm

Walakas is a meat vendor who is like a foster father to Jagal Bilawa (the character Bima, disguised as a butcher) in the country of Wiratha. Walakas appears in the *lakon*, "Adon-Adon Rajamala" [Rajamala Enters the Ring] the *Mahabharata*.

46

46. **Pandhita Srambahan**

FA.2007.40.165

Performer: Ki Purbo Asmoro:
also: Ki Puntono

Artists: Sadi Pon and Murdiyonto

Place and Date Made: Sukoharjo, 1996

Water buffalo hide and horn, water-based paint, *ancur*, bronze leaf

H: 78, W: 25 (cm)

This generic puppet portrays an aged ascetic. This particular Pandhita Sambrahan figure shows the influence of Islam: the puppet wears a turban and robe, and carries prayer beads and a purse (to collect *zakat*, or "charity").[17] This wayang figure was used by Ki Purbo Asmoro in the *lakon*, "Sinta Ilang" [Sinta Wanders Off] of the *Ramayana*.

17. Interview with Dr. Suyanto S.Kar., MA., Surakarta, June 24, 2009.

DHUDHAHAN II

This group includes the following figures: Gods, Monkey Soldiers, Animals, Armies, Weapons, *Setan* (demons and ghosts), Kayon/Gunungan, and some unconventional figures.

1. **Bathara Narada**

FA.2007.40.166

Performer: Ki Purbo Asmoro; also: Ki Sajali; Ki Kasim; Ki Kusni; Ki Kesdik

Artists: unknown

Place and Date Made: Klaten, date unknown; acquired by Ki Purbo Asmoro in Klaten, 2000

Water buffalo hide and horn, water-based paint, *ancur*, bronze leaf, wood

H: 66, W: 31 (cm)

Bathara Narada is Bathara Guru's chief advisor and he acts as a messenger between the gods in heaven and the earthly realm. Narada, who is himself a god, is an ebullient character; he never gets angry, and he often laughs and makes jokes. Narada is also wise and particularly knowledgeable about spiritual matters.

He is involved in numerous lakon about the gods and others including "Ciptoning" [Arjuna's Deep Meditation], "Sugriwa Subali" [The Story of Sugriwa and Subali]," and "Gathutkaca Jedi" [Gathutkaca is Thrown into the Cauldron], from the *Mahabharata*.

1

2. **Bathara Indra**

FA.2007.40.167

Performer: Ki Purbo Asmoro

Artists: unknown

Place and Date Made: Central Java, Kartasura Era (1680-1755); acquired by Ki Purbo Asmoro in Jakarta, 1996

Water buffalo hide and horn, water-based paint, *ancur*, gold leaf, wood

H: 82, W: 32 (cm)

Bathara Indra is god of the sky, the storms, and thunder, and this wayang kulit puppet is the oldest piece in the collection.

Indra plays a role in *lakon* about the gods, as well as other episodes like "Ciptoning" [Arjuna's Deep Meditation] and "Bima Suci" [Bima as Priest], from the *Mahabharata*.

2

3

3. Bathara Brama

FA.2007.40.168

Performer: Ki Purbo Asmoro; also: Ki Sukadi; Ki Sri Joko Raharjo

Artist unknown

Place and Date Made: Wonogiri, date unknown; acquired by Ki Purbo Asmoro in Sukoharjo, 1996

Water buffalo hide and horn, water-based paint, *ancur*, bronze leaf, wood

H: 93, W: 41 (cm)

In Java, Brama is a strong, determined, handsome—and hot-tempered—god. His state of meditation is so intense that he is said to actually disseminate heat and he is sometimes referred to as the god of fire. Mt. Bromo is a volcano in Java named for this god. In India, Brama is the god of creation.

Brama is known for his role in *Mahabharata* episodes such as "Wisanggeni Lahir" [The Birth of Wisanggeni], "Ciptoning" [Arjuna's Deep Meditation], and "Kangsa Adu Jago" [Kangsa Puts Forth an Opponent]."

4

4. Bathara Sambu

FA.2007.40.169

Performer: Ki Purbo Asmoro

Artist: Tugimin (leather carver)

Place and Date Made: Sukoharjo, 2003

Water buffalo hide and horn, water-based paint, *ancur*, bronze leaf, wood

H: 98, W: 41 (cm)

Bathara Sambu is the oldest son of Bathara Guru. This character makes a rare appearance in *lakon* involving the gods, because he is said to have a mental disorder and is not considered suitable for regular appearances. Sambu has supernatural powers that enable him to make smoke.[1]

1. Interview with Dr. Suyanto S.Kar., MA., Surakarta, June 24, 2009.

5

5. **Bathara Yamadipati, also known as Yama**

FA.2007.40.170

Performer: Ki Purbo Asmoro; also: Ki Sajali

Artist: Mentong

Place and Date Made: Klaten, date unknown; acquired by Ki Purbo Asmoro in Klaten, 2000

Water buffalo hide and horn, water-based paint, *ancur*, bronze leaf, wood

H: 107, W: 42 (cm)

Yamadipati is the god of death and the guardian of hell, and his face resembles that of a corpse. Although he may be feared because of his role in taking peoples' souls, he is not an evil character; death is natural.[2]

2. Interview with Dr. Suyanto S.Kar., MA., Surakarta, June 24, 2009.

6

6. **Bathara Mahadéwa**

FA.2007.40.171

Performer: Ki Purbo Asmoro

Artist: Tugimin (leather carver)

Place and Date Made: Sukoharjo, 2003

Water buffalo hide and horn, water-based and latex paint, *ancur,* bronze leaf, wood

H: 87, W: 36 (cm)

Mahadéwa is considered one of the "heroes" of *Kahyangan* (the heavens).[3] Mahadéwa appears in *lakon* about the gods.

3. Ibid.

7

7. **Bathara Panyarikan, also known as Bathara Sriyana**

FA.2007.40.172

Performer: Ki Purbo Asmoro

Artist: Tugimin (leather carver)

Place and Date Made: Sukoharjo, 2005

Water buffalo hide and horn, water-based paint, *ancur*, bronze leaf, wood

H: 81, W: 30 (cm)

The term *panyarikan* refers to this god's role as a secretary. (His actual name is Sriyana.[4]) Bathara Panyarikan appears in *lakon* about the gods.

4. Ibid.

8

8. **Bathara Temboro**

FA.2007.40.173

Performer: Ki Purbo Asmoro

Artist: Sukadi (painter)

Place and Date Made: Wonogiri and Sukoharjo, date unknown; acquired by Ki Purbo Asmoro in Sukoharjo, 1994

Water buffalo hide and horn, water-based paint, *ancur*, bronze leaf, wood

H: 76, W: 26.5 (cm)

This god appears as a humorous character, and usually with a sidekick, Déwa Pathuk (not included in this set). Together they are known as the "Jokesters of *Kahyangan* [the heavens]".[5]

5. Ibid.

Bathara Kamajaya is the god of love and the protector of lovers. In Java, he is believed to be the ideal of masculine beauty, and his wife, **Bathari Ratih**, the ideal of feminine beauty. Together they are considered the embodiment of marital harmony. They appear in *lakon* about the gods, and play a special role in the *lakon*, "Parta Krama" [Arjuna's Wedding].

9. **Bathara Kamajaya**

FA.2007.40.174

Performer: Ki Purbo Amoro

Artist: Tugimin

Place and Date Made: Sukoharjo, 2006

Water buffalo hide and horn, water-based paint, *ancur*, imitation gold leaf, wood

H: 78, W: 29 (cm)

10. **Bathari Ratih**

FA.2007.40.175

Performer: Ki Purbo Amoro

Artist: Tugimin

Place and Date Made: Sukoharjo, 2006

Water buffalo hide and horn, water-based paint, *ancur*, imitation gold leaf, wood

H: 62, W: 27 (cm)

10. detail

9

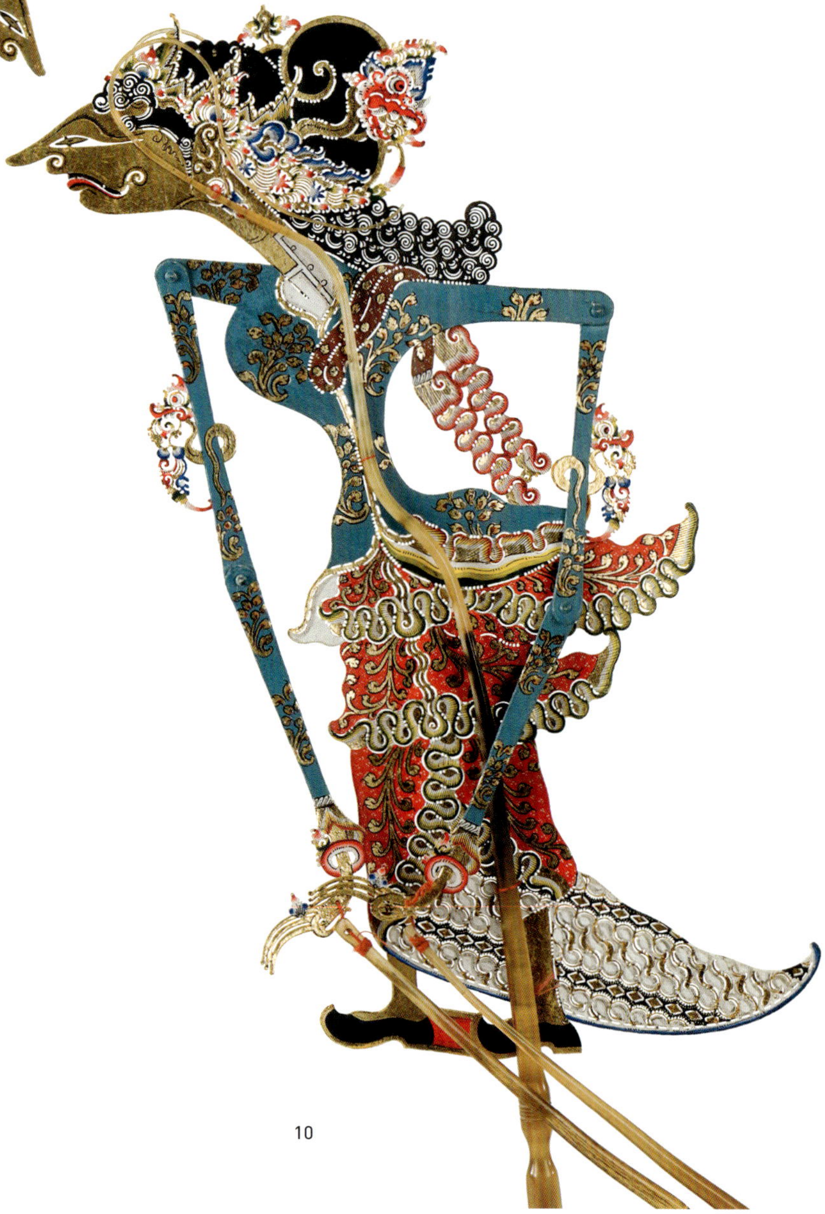

10

In the *Ramayana*, an **army of monkeys** helps Rama, Prince of Ayodya, rescue his wife Sinta who is abducted by Rahwana, the Demon-King of Alengka. The following characters are monkey soldiers in Rama's army. They appear in *lakon* such as "Rama Tambak" [Rama Bridges the Way] and other *Ramayana* episodes when the monkey armies are employed. Many of these characters continue to fight in Rama's army after he successfully returns to his Kingdom Ayodhya and becomes King Rama Wijaya (or "Rama the Great").

11. **Anggada**

FA.2007.40.176

Performer: Ki Purbo Asmoro;
also: Ki Sayoko; Ki Arif

Artists: Yatna Tentrem (leather carver), Diman (painter)

Place and Date Made: Klaten, date unknown

Water buffalo hide and horn, water-based paint, *ancur*, bronze leaf, wood

H: 82.5, W: 33 (cm)

Anggada is Subali's son and cousin to Anoman. Anggada appears in *Ramayana* episodes. His special *lakon* is "Anggada Dhuta" [Anggada Serves as Arbitrator].

11

12

12. **Anila**

FA.2007.40.177

Performer: Ki Purbo Asmoro;
also: Ki Sayoko

Artist: Pardi

Place and Date Made: Sukoharjo, 1993

Water buffalo hide and horn, water-based paint, *ancur*, imitation gold leaf, wood

H: 79, W: 31 (cm)

Anila is a blue-haired monkey that is the adored son of Bathara Narada and the Chief Minister of Pancawati. He is also a soldier in Rama's army. Anila appears in "Kembang Déwa Retna" [The Déwa Retna Flower], "Rama Tambak" [Rama Bridges the Way], and other *Ramayana* stories.

13

13. **Anggeni**

FA.2007.40.178

Performer: Ki Purbo Asmoro;
also: Ki Sayoko

Artist: Supardi

Place and Date Made: Sukoharjo, 1993

Water buffalo hide and horn, water-based paint, *ancur,* imitation gold leaf, wood

H: 80, W: 33 (cm)

The word *geni* means "fire", and this monkey has hair of fire. Anggeni is a devotee of Bathara Brama (noted in Java as the god of fire) and a soldier in Rama's army. He appears in *lakon* such as "Rama Tambak," (Rama Bridges the Way) and other *Ramayana* stories.

14

14. **Sima Ambara**

FA.2007.40.179

Performer: Ki Purbo Asmoro;
also: Ki Sayoko

Artist: Supardi

Place and Date Made: Sukoharjo, 1993

Water buffalo hide and horn, water-based paint, *ancur,* imitation gold leaf, wood

H: 76, W: 29 (cm)

Sima Ambara is a monkey soldier with the face and fur of a tiger.

15

15. **Cocak Rawun**

FA.2007.40.180

Performer: Ki Purbo Asmoro;
also: Ki Sayoko

Artist: Supardi

Place and Date Made: Sukoharjo, 1993

Water buffalo hide and horn, water-based paint, *ancur,* imitation gold leaf, wood

H: 76, W: 31 (cm)

Cocak Rawun is a monkey soldier who can fly. He is said to have wings and the face of a bird. This wayang figure does not have wings, but its face resembles a garudha bird, its body is full of feathers.

15. detail

16

16. **Kapi Wraha**

FA.2007.40.181

Performer: Ki Purbo Asmoro;
also: Ki Sayoko

Artist: Supardi

Place and Date Made: Sukoharjo, 1993

Water buffalo hide and horn, water-based paint, *ancur,* imitation gold leaf, wood

H: 75.5, W: 30 (cm)

This character is a monkey soldier with the face of a wild pig.

17

17. **Mantasthi**

FA.2007.40.182

Performer: Ki Purbo Asmoro;
also: Ki Sayoko

Artist: Supardi

Place and Date Made: Sukoharjo, 1993

Water buffalo hide and horn, water-based paint, *ancur,* imitation gold leaf, wood

H: 77, W: 32 (cm)

This character is a monkey soldier with the face of an elephant.

18. **Kethek Jaran**

FA.2007.40.183

Performer: Ki Purbo Asmoro;
also: Ki Sayoko

Artist: Supardi

Place and Date Made: Sukoharjo, 1993

Water buffalo hide and horn, water-based paint, *ancur*, imitation gold leaf, wood

H: 76, W: 32.5 (cm)

This character is a monkey soldier with the face of a horse.

18

19

19. **Janula**

FA.2007.40.184

Performer: Ki Purbo Asmoro;
also: Ki Sayoko

Artist: Supardi

Place and Date Made: Sukoharjo, 1993

Water buffalo hide and horn, water-based paint, *ancur*, imitation gold leaf, wood

H: 79, W: 33 (cm)

Janula is a green monkey soldier.

In *wayang kulit* performances, **animals** sometimes play a part in battle scenes and sometimes appear in forest scenes.

20. **Kidang**

FA.2007.40.185

Performer: Ki Purbo Asmoro

Artists: Sriyadi (leather carver), Yatna Tentrem (painter)

Place and Date Made: Wonogiri, 2007

Water buffalo hide and horn, water-based paint, *ancur*, imitation gold leaf

H: 56, W: 36 (cm)

Kidang means "deer" or "small antelope" and it is often used in forest scenes.

20

21. **Gajah**

FA.2007.40.189

Performer: Ki Purbo Asmoro; also: Ki Tristuti; Ki Puntana

Artist: Diman (painter)

Place and Date Made: Klaten, date unknown; acquired by Ki Purbo Asmoro in Klaten, 1992

Water buffalo hide and horn, water-based paint, *ancur*, bronze leaf

H: 64, W: 66 (cm)

Elephant figures can appear in forest scenes and in journey scenes. For example, some kings, such as Baladéwa, may travel by elephant. These wayang figures may also be used in battle scenes. This elephant wears chains around its ankle and carries a weapon with its trunk.

21

22

22. **Celeng**

FA.2007.40.190

Performer: Ki Purbo Asmoro

Artists: Sriyadi (leather carver), Yatna Tentrem (painter)

Place and Date Made: Wonogiri, 2007

Water buffalo hide and horn, water-based paint, *ancur*, imitation gold leaf

H: 48, W: 50 (cm)

This figure represents a wild pig.

23. **Garudha**

FA.2007.40.191

Performer: Ki Purbo Asmoro

Artists: Sriyadi (leather carver), Yatna Tentrem (painter)

Place and Date Made: Wonogiri, 2007

Water buffalo hide and horn, water-based paint, *ancur*, imitation gold leaf

H: 64, W: 60 (cm)

The Garudha is a mythical bird that supports the forces of good and the will of the gods. The figure makes an appearance in *lakon* such as "Sinta Ilang" [Sinta Wanders Off] and "Bedhahé Ayodya" [The Fall of Ayodya] of the *Ramayana*.

23

24. **Ulo**

FA.2007.40.192

Performer: Ki Purbo Asmoro

Artists: Sriyadi (leather carver), Yatna Tentrem (painter)

Place and Date Made: Wonogiri, 2007

Water buffalo hide and horn, water-based paint, *ancur*, imitation gold leaf

H: 40, W: 72 (cm)

Ulo is a snake.

24

25. **Banthèng**

FA.2007.40.193

Performer: Ki Purbo Asmoro

Artists: Sriyadi (leather carver), Yatna Tentrem (painter)

Place and Date Made: Wonogiri, 2007

Water buffalo hide and horn, water-based paint, *ancur*, imitation gold leaf

H: 58, W: 61 (cm)

A banthèng is a wild Javanese ox.

25

26

26. **Macan**

FA.2007.40.194

Performer: Ki Purbo Asmoro

Artists: Sriyadi (leather carver), Yatna Tentrem (painter)

Place and Date Made: Wonogiri, 2007

Water buffalo hide and horn, water-based paint, *ancur*, imitation gold leaf

H: 62, W: 69 (cm)

Tigers (*macan*) are sometimes found in forest scenes and can be dangerous foes for the characters that cross their paths.

27

27. **Jaran**

FA.2007.40.195

Performer: Ki Purbo Asmoro

Artists: Sriyadi (leather carver), Yatna Tentrem (painter)

Place and Date Made: Wonogiri, 2007

Water buffalo hide and horn, water-based paint, *ancur*, imitation gold leaf

H: 55, W: 60.5 (cm)

The horse puppet is used in scenes involving a grand departure or a journey, and is sometimes used in battle scenes. The puppeteer coordinates the actions of this figure with those of a human puppet character (so that it appears that the human puppet is riding the horse).

28. **Kereta**

FA.2007.40.186

Ki Purbo Asmoro Collection

Performer: Ki Purbo Asmoro

Artists: unknown

Place and Date Made: Sukoharjo, date unknown; acquired by Ki Purbo Asmoro in Sukoharjo, 2000

Water buffalo hide and horn, water-based paint, *ancur*, imitation gold leaf

H: 72, W: 94 (cm)

The kereta puppet depicts a royal carriage. The figure is used for the onstage arrival or departure of an important character, such as a king. The kereta is used in every performance.

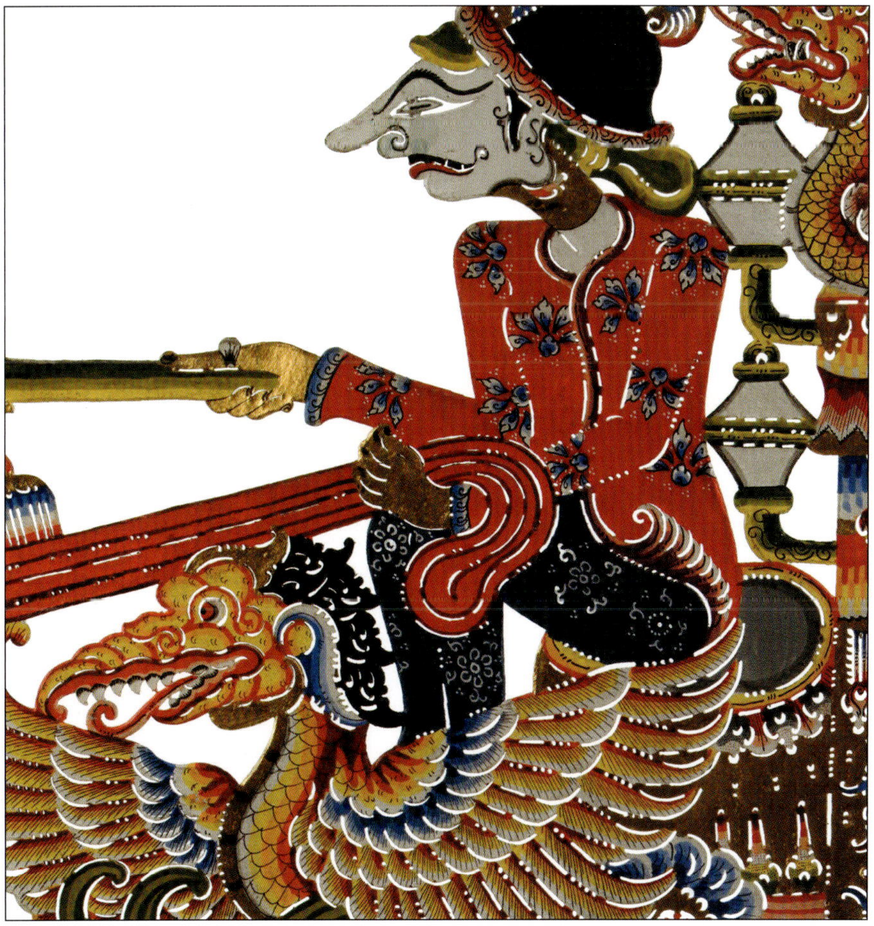

Ampyak are army figures; they portray a whole army. The *Ampyak Jawa* figure represents the Javanese army, or the human or protagonist army. The *Ampyak Buta* figure represents the ogre army or a foreign, enemy army. The Ampyak are used in every performance—for battle scenes, or for scenes showing the troops' departure.

29

29. **Ampyak Jawa**
FA.2007.40.187
Performer: Ki Purbo Asmoro
Artists: Sriyadi (leather carver), Yatna Tentrem (painter)
Place and Date Made: Wonogiri, 2007
Water buffalo hide and horn, water-based paint, *ancur,* imitation gold leaf
H: 62.5, W: 68.5 (cm)

30. **Ampyak Buta**
FA.2007.40.188
Performer: Ki Purbo Asmoro
Artists: Sriyadi (leather carver)), Yatna Tentrem (painter)
Place and Date Made: Wonogiri, 2007
Water buffalo hide and horn, water-based paint, *ancur,* imitation gold leaf
H: 62.5, W: 68.5 (cm)

30

Senjata (special weapons) and props may be used in battle or other scenes to enhance the drama of the play.[6]

6. Individual weapons identified by Dr. Suyanto S.Kar., MA. and Honggo Utomo.

31. (a-n) **Senjata (weapon)**

Performer: Ki Purbo Asmoro

Artists: unknown

Place and Date Made: unknown

Water buffalo hide, wood, water-based paint, *ancur*

Measurements vary

a. Druasa—a weapon used by Karna's son
FA.2007.40.196

b. Jamus Kalimasada—a letter or document
FA.2007.40.197

c. Naga Mangsa—a weapon used by Indrajit that shoots out poisonous snakes
FA.2007.40.198

d. Cis or Patrem—a weapon for female characters, such as Srikandhi
FA.2007.40.199

e. **Keris**—a weapon with special power; it also has special significance to Javanese identity and heritage
FA.2007.40.200

f. **Wadung**—a weapon carried by Gareng
FA.2007.40.201

g. **Wijaya Kusuma**—Great Flower; a special heirloom flower belonging to Kresna
FA.2007.40.202

h. **Bendho**—a generic weapon
FA.2007.40.203

i. Mosala— a generic weapon
FA.2007.40.204

j. Cakra Baskara—Kresna's special weapon
FA.2007.40.205

k. Arda Dadali—Arjuna's special weapon; a gift he received from Durna
FA.2007.40.206

l. Limpung—a special weapon used by Rahwana
FA.2007.40.208

m. Alu—this is Petruk's special weapon
FA.2007.40.209

n. Bima's Gada—a gada is a commonly used weapon, but Bima's special gada is particularly large.
FA.2007.40.210

Setan are (unseen) evil spirits. These figures generally distract people from their tasks and disrupt or thwart their meditations.

32. **Setan**

FA.2007.40.211 - 216

Performer: Ki Purbo Asmoro

Artists: unknown

Place and Date Made: unknown

Water buffalo hide and horn, water-based paint, *ancur*

Measurements vary

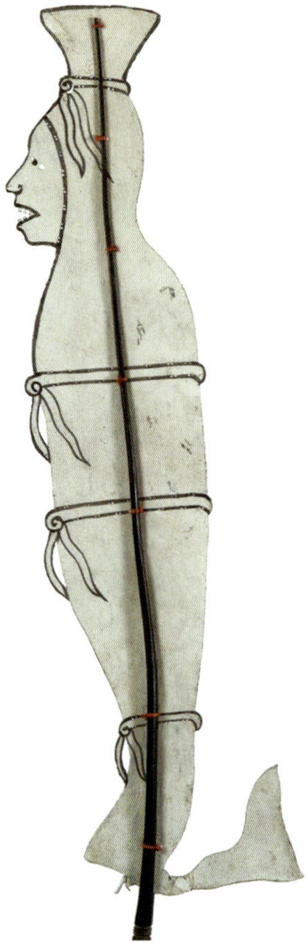

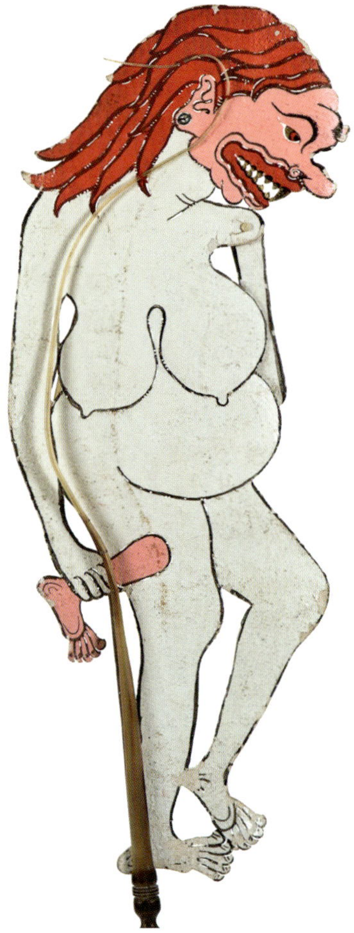

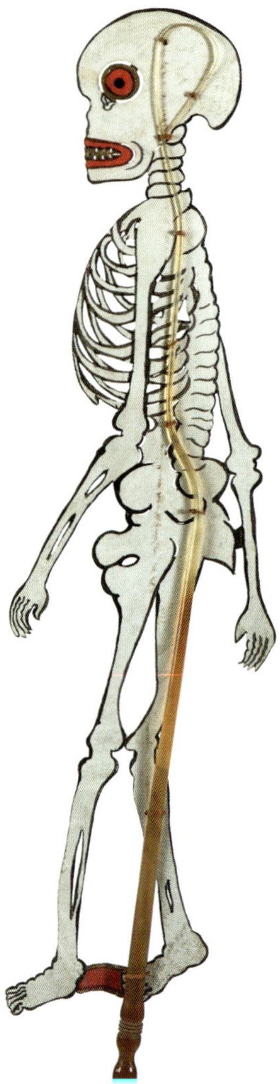

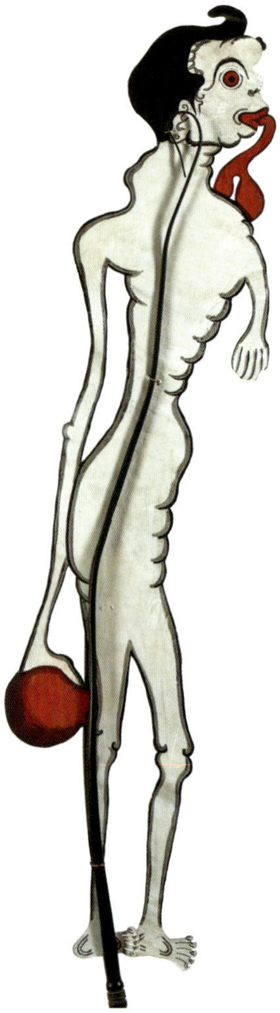

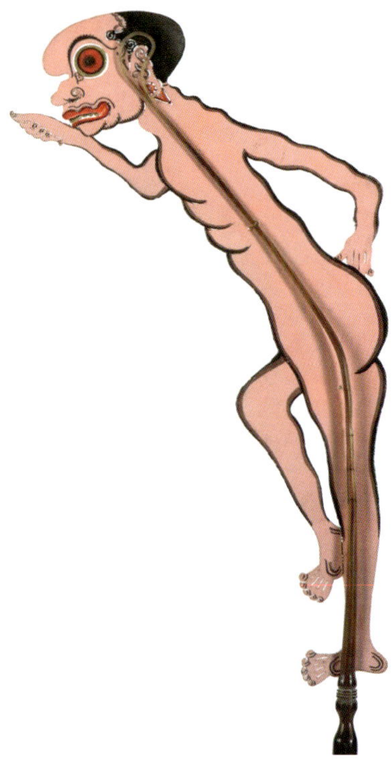

The Tree of Life (Kayon) figure is also known as a Cosmic Mountain (Gunungan). The terms *Kayon* and *Gunungan* are used interchangebly. These mountain-shaped figures are used in every performance to begin and end the show, as well as for other purposes: to mark scene divisions; to represent the natural elements; natural storms; or extreme emotions. The gunungan/kayon may also represent a palace, home, forest, or other physical locations. Today, many performers choose to utilize several gunungan/kayon at one time to enhance the visual impact that these wayang figures can create.

These are the only wayang figures that are painted differently on each side. The front usually includes a tree of life with animals in its branches and it may portray guardian figures in front of a home, a palace, or a mosque, or it may depict a water motif (such as a pond). The back side of the shadow puppet usually portrays water and wind or fire elements, often with the face of a *barong* or *mankara* (a protective guardian figure that provides strength).

33. **Gunugan Gapuran, also known as Kayon Gapuran**

FA.2007.38.1

Performer and Designer: Ki Enthus Susmono

Artist: Rasimin

Place and Date Made: Solo, 1992

Water buffalo hide and horn, water-based paint and dyes, *ancur*, gold leaf

H: 110, W: 49.5 (cm)

Gunugan Gapuran is associated with the masculine lingam form, and typically features a place (home, palace, or mosque) with guardian figures and a tree of life.

33. front

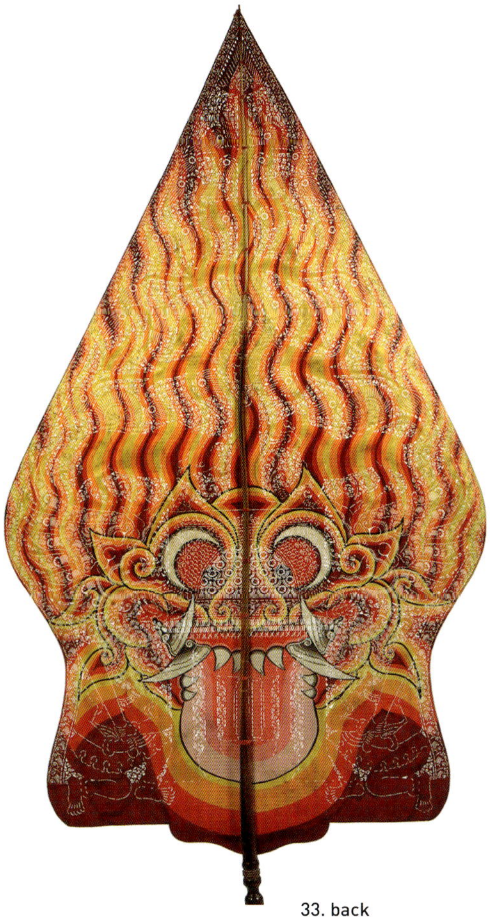

33. back

34. back

34. front

34. silhouette

34. detail

34. **"Kayon Siwa"**

FA.2007.18.1

Performer, Designer and Artist: Ki Sukasdi

Assistant Artists: Pramono (leather carver) and Makmur (painter)

Place and Date Made: Sukoharjo, 2007

Water buffalo hide and horn, water-based paint, *ancur*, gold leaf

H: 117, W: 52.5 (cm)

The artist gave this gunungan/ kayon figure the title, *"Kayon Siwa,"* which refers to the Hindu god, Siwa (also known as Bathara Guru), who is depicted on the front side of this wayang figure. The Siwa imagery is considered a special innovation by the artist and is not traditionally found on these puppet forms. To the artist, the Hindu gods are an important part of Javanese culture and Siwa is a high god; he is particularly important. Also featured is a classic, though exceptionally detailed, tree of life. On the back of the piece is the traditional image of *mankara*, a guardian-protector who gives strength.

This piece was acquired directly from the artist, who is also trained as a dhalang. He used this gunungan/ kayon in only a few of his own performances. This extraordinary artistic creation took Ki Sukasdi five months to make, including help from assistant artists.

34. detail

35. front

35. **Gunugan Blumbangan, also known as Kayon Blumbangan**

FA.2007.38.2

Performer and Designer: Ki Enthus Susmono

Artist: Rasimin

Place and Date Made: Solo, 1992

Water buffalo hide and horn, water-based paint and dyes, *ancur*, gold leaf

H: 100, W: 46 (cm)

Gunugan Blumbangan features a tree of life with a water motif that is associated with femininity. Water is the source of life and represents the female yoni.

35. back

36. **George W. Bush, Saddam Hussein, and a missile** from the series, "Wayang Planet"

FA.2007.39.1&2; 2008.4.1

Performer and Designer: Ki Enthus Susmono

Artist: Rasimin

Place and Date Made: Solo, 2001

Water buffalo hide and horn, water-based paint and dyes, *ancur*, gold leaf, wood

H: 106, W: 47 (cm) (human figures are approximately the same size)

These George W. Bush and Saddam Hussein wayang figures made appearances in numerous classical wayang performances by the dhalang and designer of these figures, Ki Enthus Susmono. Ki Enthus used these wayang kulit to encourage his audience to contemplate the effects of war; he would present the issues in a short, satirical scene.

For example in the *lakon* "Gathutkaca Gugur" [The Death of Gathutkaca] from the *Mahabharata*, Gathutkaca tells Kresna about his reluctance to continue his fight against his blood relatives, the Kurawas. When a missile flies overhead, the characters (Gathutkaca and Kresna) follow its path. They discover George W. Bush chasing Saddam Hussein in a madcap routine. Kresna and Gathutkaca look at the land of Iraq to see all the suffering and destruction caused by war, and they discuss the meaning of it all. Kresna explains that despite the pains of war, Gathutkaca must continue the battle against his cousins to prevent them from taking over the world—continuing the fight and winning the battle will help restore the forces of good and carry out the will of the gods.[7]

Written when the Museum purchased the George W. Bush wayang, Ki Enthus stated:

I extradite wayang "George W. Bush" from the world of Wayang Planet. It is my hope that in his time living with other wayang, together in one kothak, he has learned from Javanese culture and has a greater appreciation for humanity"
July 2, 2007

These wayang figures are innovations of Ki Enthus Susmono, and they do not appear in typical sets of classical wayang kulit.

7. Honggo Utomo, E-mail communication, February 25, 2008

Bibliography

Anderson, Benedict R. O'G. *Mythology and the Tolerance of the Javanese*. Ithaca, N.Y.: Modern Indonesia Project; Southeast Asia Program, Department of Asian Studies, Cornell University, 1965.

Brandon, James. *On Thrones of Gold*. Cambridge: Harvard University Press, 1970.

Brinner, Benjamin. *Music in Central Java: Experiencing Music, Expressing Culture*. New York: Oxford University Press, 2008

Chandler, David P., et al. *In Search of Southeast Asia: A Modern History*. Edited by David Joel Steinberg. Honolulu: University of Hawaii Press, 1987.

Geertz, Clifford. *The Religion of Java*. Chicago: University of Chicago Press, 1960.

Guritno, Pandam, Haryono Guritno, Teguh S. Djamal, and Molly Bondan. *Lordly Shades: Wayang Purwa of Indonesia*. Jakarta: PT Jayakarta Agung Offset. 1984.

Haryana, Timbul. "Historiografi Seni Masyarakat Jawa Kuna dalam Prespektif Arkeologis: Studi Kasus Seni Pertunjukan." In *Seni pertunjujkan Indonesia: Menimbang Pendekatan Emik Nusantara*. Surakarta: Program Pendidikan Pascasarjana Sekolah Tinggi Seni Indonesia Surakarta, 2005.

Irvine, David. *Leather Gods and Wooden Heros: Java's Classical Wayang*. Singapore: Marshall Cavendish International (Asia) Private Limited, 2005.

Kattsoff, Louis O. Elements of Philosophy. Translanted by Soejono Soemargono.Yogyakarta: Tiara Wacana, 2004.

Keeler, Ward. *Javanese Shadow Plays, Javanese Selves*. Princeton: Princeton University Press, 1987.

Mangkunagoro, K.G.P.A.A. VII. *On the Wayang Kulit (Purwa) And its Symbolic and Mystical Elements*. Translated from the original Dutch by Claire Holt. Southeast Asia Data Paper no. 27. Ithaca, N. Y.: Cornell University, 1957.

Mellema, R. L. *Wayang Puppets: Carving, Coloring, and Symbolism*. Amsterdam: Royal Tropical Institute, 1954.

Mrázek, Jan. *Phenomenology of a Puppet Theatre: Contemplations on the Art of Wayang Kulit*. Leiden: KITLV Press, 2005.

__________. "Javanese Wayang kulit in the times of comedy: Clown scenes, innovation, and the performance's being in the present world, Part One." *Indonesia* 68 (1999): 38-128.

__________. *Puppet Theatre in Contemporary Indonesia: New Approaches to Performance Events*. Ed. by Jan Mrázek. Ann Arbor: U of Michigan Press, 2002.

Peacock, James L.. *Purifying the Faith: The Muhammadijah Movement in Indonesian Islam.* Monographs in Southeast Asian Studies, Program for Southeast Asian Studies. Arizona State University, 1992.

Reid, Anthony. *Southeast Asia in the Age of Commerce 1450-1680.* Vol. 1: *The Lands below the Winds*. New Haven: Yale University Press, 1988.

Sears, Laurie Jo. "Epic Voyages: The Transmission of the *Ramayana* and *Mahabharata* from India to Java." In *Aesthetic Tradition and Cultural Transition in Java and Bali*. edited by Stephanie Morgan and Laurie Jo Sears,1-30. Madison: Center for Southeast Asian Studies. 1984.

Sumarsam. "Gendèr Birung: Its Technique and Function in the Context of Javanese Art." *Indonesia* 20 (1975): 161-171.

__________. "Gamelan Music and the Javanese Wayang Kulit." In *Aesthetic Tradition and Cultural Transition in Java and Bali*, edited by Stephanie Morgan and Laurie Jo Sears, 105-116. Madison, WI: Center for Southeast Asian Studies, 1984.

__________. *Gamelan: Cultural Interaction and Musical Development in Central Java*. Chicago: University of Chicago Press, 1992.

UNESCO. *Wayang Indonesia Performance*. Livret Program Book. Jakarta: SENAWANGI & PT Gramedia, 2004.

Widodo, Ki Marwoto Panenggak. *Tuntunan Ketrampilan Tatah Sungging Wayang Kulit*. Surabaya: PT. Citra Jaya Murti, 1990.

Wirastodipuro, K. R. M. H.. *Ringgit Wacucal, Wayang Kulit, Shadow Puppet*. Surakarta: Press Solo, 2006.

Wiryamartana, Kuntara I. *Arjunawiwaha*. Yogyakarta: Duta Wacana University, 1999.

Zoetmulder, P. J. "The Wayang as a Philosophical Theme." *Indonesia* 12 (1971): 85-96.

__________. *Kalangwan Satra Jawa Kuno Selayang Pandang*. Jakarta: Djambatan, 1983.

__________. *Manunggaling Kawula Gusti Pantheisme dan Monisme dalam Sastra Suluk Jawa*. Jogyakarta: Kanisius,1990. </>

Index